TRADE
U.S. POLICY SINCE 1945

TRADE

U.S. POLICY SINCE 1945

Congressional Quarterly Inc.
1414 22nd Street N.W., Washington, D.C. 20037

Congressional Quarterly Inc.

Congressional Quarterly Inc., an editorial research service and publishing company, serves clients in the fields of news, education, business and government. It combines specific coverage of Congress, government and politics by Congressional Quarterly with the more general subject range of an affiliated service, Editorial Research Reports.

Congressional Quarterly publishes the *Congressional Quarterly Weekly Report* and a variety of books, including college political science textbooks under the CQ Press imprint and public affairs paperbacks designed as timely reports to keep journalists, scholars and the public abreast of developing issues and events. CQ also publishes information directories and reference books on the federal government, national elections and politics, including the *Guide to Congress*, the *Guide to the Supreme Court*, the *Guide to U.S. Elections* and *Politics in America*. The *CQ Almanac*, a compendium of legislation for one session of Congress, is published each year. *Congress and the Nation*, a record of government for a presidential term, is published every four years.

CQ publishes *The Congressional Monitor*, a daily report on current and future activities of congressional committees, and several newsletters including *Congressional Insight*, a weekly analysis of congressional action, and *Campaign Practices Reports*, a semimonthly update on campaign laws.

CQ conducts seminars and conferences on Congress, the legislative process, the federal budget, national elections and politics, and other current issues. CQ Direct Research is a consulting service that performs contract research and maintains a reference library and query desk for clients.

Library of Congress Cataloging in Publication Data

Main entry under title:

Trade: U.S. policy since 1945.

    Bibliography: p.
    Includes index.
    1. United States — Commercial policy — History — 20th century. I. Congressional Quarterly, inc.
HF1455.T67   1984   382'.3'0945   83-25246
ISBN 0-87187-282-X

Editor: Margaret C. Thompson

Major Contributors: Nancy A. Blanpied, Mary H. Cooper, Alan Murray, Michael D. Wormser

Contributors: Nancy Lammers, Marc Leepson, Mary L. McNeil, John L. Moore, Steven Pressman, Elizabeth Wehr

Designer: Mary L. McNeil

Cover Design: Richard A. Pottern

Graphics: Robert Redding

Photo Credits: Cover—Jerry Wachter/FOLIO; p. xii, Cris Cross/UNIPHOTO; p. 96, Wide World; p. 134, National Film Board of Canada; p. 148, Kearney & Trecker Corporation; p. 170, Doug Wilson, U.S. Department of Agriculture; p. 186, Connecticut Yankee Power Company, Boeing Commercial Airplane Company, Bell Labs; p. 198, General Motors; p. 216, Chrysler Motor Co.

Indexer: Jodean Marks

Table of Contents

Tables and Graphs

PREFACE

United States trade policy in the first decades after World War II was founded on the premise that eliminating barriers to the free exchange of goods among nations would benefit not only this country but others as well. Reducing tariffs, quotas and similar trade restrictions made economic sense to U.S. policy makers. The industrialized world had been ravaged by war, except for the United States, which had emerged stronger than ever, with a surfeit of manufactured goods and food to export — products that the rest of the world desperately needed.

Guided by those facts, the United States, during the 1940s, 1950s and 1960s, led a largely successful assault on breaking down the most blatant obstacles to trade among free world nations. Those roadblocks primarily were tariffs, the first target of the original 23 signatories to the General Agreement on Tariffs and Trade (GATT), formed in 1947. The GATT members pledged to negotiate multilateral agreements that would reduce tariffs and eliminate other impediments to free economic interchange. By the end of 1983, 90 governments had subscribed to GATT, and most other Western nations that did not belong informally adhered to its principles.

Perhaps the very success of GATT, evidenced by the results of several rounds of trade negotiations that dramatically reduced tariff levels, laid bare the more intractable barriers to trade. These nontariff restrictions included not only quotas on imports but often more fundamental practices of national governments such as subsidies to exporting sectors of the economy and industrial policies designed to promote certain growth industries, often at the expense of foreign competitors. The whittling away of tariffs, ironically, even may have caused governments to strengthen other protectionist measures, particularly during a time of worldwide inflation, recession and crises in energy supplies.

These pressures took their toll on the pursuit of free trade.

Increasingly during the late 1960s and 1970s protectionism crept into the shaping of trade policy throughout much of the world. The concept of reciprocity assumed a new meaning. Previously the cornerstone of a doctrine that rested on extending mutual trade concessions, reciprocity by the 1980s had come to be linked with pursuit of measures designed to counter, or retaliate against, what were seen as unfair or restrictive trade practices by other nations.

Trade: U.S. Policy Since 1945 traces the evolution of U.S. trade relations in the postwar decades. The book highlights the difficult issues confronting the United States as it attempts to deal with persistent trade and balance-of-payments deficits caused by overseas competition and an overvalued dollar (which made U.S. products more expensive, and therefore less attractive, for foreigners to purchase).

An introductory chapter provides an overview of the major challenges confronting U.S. trade policy in the 1980s, followed by background chapters on the development of U.S. economic relations with the industrialized nations, the third world of developing nations and communist countries, particularly the Soviet Union and the People's Republic of China. Separate chapters examine U.S. trade relations with Japan and Canada, controls on high-technology transfers, export subsidies and the role of the Export-Import Bank, America's large agricultural trade and proposals to fashion a comprehensive industrial policy to orchestrate an effective trade and growth effort.

Chapters 1 through 4, 7, 8, and 9 were compiled and written by Margaret C. Thompson and chapters 5, 6 and 10 by Nancy A. Blanpied. Material for the chapters was based in large part on Congressional Quarterly's *Congress and the Nation*, vols. I-V, articles appearing in the *Congressional Quarterly Weekly Report* and reports written by the staff of CQ's *Editorial Research Reports*.

Margaret C. Thompson
January 1984

TRADE

U.S. POLICY SINCE 1945

One of the most difficult issues that confronted U.S. policy makers in the early 1980s was how to deal with competition from foreign manufacturers while continuing to adhere to free-trade principles.

Chapter 1

U.S. TRADE POLICY: ISSUES IN THE 1980s

President Ronald Reagan's speech to the nation Jan. 25, 1983, made it clear that, in economic terms, the state of the union was more closely entwined with the state of the world than ever before. "Every American has a role and stake in international trade," Reagan told the nation. "One out of every five jobs in our country depends on trade. We export over 20 percent of our industrial production, and 40 percent of our farmland produces for export."

The theme was woven throughout the president's State of the Union address. "In at least half the pages of his text, he made references to programs that impact on trade," noted U.S. Trade Representative William E. Brock III, the administration's chief trade negotiator with foreign governments. The reason, said Brock, was that the 1982 decline in trade contributed greatly to unemployment in the United States. "The very essence of trade is to deal with that problem," he said.

Reagan was not alone in emphasizing trade. The Senate Finance Committee had met earlier in the day to discuss the same issue. "I really believe trade is going to be the most important issue we face this year," said Sen. Lloyd Bentsen, D-Texas. In their response to Reagan's speech, congressional Democrats also staked out international trade as important ground. "It's time the United States began to deal with the reality of the international economy that we live in today," said Senate Minority Leader Robert C. Byrd, D.-W.Va. "America must get just as tough on trade as our world competitors. . . . That could be the difference in thousands and thousands of jobs a year."

The world recession, which caused global trade to drop in 1982 and 1983, drove home the full implications of the United States' increased dependence on trade. And the effects of recession were exacerbated by a new reliance on mercantilism in the world, with governments adopting extreme measures to increase exports and decrease imports. Because one nation's imports were another's exports, the conflicts of this strategy were clear, if difficult to escape.

The United States officially continued to preach the virtues of free trade. "As the leader of the West and as a country that has become great and rich because of economic freedom, America must be an unrelenting advocate of free trade," Reagan said in his address. But even as he spoke, labor and business leaders as well as members of Congress were looking abroad for the culprit responsible for the nation's economic woes. They maintained that America's trading partners and traditional allies, by applying aggressive export policies and limiting U.S. imports to their own markets, were in effect exporting domestic unemployment to the United States.

Reagan's critics said that a more realistic trade policy than the "free-trade" approach favored by the administration was what America needed to get its ailing industries back on their feet and American workers back on the job.

Rising Trade Deficit, Unemployment

Ten years earlier, trade issues did not receive such attention. But in 1973 trade accounted for only 6 percent of the U.S. gross national product (GNP). By 1983 it represented more than 12 percent. Although the U.S. economy was less dependent upon foreign trade for its health than those of most industrialized nations, a number of key domestic industries relied heavily on export sales of their products for survival, while others were particularly vulnerable to imported products with which they had to compete on the domestic market. Brock pointed out in January 1983: "In recent years four out of five of the new U.S. jobs in manufacturing have been created by international trade. One out of every three acres planted by American farmers is producing crops for export. Two trillion dollars of goods and services currently are being traded internationally and the potential for growth is unlimited."

In spite of a 15.6 percent drop in oil imports in 1982, the United States registered a record trade deficit of $42.7 billion, after posting a $39.7 billion deficit the previous year. While the trade statistics indicated a lack of growth on both sides, with a 7 percent decline in imports and a 9 percent fall in exports, the overall deficit underscored the plight of ex-port-dependent industries. Preliminary figures for 1983 did not look any brighter. In the second quarter of the year the deficit in the U.S. current account (the balance of exports and imports of goods and services) rose

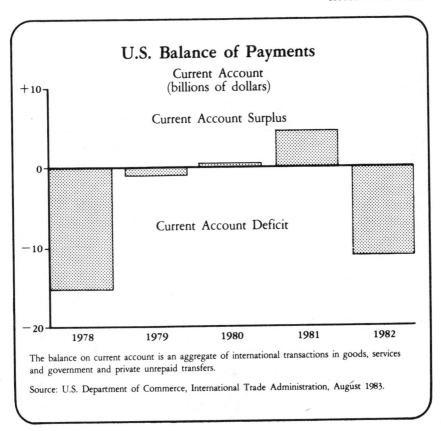

U.S. Balance of Payments

Current Account
(billions of dollars)

Current Account Surplus

Current Account Deficit

+10

0

−10

−20

1978   1979   1980   1981   1982

The balance on current account is an aggregate of international transactions in goods, services and government and private unrepaid transfers.

Source: U.S. Department of Commerce, International Trade Administration, August 1983.

to $9.7 billion from $3.6 billion, largely as a result of a widening of the merchandise trade deficit to $14.7 billion from $8.8 billion in the first quarter of the year. Commerce Department officials expected a total trade deficit of between $65 billion and $70 billion for 1983 and warned that it could be as high as $174 billion by 1990.

Lower exports and higher imports also meant job losses. In September 1983 the seasonally adjusted unemployment rate for all civilian workers stood at 9.5 percent. According to Alfred E. Eckes, chairman of the U.S. International Trade Commission (a non-partisan government advisory agency), each $1 billion change in the trade balance affected at least 25,000 jobs. Thus an increase in the deficit of $60 billion might put 1.5 million Americans out of work. Many of those lost job opportunities would be in manufacturing, where the deficit was widening rapidly. Between 1979 and 1982, employment fell by 39 percent in the U.S. auto industry, 47 percent in steel, 19 percent among shoe manufacturers and 17 percent in the apparel industry.

On the other hand, protectionist measures to save jobs often were self-defeating and costly, particularly for consumers. According to a study by C. Fred Bergsten and William R. Cline, in the late 1970s U.S. consumers paid an estimated $58,000 annually per job saved by protecting domestic manufacturers of specialty steel, television sets and footwear. That would amount to about $92,000 annually per job at 1982 prices.

Decline in Agricultural Exports

Over the past decade Americans have been able to pay their foreign energy bills thanks largely to a significant increase in agricultural exports, which rose from $7.3 billion in 1970 to $43.3 billion in 1981. In 1982, however, agricultural exports, while maintaining a comfortable surplus over imports, had fallen to $36.6 billion and were expected to decrease still further in 1983. The reasons for this decline, according to Jim Donald, chairman of the Department of Agriculture's World Food and Agricultural Outlook and Situation Board, were "very weak world economic conditions, along with the strength of the dollar." Due to the increased value of the dollar over nearly all major currencies in 1982 and 1983, U.S. agricultural commodities tended to be priced higher in overseas markets than comparable products of other countries. *(Dollar's strength, box, p. 12)*

Other analysts pointed to the U.S. embargo on grain sales to the Soviet Union, imposed in 1980 in response to the Soviet invasion of Afghanistan, as a crucial factor in diverting foreign buyers to other, more reliable, grain suppliers, in particular Argentina and Canada. At the same time, favorable weather conditions among grain exporting nations and weak demand due to the recession caused sizable surpluses of grain stocks. This further depressed prices for those commodities, which account for almost half of all U.S. agricultural exports. *(For further discussion, see chapters on U.S. Farm Exports and Trade With Communist Nations.)*

Plight of Auto and Steel Industries

In addition to declining exports, many sectors of the U.S. economy faced steep competition from imported goods. Chief among these was the auto industry, which continued to lose its share of the domestic car

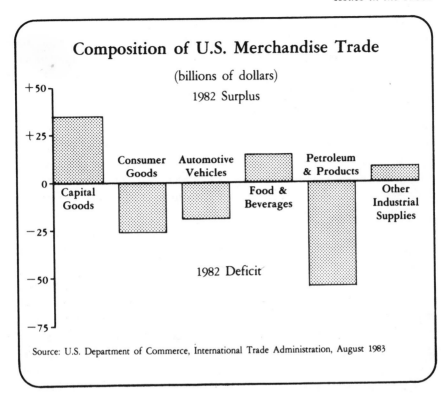

Composition of U.S. Merchandise Trade

(billions of dollars)

market in 1982, when the value of auto imports rose to $20.6 billion from $18.4 billion the year before. Imports in 1982 accounted for 27.9 percent of all cars sold in the United States. If the trend continued, said Eugene I. Casraiss, Jr., legislative representative of the United Auto Workers (UAW), imports could account for 35 to 40 percent of the U.S. automobile market by the end of the 1980s. This, he said, would have a disastrous effect on jobs. By the fall of 1983, however, there were signs that the industry was recovering, although the strength and longevity of that recovery were uncertain. *(Competition from Japan, p. 150)*

Another basic industry troubled by the recession and foreign competition was steel. While iron and steel imports fell by $1.3 billion in 1982 to $9.9 billion — partly as a result of a 1982 agreement with European Economic Community (EEC) producers setting quotas on imports to the United States — domestic steel mills operated at only 40 percent capacity and reported a staggering 50 percent unemployment rate for the year.

The steel industry as a whole was faced with an urgent need to replace outmoded equipment — and quickly — if it was going to have any chance of competing successfully against highly efficient manufacturers in Japan, subsidized producers in Europe and cheap-labor mills in developing nations. But industry representatives said that companies could not afford to make costly investments in modern equipment unless they were protected in the meantime against imports, which foreign producers allegedly were "dumping" on the U.S. market at prices that were below cost. While U.S. steel spokesmen conceded that new tax laws and revised environmental regulations had provided significant incentives for investment, they said that protection from unfair foreign competition also was a prerequisite for modernization.

Responding to pressure from U.S. steel producers and members of Congress from steel-producing states, President Reagan July 5, 1983, raised tariffs and set quotas on specialty steel imports. The decision placed an extra 10 percent tariff on imports of stainless steel sheet and strip, declining to 4 percent over a four-year period; on stainless steel plate imports, the tariff started at 8 percent and would decline to 4 percent. The new tariffs were in addition to existing tariffs on stainless steel products, which ranged from 7 to 11.5 percent. The president also set quotas on imports of stainless steel bars and rods and on alloy tool steel.

The action followed a ruling by the U.S. International Trade Commission in June that U.S. steel makers had suffered injury from European steel imports. European and Canadian officials, however, complained that the tariffs and quotas violated a commitment made at the May 1983 summit meeting in Williamsburg, Va., of the heads of leading industrial nations to resist protectionism. But Trade Representative Brock said the move was designed to promote free trade by combating the "serious distortions" in foreign steel trade practices.

Structural Changes in the World Economy

The problems confronting U.S. industries, both domestically and abroad, as well as the general global recession, had parallels in the international economic climate that prevailed after World War I. That period, too, was marked by intense competition from foreign-made goods, and the result was similar — mounting domestic pressure for protecting American jobs. Tariff rates were raised in 1922 to the highest levels since 1897, thus making it difficult for the European allies to repay their war debts to the United States. It is generally agreed that the tariff policies of the 1920s contributed to the Depression of the 1930s.

As early as 1921 the Baltimore *Evening Sun* warned: "A tariff wall that keeps foreign goods out may also keep American goods in; that unless we buy from the outside we cannot sell to the outside." But most Americans ignored such prophets of doom. "The American people . . .," wrote historian Thomas A. Bailey in *A Diplomatic History of the American People* (1969), "continued to believe that imports were basically bad." This prejudice toward imports was embodied in the Smoot-Hawley Tariff of 1930, which raised tariffs on imported durable goods to a record high level of 59 percent by 1932.

A turnabout in American tariff policy was inaugurated with the Reciprocal Trade Agreements Act of 1934. The movement toward lower tariffs was led by Secretary of State Cordell Hull, a Tennessean committed to the position long popular in the South that low tariffs were good for the country. The 1934 act gave the president authority to negotiate trade agreements with individual countries and greatly reduced duties in return for similar concessions on their part. *(For further background discussion, see pp. 31-33.)*

Foreign Challenges to U.S. Markets

After World War II the United States took the lead in trying to establish a broader approach to tariff reduction and trade liberalization. It was due largely to American initiative that 23 countries in 1947 signed the General Agreement on Tariffs and Trade (GATT).

Although GATT represented a multilateral attempt to mediate differences among the contracting nations over changing trade patterns, many observers believed more attention should be paid to the structural changes that had brought about those shifts, so that a more coherent and effective international trade strategy might be devised for the future. For example, the postwar reindustrialization of Western Europe and Japan, as well as the emergence of newly industrialized nations, had an enormous impact on trade.

Before the oil shortage shocks of the mid- and late-1970s, postwar international trade had grown about 7 percent a year, due in part to the removal of barriers during several rounds of multilateral GATT negotiations that substantially reduced tariffs and import quotas. The undisputed winner during this period was the United States, which claimed in the economic boom years of the 1950s and 1960s about one-fourth of the world market in manufactured goods. By 1979 the U.S. share had fallen to approximately 17 percent.

By the late 1970s South Korea, Taiwan, Hong Kong, the Philippines, Mexico and Brazil had emerged as efficient producers of synthetic textiles, footwear, automobile components and simpler consumer products; they also moved into steel production and shipbuilding (South Korea, for example, developed one of the world's largest shipyards). Advances in transportation and communications, along with an adaptable international financial structure, meant that the manufacture of more and more products could be parceled out around the globe to where they could be produced most efficiently. This growth of multilateral corporations and U.S. foreign subsidiaries adversely affected the U.S. balance-of-payments picture because goods previously manufactured for export now were being produced abroad.

While U.S. domestic industries were ceding some of their power to Japan, Western Europe and, increasingly, to the newly industrialized nations of East Asia and South America, the services sector began to grow. As early as the mid-1950s, the number of American workers employed in the services sector began to exceed those in the blue-collar industries. As a result of this "deindustrialization" process, seven out of every 10 non-agricultural workers in the United States were employed in the services sector in 1983, and the number was expected to grow. "The millions of jobs that are going to be created in this world in the next 20 or 30 years — most of them are going to be in the services area," said Brock, shortly before a November 1982 GATT ministerial meeting that addressed trade in services.

At the same time, the growing participation of the third world nations in the international economy emphasized nations' interdependence. In 1982 alone, the less developed countries (LDCs) bought more than 40 percent of all U.S. exports and more than one-quarter of total exports from the 24 members of the Organization for Economic Cooperation and Development (OECD), a group of Western industrialized nations.

In an article appearing in the Spring 1983 issue of *Foreign Affairs*, Robert B. Reich, professor of business and public policy at Harvard University, described the changes in the world economy confronting the United States in the 1980s. The rapidly industrializing nations had become major producers of complex products such as automobiles, color televisions and small computers. At the same time, some of the less developed countries began to take over production of clothing, footwear

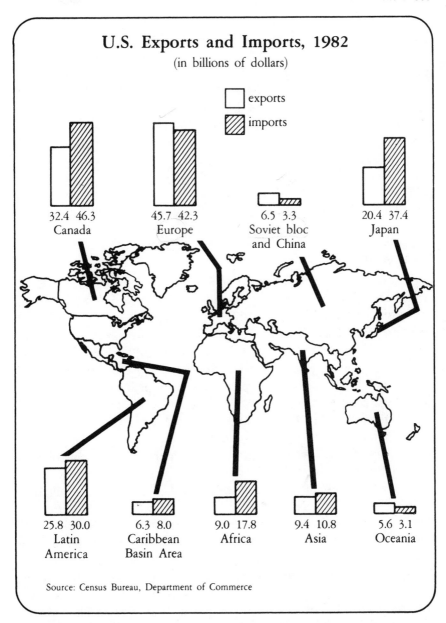

U.S. Exports and Imports, 1982
(in billions of dollars)

□ exports

▨ imports

32.4 46.3
Canada

45.7 42.3
Europe

6.5 3.3
Soviet bloc
and China

20.4 37.4
Japan

25.8 30.0
Latin
America

6.3 8.0
Caribbean
Basin Area

9.0 17.8
Africa

9.4 10.8
Asia

5.6 3.1
Oceania

Source: Census Bureau, Department of Commerce

and small electronics.

Robots and computers were substituting for semiskilled labor in many countries; as a result, Japan, West Germany, France and other highly industrialized countries began to emphasize production of exports requiring highly skilled labor, such as precision castings, specialty steel, special chemicals and sensors and large-scale integrated circuits. *(For a further discussion, see Chapters 6 and 10.)*

One result of these changes was that governments were working with labor to shift their countries' economic base to products in which they had an international trade advantage. At the same time, they selectively raised entry barriers, reduced production costs, retrained workers and provided investment incentives for development of new industries. The dilemma for the United States was how to fashion a policy that preserved jobs while changing to more efficient production techniques in sectors of the economy where it had a competitive advantage on the world market.

Competition From Japan

Responding to the fall in the volume of world trade and the rise in protectionist sentiment among U.S. trading partners in the 1980s, Reagan administration officials — notably Trade Representative Brock and Commerce Secretary Malcolm Baldrige — began to call for strengthening U.S. and international trade rules. Although GATT had been largely successful in reducing import quotas and tariffs, by the 1980s a number of potentially explosive trade disputes had developed, particularly among the United States, Japan, Western Europe and Canada.

With the contraction of economic growth and exports brought on by the global recession, numerous conflicts erupted among the principal trading blocs, which were locked in increasingly fierce competition to maintain their overseas markets while protecting their domestic ones. Japan, the strongest of these, enjoyed a surplus of nearly $30 billion in 1982 in its trade with the United States and the EEC (also called the European Common Market). It was an embarrassment of riches for Japan, which was accused by its trading partners of building its surplus by unfairly excluding many of their goods from the Japanese market.

The Japanese Ministry of International Trade and Industry maintained that the trade imbalance was due to factors other than tariffs or nontariff barriers (such as import quotas and stiff quality-control standards). It pointed out that the Japanese economy also was troubled by rising unemployment and a slowdown of its basic industries, including steel and autos. Japan's exports in fact fell by more than 13 percent in the second half of 1982. Officials in Tokyo, fearing isolation by Japan's trading partners, pointed to tariff cuts on hundreds of imported items, but U.S. and EEC officials responded that Japan needed to go further in reducing its trade barriers. *(Details, see Chapter 6.)*

While previous conflicts between the United States and Japan centered on Japanese textiles, color television sets and steel, problem areas in 1983 were Japanese auto exports and U.S. access to Japanese markets, especially for citrus fruits and beef. Japan agreed in 1981 to impose "voluntary" quotas on its exports of automobiles to the United States (the agreement later was extended several times; as of the end of 1983 it was due to expire in April 1985). But Japanese imports still accounted for more than 20 percent of the new car sales in the United States. On the other hand, the American suggestion that Japan open its markets to a greater share of U.S. beef and citrus products provoked mass demonstrations in the streets of Tokyo by Japanese farmers, who protested that the Japanese market already absorbed about half of all U.S. exports of these items.

West European countries also were pressing for greater access to Japanese markets. France, in particular, retaliated by erecting nontariff barriers of its own to Japanese products. For example, the French government required that all Japanese videotape recorders be processed through a small, provincial customhouse and that all documents and instruction manuals accompanying imports be translated into French. In late 1982 the EEC filed a complaint in GATT against a broad array of Japanese trade practices.

U.S. Relations With Developing Nations and the EEC

For its part, Japan by the 1980s found itself increasingly vulnerable to competition from the newly industrialized centers of Hong Kong, Singapore, South Korea and Taiwan, which were following Japan's example of promoting an export-dependent economy by specializing in such labor-intensive industries as steel and textiles. But even these "new Japans," with their 10 percent average economic growth in the 1970s, were finding that the global recession and subsequent contraction of world markets prevented them from transforming their industrial bases into the high-technology industries necessary for their future economic development.

While the 10 member countries of the EEC (Great Britain, France, West Germany, Italy, the Netherlands, Belgium, Luxembourg, Ireland, Denmark and Greece) focused their complaints of unfair trade practices

Global Currency Misalignment...

While the falling demand for U.S. exports in the early 1980s was attributable largely to the dampening effects of the worldwide recession, much of the blame for the adverse U.S. trade balance — the ratio of imports to exports — was due to the high valuation of the dollar on foreign exchange markets. Beginning in 1983, the dollar climbed to record levels in relation to the currencies of major U.S. trading partners and stood at about 50 percent above its value in 1980.

Although Americans traveling abroad found the dollar could buy more than it had in many years, most observers seemed to agree that the strong dollar's ill effects on the U.S. trade position far outweighed its benefits for foreign travel. Lawrence B. Krause, senior fellow in economics at the Brookings Institution in Washington, D.C., estimated that the blame for the trade deficit lay "50-50 between the recession and the strong dollar." Other economists, including C. Fred Bergsten, director of the Institute for International Economics, placed even greater emphasis on the dollar's role. According to Treasury Department statistics, the dollar appreciated 20.4 percent from the beginning of 1981 through January 1983 against the currencies of the 23 other countries belonging to the Organization for Economic Cooperation and Development (OECD). With each successive appreciation of the dollar's value, U.S. exports become more costly to overseas buyers and less competitive with similar goods produced abroad. Dollar appreciation also made domestically produced goods less attractive to American consumers than relatively cheap imports.

Some observers, however, believed the strong dollar's role in widening the trade deficit was overstated. A September 1983 study by the U.S. International Trade Commission concluded, ". . . [I]t is extremely difficult to determine with certainty the extent to which changes in exchange rates affect trade, because other factors, such as international

on Japan, they in turn were the object of similar complaints from Washington. While the United States still enjoyed a $5.3 billion trade surplus with the combined economies of the Common Market nations in 1982, its margin of advantage shrank that year from a 1981 surplus of $9 billion. U.S. steelmakers accused their European counterparts of seeking

. . . Impact of Strong Dollar on Trade

price competitiveness, technological leadership and new supplying countries, are simultaneously affecting trading nations' competitiveness and
trade levels." Commerce Secretary Malcolm Baldrige, however, said in
releasing U.S. trade statistics for July 1983, "Although growth abroad
is beginning to follow our recovery and will result in some increases in
our exports, the high value of the dollar will continue to cut into the U.S.
share of any increase in world trade." As the recovery picked up steam,
U.S. consumer demand also was expected to increase, and late 1983 trade
figures showed that imports were satisfying an ever-larger share of that
demand.

Writing in July 1983, Data Resources economist Sara Johnson said,
"[T]he dollar's appreciation, by lowering import prices and raising the cost
of American goods on foreign markets, is gradually shifting production
abroad. Over the past two years, the dollar's rise has cost the U.S. economy
over a million jobs, and economic performance will remain far below
potential for several years to come."

Because of the dollar's role as the world's premier reserve currency,
the impact of the strong dollar has not been limited to the United States.
Dollar overvaluation raised the cost of commodities, especially oil, whose
price was pegged to the dollar. Although OPEC oil prices had declined,
foreign consumers had to pay more for imported oil because they had to
buy it with expensive dollars. Third world borrowers, which must pay
interest on their staggering debts (estimated at $600 billion to $700 billion)
in dollars, were particularly hard hit by the U.S. currency's appreciation.
Faced with enormous difficulties in repaying their debts, developing
countries were forced to impose severe austerity measures. One result was a
sudden cutback in their purchases of American exports, further widening
the U.S. trade deficit.

to solve their own problems by dumping steel on the U.S. market. EEC
steel imports accounted for about 25 percent of all steel used in the
United States. This was made possible, U.S. firms said, by government
subsidies to the European steel industry, enabling manufacturers to sell
their products in the United States at below the cost of production. The

Carter administration's attempt in late 1979 to solve the problem with the "trigger-price" mechanism was followed in 1982 by a bilateral agreement to limit exports of certain categories of European steel products to the United States. (The "trigger price" mechanism established a minimum price for which steel imports could be sold on the U.S. market. Sale of imported steel below the "trigger price" allowed U.S. steelmakers to initiate anti-dumping suits against the offending producers.)

While 1982 saw a partial resolution of the steel dispute, the battle still raged over the EEC's subsidization of agricultural exports, which U.S. farmers blamed for their own falling exports. Twenty cents out of every dollar of Common Market food exports represented a government grant. The United States filed a series of petitions against European export subsidies for wheat, flour and pasta. To the U.S. complaint the Europeans replied that their trade deficit with the United States in agricultural products had continued to rise. They attributed the American decline in world agricultural trade not to European subsidies but rather to the increased value of the dollar, high U.S. interest rates, reduced U.S. grain sales to the Soviet Union, and record harvests at a time of contracting overseas markets.

This deepening trade conflict was intensified by European condemnation of the Reagan administration's imposition of sanctions against European subsidiaries of U.S. companies selling equipment to the Soviet Union for use in construction of the Siberian gas pipeline. Those sanctions were imposed in December 1981 and lifted in November 1982. The EEC also was unhappy over the Reagan administration's January 1983 agreement to subsidize U.S. exports of wheat flour to Egypt, a market previously dominated by subsidized EEC flour.

GATT's Capabilities Questioned

These and other strains (for example, U.S. dissatisfaction with Canada's tough restrictions on foreign investment) led many trade experts to fear that GATT could collapse under the barrage of trade complaints, dealing a severe blow to the international trading system and creating a 1930s-type depression. They pointed out that GATT, whose members accounted for 90 percent of non-communist trade, was being asked to do more than its structure could handle. Moreover, its very success in reducing import quotas and tariffs had led nations to turn to other methods to obtain trade advantages, such as production subsidies, restrictive quality standards and other barriers that were more difficult to identify and police. According to an Oct. 28, 1983, article in *The Christian Science Monitor*, a confidential GATT report estimated that $23.7 billion worth of trade was subjected to special curbs and restraints outside the purview of the GATT framework.

In addition, a number of experts questioned GATT's ability to settle today's complex trade disputes. Observers pointed to the essentially political nature of the issues and the deeply entrenched positions of the leading participants. The organization's large (and still growing in 1983) membership made it a rather unwieldy forum for hard negotiations. Moreover, GATT did not control the activities of public corporations (the government's share in certain major industries was substantial in many countries) or transfers within multinational corporations.

Faced with those challenges a number of experts called for revamping GATT's structure. "What's wrong with GATT is that the [free trade] consensus underlying the original compact no longer exists," said Hugh Corbet, the director of the London-based Trade Policy Research Centre, in 1982. Corbet suggested establishing a high-level international group to recommend possible changes.

Disappointing GATT Ministerial Meeting

It was in this atmosphere that, for the first time in nine years, the 88 members of GATT (the number of members had risen to 90 a year later) held a ministerial level meeting in Geneva on Nov. 24-29, 1982. Convened largely at the insistence of the United States, the meeting, attended by about 3,000 delegates, had an ambitious agenda: to further liberalize international trading rules, to impose on service sector exports (which include such industries as banking, insurance, telecommunications and engineering and design) the same regulations already applying to manufactured goods, to stem the wave of protectionist measures imposed by member governments, and to liberalize trade restrictions on agricultural products.

But the GATT ministerial meeting served principally to underscore the growing rift among the main trading blocs, especially between the United States and the EEC over agricultural policy.

Congressional members of the U.S. delegation came back disillusioned with the GATT and angry with the unwillingness of some major nations to work toward the elimination of trade barriers. The administration and congressional advocates of free trade originally had hoped they would be able to use a new GATT agreement to fight restrictive trade legislation pending in Congress. But the flimsy accord signed in Geneva did not dampen the surge of protectionism in the United States and abroad.

Highlights of the GATT meeting included:

• Agricultural Subsidies. The United States failed completely in its attempt to freeze and then gradually to roll back the heavy subsidies that the EEC was using to gain a growing share of the world's agricultural export markets. The Europeans, particularly France, were intransigent.

• Dispute Settlement. The United States' major victory at the conference — an agreement on the dispute settlement process — was a thin one. U.S. trade officials were anxious to improve the way in which disputes between nations were settled under the GATT structure. Existing procedures made obstruction easy, and allowed a nation that lost a dispute to simply veto a GATT finding.

The agreement did not eliminate that veto power, but it did commit members to avoid "obstruction" in the dispute settlement process. "We will see what that means in practice," said Brock.

• GATT Expansion. The U.S. delegation convinced the GATT conference to take a very preliminary look at the problems of trade in services. But it could obtain no agreement for a study of high-technology trade or of certain countries' trade-distorting investment regulations.

• Safeguards. The United States had hoped for an agreement to improve the "safeguard" measures nations would be allowed to take to protect domestic industry from severe damage caused by import competition.

The trade ministers failed to agree on an approach for negotiations between the industrial and developing nations to reduce tariff and nontariff barriers. They also failed to make any progress on counterfeit production of brand-name goods.

In their final declaration, the participants agreed only to "resist protectionist pressures" and to "refrain from taking or maintaining any measures inconsistent with GATT." The pressing issues of expanding GATT rules to include trade in services and liberalizing trade in agricultural goods were relegated to further study. While Brock, who led the U.S. delegation to the Geneva meeting, gave the conference a "grade of C" at its conclusion, he said in January 1983 that "given the economic atmosphere in which the ministerial took place, perhaps our most important achievement was in keeping the GATT system together and moving in a positive direction."

In spite of the unimpressive scorecard, participants in the talks insisted it was a step forward, if a small one, for the world trading system. "I think it is important to have realistic expectations about something like this," said Sen. John C. Danforth, R-Mo., chairman of the Finance Subcommittee on International Trade. "It is a conference that lasted only a few days. It involved . . . countries with widely different views trying to act by consensus in the depth of a depression."

The IMF and Third World Debt

Besides the problems that surfaced during the GATT meeting, international trade was suffering from major financial difficulties between the West and the developing nations. Sluggish growth in the industrialized nations depressed demand for the commodities produced by the less developed countries, whose lack of industrial infrastructure made them dependent upon the exports of raw materials such as iron ore, copper and bauxite. With the exception of the oil-exporting countries, the LDCs were faced with a staggering combined external debt of more than $600 billion in 1983, which they were unable to repay for lack of export-generated income. Unable to export commodities, the LDCs reduced their imports. For the United States, which directed a large share of its exports to third world nations, the effect of the debt crisis in these countries was a further deepening of its own trade deficit.

The developing countries, for their part, frequently accused GATT of being a "rich man's club." They argued that the global economic system was heavily weighted in favor of the West, which enjoyed a massive balance-of-trade surplus in manufactured products with the third world ($168 billion in 1980). In addition, Western nations imposed highly protectionist measures against the LDCs' most competitive products such as textiles and agricultural produce. For example, the LDCs were highly critical of the EEC's practice of applying "safeguards" against cheap imports that might hurt the Europeans' domestic industries. They also complained about the U.S. decision to impose a new (higher) tariff rate on products entering the United States from newly industrialized countries. In addition, the United States was insisting that the more advanced developing nations such as Brazil, India, and South Korea as well as Singapore, lower their import tariffs. But they responded that they could not be expected to do so in the face of massive debts.

One of the few areas of agreement between the United States and its industrialized trading partners was over the threat posed to international trade by the growing external debt of the less developed countries. In a striking policy reversal, the administration agreed in mid-January 1983 to support an increase in the special emergency fund that the International Monetary Fund (IMF) made available to borrowing nations to help repay their debts. While considerable opposition to increased funding came from the U.S. Congress because of members' concern about ballooning budget deficits, the move in favor of the additional funding by the Reagan administration, which had previously espoused the notion that third world development could best be handled by the "magic of the marketplace," was an indication of the heightened level of concern in official circles.

The United States was the largest contributor to the IMF, and a failure by Congress to approve the $8.4 billion U.S. share of the nearly $32 billion proposed increase in IMF funding would be a disastrous blow to the international institution. Throughout most of 1983, however, legislation implementing the increase had been held up in Congress. Reagan outlined the problem in stark terms during a Sept. 27 speech in Washington, D.C., at a meeting of finance ministers and central bankers from 146 nations. "If the Congress does not approve our participation, the inevitable consequence would be a withdrawal by other industrial countries from doing their share. At the end of this road could be a major disruption of the entire world trading and financial systems — an economic nightmare that could plague generations to come."

Congress finally responded, clearing authorization for the IMF contribution on Nov. 18, just before adjourning the session.

Reagan Policies and Protectionism

While President Reagan had to bend somewhat to protectionist pressures from voters and members of Congress, he remained basically committed to a free-trade policy. This was made clear in the economic report Reagan sent to Congress Feb. 2, 1983, in which he said he was "committed to a policy of preventing the enactment of protectionist measures in the United States." The president continued:

> While the United States may be forced to respond to the trade distorting practices of foreign governments through the use of strategic measures, such practices do not warrant indiscriminate protectionist actions, such as domestic content rules for automobiles

sold in the United States. Widespread protectionist policies would hurt American consumers by raising prices of the products they buy, and by removing some of the pressures for cost control and quality improvement that result from international competition. Moreover, protectionism at home could hurt the workers, farmers and firms in the United States that produce goods and services for export, since it would almost inevitably lead to increased protectionism by governments abroad.

Reagan's position did not quell calls for more specific measures aimed at protecting domestic industries and workers in need of help. To the administration's appeal for "free trade," spokesmen for ailing U.S. businesses and labor unions responded with calls for "fair trade." The AFL-CIO's 1983 platform contained an entire section on the trade issue, in which the "simplistic dialogue of 'free trade' vs. 'protectionism' " was condemned. Since other governments routinely intervened in the flow of trade, it stated, so, too, did "the United States [need] clear limits on certain imports until the nation's future is assured."

Labor and Domestic Content Legislation

The labor document went on to describe the AFL-CIO's chief trade priorities for the year: temporary restrictions on "harmful imports"; enactment of a "domestic content" law that would compel foreign automakers selling to American consumers to build up to 90 percent of each auto with U.S parts and labor or face import quotas; and to win assurances that a greater portion of U.S. raw materials would be processed domestically before exportation. "Reciprocity should have some teeth in it . . . ," stated AFL-CIO President Lane Kirkland in January 1983. "We ought to play by the same ground rules as our competitors and negotiate from that basis."

The UAW pressed for passage of a domestic content bill in 1983, despite the fact that the Japanese agreed to continue their voluntary restraints on auto exports to the United States. The House passed a domestic content bill in December 1982, but the Senate did not act on it. The bill was reintroduced in the 98th Congress and was again approved by the House, in November 1983. Once again, the Senate failed to act on the proposal.

Expressing the administration's opposition, Brock said, "This bill would raise the price of every car, cost jobs and start a trade war. It is the worst piece of economic legislation in a decade." Brock predicted "this bill will never become law." Indeed, with the domestic auto industry enjoying a recovery by the fall of 1983, support for the measure had eroded somewhat. And the bill's opponents, including farmers and exporters who feared they might be subjected to retaliation by foreign nations, increased their lobbying efforts against the measure. *(For further discussion of domestic content, see Chapter 6, p. 151.)*

'Reciprocity' and Other Protectionist Measures

The domestic content bill was just one of the measures considered by the 97th and 98th Congresses to protect U.S. industries from further import competition. One of the first to be enacted, on Oct. 1, 1982, was a bill designed to encourage creation of export trading companies, previously barred by antitrust laws, to facilitate small business exporting. More significant was a "reciprocity" bill, devised in large part by Missouri's Senator Danforth, that sought to impose trade restrictions on countries limiting access of U.S. exports to their markets. While neither this nor any other version of the reciprocity proposal was cleared by Congress in 1982, similar legislation was reintroduced in 1983. Such measures received a more favorable reception from former free-trade advocates, many of whom appeared to modify their position under pressure from constituents, especially those in districts hard hit by factory closings and rising unemployment. The Senate approved a reciprocity bill in April 1983, and in September the House Ways and Means Committee, formerly a bulwark of free trade in the House, approved a similar moderate reciprocity measure.

While Brock condemned the "dollar for dollar" interpretation of reciprocity espoused by some hard-line protectionists, the milder wording of the Danforth and Ways and Means initiatives, which strengthened the president's authority to negotiate trade agreements and to retaliate against unfair trading practices, was praised by Brock because it also respected the administration's definition of desirable trade policy as one creating "a global trading system in which benefits are mutually shared and concessions are mutually made."

As approved by the Ways and Means committee, the reciprocity bill expanded the president's authority to deny licenses to, or otherwise restrict, dealings with foreign service companies from nations that had barriers to U.S. services exports (banking, insurance, data processing, etc.). The bill also allowed the president to retaliate against nations that blocked trade-related foreign investment. And it authorized the Office of

Proposals for New Trade Department

The Reagan administration, with the backing of several influential members of Congress, in 1983 proposed consolidating all federal trade functions into an expanded Commerce Department, to be renamed either the Department of Trade and Commerce or the Department of International Trade and Industry. Eight different departments, offices and agencies have statutory roles in international trade. (The Commerce Department, for example, administers import and export controls, along with the State and Defense departments; the Treasury Department enforces them through the U.S. Customs Service; the Agriculture Department promotes U.S. farm exports; the International Trade Commission determines whether imports have injured U.S. industries; and the Office of the U.S. Trade Representative in the Executive Office of the President is responsible for negotiating bilateral and multilateral agreements.)

Plans for a new "lean and mean" trade department were promoted vigorously by Sen. William V. Roth Jr., R-Del., a member of the Senate Finance Committee's International Trade Subcommittee and the Senate Governmental Affairs Committee, and Commerce Secretary Malcolm Baldrige. Under Roth's bill, the new department would include the Office of the U.S. Trade Representative as well as much of the existing Department of Commerce. The secretary of the new department would be the president's principal adviser on international trade policy and would assume most of the responsibilities of the current secretary of commerce and the U.S. trade representative.

The Senate Governmental Affairs Committee approved the measure Oct. 4, 1983, but only after committee Democrats tacked on an amendment providing for creation of a council on industrial policy. A similar bill was introduced in the House by Rep. Don Bonker, D-Wash. Neither measure was passed in 1983, and their fate in 1984 was uncertain. *(For further discussion, see chapter on Industrial Policy.)*

Sen. John C. Danforth, R-Mo., chairman of the Finance Committee's Subcommittee on Trade, was a leading opponent of a new department. Praising the effectiveness of the existing institutional arrangement, he said the bill "would be a step backward in U.S. trade policy."

the U.S. Trade Representative to initiate investigations into potential unfair foreign trading practices on its own. The bill required the president to seek international negotiations to eliminate barriers to trade in services and high-technology products, as well as barriers to foreign direct investment. As noted on p. 16, the United States had pressed for this at the November 1982 GATT meeting but received a lukewarm response. (GATT has dealt primarily with barriers to trade in manufactured goods.) *(For further discussion on reciprocity, see Chapter 6, p. 160.)*

The 98th Congress also was considering other controversial trade issues, including the advisability of formulating an official federal industrial policy similar to Japan's export policy. Such a policy would involve short- and long-term overall economic planning, with the aim of improving the U.S. competitive position in world markets. Related to the industrial policy issue were proposals to consolidate U.S. trade policy making in a single new trade department. *(Trade department, box, p. 21; for further discussion of industrial policy, see Chapter 10.)*

The Export Administration Act, which expired Sept. 30, 1983 (but was kept alive by executive order), was the subject of lively debate both in Congress and in the administration. The law empowers the president to limit exports for foreign policy or national security reasons. The administration wanted to maintain and even strengthen the restrictions, but business interests pressed for a relaxation of the terms of the existing law and for a provision honoring the sanctity of existing contracts. They argued that excessive controls on high-technology items not only had eroded the U.S. export position but also were ineffectual, particularly when similar items were available from other nations. And the imposition of embargoes in the name of foreign policy considerations undermined the United States' reputation as a reliable supplier, critics of the controls contended. That the issues involved were extremely complex and controversial was evidenced by the fact that a divided Congress failed to agree on revisions to the existing law in 1983. *(Details, Chapter 9)*

Also up for renewal in 1983 was extension of lending authorization for the Export-Import Bank, which provides low-interest loans to foreign nations and companies purchasing U.S. goods. President Reagan, in his Jan. 25 State the Union message, reversed his previously stated intention to reduce the bank's lending authority and proposed instead to increase the overall ceiling on loans it could guarantee to foreign countries buying U.S. exports. *(See Chapter 8.)*

That reversal, as well as the administration's decision to subsidize

Trade Adjustment Aid Extended

A program to provide benefits to workers who have been laid off from industries harmed by import competition was extended for two years by Congress on Sept. 30, 1983, just hours before the program was set to expire.

The trade adjustment assistance program was started in 1962 and expanded under the Trade Act of 1974. In 1981 Congress extended the program through Sept. 30, 1983, but drastically curtailed eligibility for benefits. *(1962 act, p. 55; 1974 act, p. 82)*

The Reagan administration had wanted to end the program, but high levels of unemployment convinced a majority in both houses of Congress that the benefits should be continued. The House-passed version would have greatly expanded the program at an estimated cost of $217 million in fiscal 1984, but the Senate Finance Committee rejected the House changes and approved instead a simple two-year extension of the existing program, expected to cost $95 million in fiscal 1984. The House accepted the Senate's more modest version, clearing the bill.

wheat exports to Egypt and its position on reciprocity legislation, indicated that the White House's support for free trade had been tempered by growing trade deficits and other seemingly intractable international problems, not the least of which were restrictive trade practices on the part of other nations. Evidence of that change of heart was provided in the February 1983 report of the president's Council of Economic Advisers, long a supporter of free trade, which concluded, "even though costly to the U.S. economy in the short run [retaliation] may . . . be justified if it serves the *strategic* purpose of increasing the cost of [trade interventions] by foreign governments."

Lack of Consensus on Solutions

Although the voices being raised in Washington in favor of protectionism had the makings of a mighty chorus, it apparently was not a harmonious one. Purveyors of protectionism included a wide variety of industries and groups, but there was no single protectionist coalition.

The chorus remained a collection of soloists at the end of 1983. Each group pushed for its own particular relief measures, with little regard for the interests of others. As a result, the first session of the 98th Congress, which some had predicted would produce the largest crop of protectionist legislation since the 1930 Smoot-Hawley Act, did surprisingly little to impede international free trade.

To be sure, some new trade barriers were erected on steel, textiles and other products, and protectionists in Congress whittled away many trade benefits of Reagan's Caribbean Basin trade initiative and attached "Buy American" provisions to a number of bills. But far tougher measures could have been taken.

The failure of protectionist groups to join forces resulted in part from the nature of trade. Tariffs on one item frequently were the equivalent of a tax on another good that used that product. Getting conflicting groups to agree on a common set of trade restrictions was no easy task. Furthermore, the committee structure in Congress hindered the progress of any quota or tariff bill designed to meet the varying demands of those groups. "The same trade rules that apply to autos do not apply to textiles or machine tools," said United Auto Workers lobbyist Gene Casraiss. "As a result, you would wind up with a 200-page bill in five committees."

Such a massive bill could easily be blocked by dedicated free traders in Congress, who held important leadership positions and were particularly adept at combating legislation thought to impede world trade unduly. Furthermore, the number of free traders in Congress probably was larger than it seemed. Members sometimes introduced and publicly supported protectionist measures to curry favor with constituents, but many of them nevertheless remained philosophically opposed to trade restrictions and even worked against them behind the scenes. Former U.S. trade official Harald B. Malmgren called this phenomenon "Lyndon Johnson's iron law of trade: 'Be a free trader, but don't tell a soul because there are not votes in it.' "

Free trade, of course, was not entirely without a political constituency, particularly among farmers, multinational corporations and consumer groups. Nevertheless, if they worked in unison, the many interests seeking import protection probably would have little difficulty overwhelming their free-trade opposition.

Efforts were made in the early 1980s to create a coalition of groups interested in trade legislation. UAW President Douglas A. Fraser attempted in 1981 to convince representatives of various industry and labor groups to agree on common legislative goals. That effort, however, met with little success. In 1982 a group of industries — ranging from steel and textiles to color televisions and leather handbags — formed the Trade Reform Action Coalition to propose revisions in the trade laws. But "TRAC" was loosely organized around a single issue: reform of the existing import relief procedures. Getting agreement on that narrow issue was difficult enough, and members continued to disagree fervently on other trade matters.

Chrysler Chairman Lee A. Iacocca in 1983 led an attempt to form a broader coalition. He started a group called the U.S. Trade Policy Council, with members from steel, auto, textiles, aviation and other industries. In general terms their goal was to seek a "level playing field" — the rallying cry of those who believed that if foreign nations did not lower their trade barriers, the United States should reciprocate in kind.

The ironies and difficult choices in the free trade vs. protection debate were perhaps best summarized by Brock. "Everyone is against protectionism in the abstract," he said in an interview in the Nov. 13, 1983, *New York Times Magazine*. "That is easy. It is another matter to make the hard, courageous choices when it is your industry or your business that appears to be hurt by foreign competition."

Trade Politics and Future Policy

Ultimately, the success of protectionist measures in Congress depended on the mood of the public. With the 1984 election campaigns approaching, members in many districts would have to keep their eyes on their constituents' concern about import competition. In any case, the various debates on international trade were certain to influence the campaign for the 1984 presidential election, with Reagan's Democratic critics and potential opponents gearing up for battle over trade policy.

President Reagan also was challenged on trade policy by conservatives within his own party. Conservative commentator Kevin Phillips, in an article published Jan. 23, 1983, in *The Washington Post*, took the administration to task for failing to formulate a coherent trade policy.

Throughout 1984 it was likely that the issue of "protectionism" vs. "free trade" would continue to unfold in congressional debate. To a large extent, the outcome depended on the pace of economic recovery and the prospects for employment of American workers. Meanwhile, the growing trade deficit could continue to fuel protectionist fires even as the economy recovered.

While the predictability of economic trends has been spotty at best, economic forecasters in 1983 were almost unanimous in their assessment that the recession had "bottomed out" in the United States. But although domestic business activity picked up in 1983, the problems in export-dependent industries were likely to continue for some time, as countries that imported U.S. products continued to be plagued by high unemployment and slow growth. Because unemployment in the United States was expected to remain high, industries already hurt by imports likely would continue to experience difficulties and press for special concessions from Washington.

As debate continued in the United States, a number of trade experts were suggesting that Washington should begin to rethink its trade policy. One of them was Harvard Professor Reich, who suggested that the United States might learn from the practices of Japan, EEC nations and others. "To dismiss all ... interventions as lamentable 'distortions' is neither economically illuminating nor politically compelling," Reich wrote.

> Free trade is not an end in itself, but a means to a higher living standard for the world's people. Government interventions that make economic transitions smoother, more equitable, and more efficient can serve precisely this purpose.
>
> What is the proper end of U.S. trade policy? The issue no longer can be weighed on the familiar scales of free trade versus protection. Our failure to craft a national strategy for responding to the structural changes occurring in the world's economy confines us to a confused and contradictory trade policy. Our trading partners do not know what we want because we have failed to articulate it, or even to acknowledge the choices we face. By default, we are adopting a trade policy that preserves our old industrial base, and freezes structural change and progress in the United States and around the globe.

Reich cautioned, however, that the United States' freedom of action was limited by its size and influence. Accounting for more than one-fifth of global production and one-half of total exports, and with the dollar the medium of exchange for 80 percent of non-communist trade, any major change in U.S. trade practices would have a far-reaching economic and political impact on the rest of the world.

As the United States sought to refashion its trade policy in the

1980s, International Trade Commissioner Eckes offered this assessment in an Aug. 31, 1983, speech, "[I]mports will continue to challenge United States firms at home and abroad. No industry is immune. . . . [R]ising imports make it imperative for American industry and labor to become internationally competitive again. Only in this way can we maintain a viable manufacturing sector. We as a nation have not yet proven that we can meet that challenge."

Throughout the first two decades after World War II the United States led the movement to eliminate barriers to trade among the Western industrialized and developing nations.

Chapter 2

TRADE LIBERALIZATION, 1945-68

The removal of barriers to the free flow of international trade was a principal goal of American foreign policy throughout more than two decades following World War II. With little variation, Presidents Harry S Truman, Dwight D. Eisenhower, John F. Kennedy and Lyndon B. Johnson held that a liberal trade policy, no less than foreign aid, was an essential means to establish a more secure and prosperous world. Each was forced to do battle, however, with an array of protectionist interests whose pressures on Congress complemented a historic legislative view that tariffs were a domestic matter, not to be subordinated to foreign policy objectives.

From these encounters some important compromises ensued. Successive extensions of the basic legislative mandate to cut tariffs — the Trade Agreements Act of 1934 — were accompanied by increasingly restrictive provisos. Import quotas and other concessions to protectionism were granted to such politically influential interests as independent petroleum producers, lead and zinc miners and textile manufacturers. American agriculture, bound up in a web of government controls and subsidies, was largely exempted from the pressures of competitive imports, although this was to change by the 1970s. *(See chapter on agriculture trade.)*

But the main thrust of national trade policy — and the preponderance of economic advantage — continued to lie with liberalization throughout the era. Thanks in some measure to the reciprocal removal of restraints on trade, American exports of merchandise had climbed from $9.8 billion in 1945 to $25.1 billion by 1964; imports, over the same span, rose from $4.2 billion to $18.6 billion. More significantly, the initiative taken and maintained by the United States in trade liberalization — together with the financial aid extended to the nations of Western

Europe and Japan — enabled those countries to rebuild their war-shattered economies and achieve, by the late 1950s, a remarkable degree of economic strength and political stability in a world riven by East-West conflict.

Pressure for Freer Trade

By 1962, however, there were new and compelling reasons for the United States to champion the free flow of trade. Although exports and imports remained small in relation to a gross national product (GNP) of more than $500 billion, they occupied an increasingly important role in an economy beset by a slow rate of growth. Moreover, despite its substantial and continuing surplus of exports over imports, the United States was experiencing severe deficits in its total international accounts because of heavy expenditures abroad for military and other purposes. Of the several alternatives for bringing the payments' deficit under control, a rapid expansion of exports was in many ways the most desirable.

But the expansion of exports rested, in turn, upon the reversal of a new trend to protectionism abroad, as evidenced in the common tariff wall constructed by the six-member European Economic Community (EEC) in 1957, an event that may have encouraged the formation of other trade blocs. With a large economic stake in the freest possible access to world markets, in addition to the United States' overriding political interest in building a strong and interdependent free world, Congress in 1962 authorized President Kennedy to take a new initiative in behalf of trade liberalization. For all the concern voiced by and for those unable or unwilling to compete with the products of other nations, the Trade Expansion Act of 1962 reflected the majority view that freer trade was no longer a choice but a necessity for the United States.

By the late 1960s and early 1970s, however, that thinking had changed markedly. A report prepared in 1970 by the General Agreement on Tariffs and Trade (GATT), the principal instrument for negotiating multilateral trade agreements, concluded that protectionist influences were being felt throughout much of the world more strongly than at any time since the early 1930s.

In the United States, protectionism was a response to the growing tide of imports that exacerbated the woes of domestic industries already troubled by inflation. From an overall balance of trade surplus of $6.8 billion in 1964, the U.S. trade balance ledger recorded a postwar low surplus of $837 million in 1968.

Historical Development of Trade Policy

The surge of protectionism in world trade by the end of the 1960s called to mind the rise of mercantilism in Europe at the close of the Middle Ages. The doctrine of mercantilism held that each country's interest was to export to its utmost capacity and import as little as possible. Such a favorable trade balance would bring gold and silver into the country. It was the accepted wisdom of the day that a nation, or an individual, could prosper only at the expense of another. Swedish historian Eli F. Heckscher, in his study *Mercantilism* (1955), defined mercantilism as the philosophy and practice of state power.

That philosophy was well entrenched in the 17th century when Charles D'Avenant, the English mercantilist, wrote: "It is to the interest of all trading nations that their consumption should be little . . . and their own manufactures should be sold at the highest markets and sent abroad, since by what is consumed at home, one loseth only what another gets and the nation in general is not at all the richer, but all foreign consumption is a clear and net profit."

Adam Smith and Economic Liberalism

It was only in the late 18th century that mercantilism began to give way to economic liberalism. David Hume, the Scottish philosopher, was one of the first to attack the monetary concepts of the day, particularly the idea that a nation could prosper by selling but not buying abroad. Adam Smith, Hume's economist friend, showed that trade between countries was productive of itself. Smith's *Inquiry into the Nature and Causes of the Wealth of Nations*, published in 1776, became the foundation for the study of political economy. Smith's basic contention was that progress was best achieved by freedom of private initiative within the bounds of justice. The *Wealth of Nations* pointed out that a nation seeking to enrich itself by trade "is certainly most likely to do so when its neighbors are all rich, industrious and commercial nations."

Smith's theories converted most of the economists of his day, but it was not until midway through the 19th century that free trade was accepted as desirable and nations discarded policies actively designed to impoverish their neighbors. Prime Minister Robert Peel caused Parliament to repeal protective duties on food in 1846, making Britain the first free-trade country in the world. Under free trade, British exports flourished and Britain became the world's foremost industrial nation.

While the price of food was greatly reduced, the wages of the British working classes did not fall, as the classical economists had expected. Instead, they rose markedly because of the increased prosperity of the country.

U.S. Sectional Divisions on Tariffs

The United States had a mixed attitude toward trade policy in the early years of the republic. The Tariff Act of 1789 was the first legislative measure enacted by the new federal government. Protectionists have pointed to it as showing a disposition of the First Congress to adopt at once a policy of protectionism; free traders have pointed to it as showing a predilection for their own thinking. It has been suggested that both groups are right: The spirit of the act was protective, but, compared with subsequent legislation, duties imposed by the act were relatively mild.

A duality of thought persisted in America, then as now, about free trade. The colonies had chafed under Britain's Trade and Navigation Acts (1650-1767), which prohibited virtually all trade except with the mother country. Their defiance (symbolized by the Virginia Assembly's declaration in 1655 that freedom of trade would be maintained) was born in trade but spread to other areas of discord and finally flared into the American Revolution. Yet once independence was achieved, Yankee manufacturers demanded and got protective tariffs. By 1828, to their satisfaction, the so-called "tariff of abominations" established almost prohibitive duties on woolen and cotton goods — to the consternation of the South where growers of cotton, tobacco and rice feared it would kill their profitable sales to England.

For the next half-century, tariff rates seesawed as first one section and then the other gained influence in Congress. Some of the sectional bitterness that grew out of these tariff fights was considered a contributing cause of the Civil War.

Reversing Protectionism: The 1934 Trade Act

America's explosive industrial development after the Civil War, especially after 1890, was attributed by protectionists to the benefits of high tariffs and by those favoring low tariffs to the country's abundance of natural resources.

Democrats tried to remove tariff barriers and Republicans continued to raise them throughout the remainder of the 19th century. The Dingley Tariff of 1897 pushed rates to a new high — to an average of 57 percent — and expanded the list of dutiable items. As Treasury surpluses grew — customs accounted for half of all federal revenues until the end of the 19th century — sentiment developed for lower tariffs, and early in the new century both major political parties declared themselves in favor of revising the prohibitive rates set by the Tariff Act of 1897. The Payne-Aldrich Tariff of 1909 and its successor, the Underwood Tariff of 1913 (the latter enacted at the request of President Woodrow Wilson) reversed the trend, lowering the average rates from about 40 percent to 29 percent. But a new surge of protectionist sentiment drove the rates up again after World War I.

That round of tariff making started as an effort to give greater protection to depressed farm prices in the 1920s, but manufacturers succeeded in protecting many of their products as well. Tariff rates were again increased, first in 1922 and later under the Smoot-Hawley Act, named for Sen. Reed Smoot, R-Utah (1903-33), and Rep. Willis C. Hawley, R-Ore. (1907-33). Enacted in 1930 at the onset of the Great Depression, U.S. tariffs were set by Congress for the last time and raised to the highest level in American history. Tariffs on dutiable imports averaged 59 percent of value in 1932, a year in which total imports of $1.3 billion were at their lowest level since 1909, while exports of $1.6 billion barely exceeded those of 1905. Smoot-Hawley and the Depression had worldwide repercussions; restrictions on trade multiplied everywhere. Economic activity stagnated and by 1932 world trade had sunk to about one-third of the 1929 level.

Free Trade Expanded Under Roosevelt and Truman

To reverse this flight to economic isolationism, and more specifically to assist economic recovery at home by expanding American exports, the administration of Franklin D. Roosevelt proposed that Congress delegate some of its constitutional power to "regulate commerce with foreign nations" to the president by authorizing him to negotiate trade agreements with other nations. The administration sought to cut U.S. tariffs by as much as 50 percent in return for equivalent concessions from other governments. Prodded and persuaded by Secretary of State Cordell Hull, the Democratic-controlled 73rd Congress — over the nearly unanimous opposition of Republicans — made this grant of authority in the Trade Agreements Act of 1934 (also known as the Hull Act).

By 1939 the United States had negotiated more than a score of reciprocal trade agreements; exports had risen to $3.1 billion, imports to $2.3 billion. But with the start of World War II normal trade relations went out the window; military and other non-commercial criteria determined the flow of exports and imports. Six years later, much of Europe and the Far East lay in ruins while the United States, unscathed, emerged as the world's foremost economic as well as military power. Economic experts recognized that such an imbalance of resources was potentially disastrous to future world trade.

Large-scale financial assistance became the first order of business. But economic recovery could not proceed, in the U.S. view, without the early resumption of normal trading relationships. This would require, in turn, a concerted attack on trade barriers.

Extension and Revision of the Trade Act

A multilateral approach to trade policy was envisioned by the United States well before President Roosevelt, early in 1945, won new tariff-cutting authority from Congress in a three-year extension of the Trade Agreements Act. The measure, which had been extended in 1937, 1940 and 1943, was due to expire June 12, 1945. On March 26, shortly before his death, Roosevelt urged Congress to amend and extend the act as an "essential" tool of postwar policy that had been "tested and perfected by 10 years of notably successful experience."

Agreements had been signed with 28 countries. In the process, however, much of the president's original authority to reduce the rates of 1934 by as much as 50 percent had been exhausted. Thus, Roosevelt asked that "the 50 percent limit be brought up to date by an amendment that relates it to the rates of 1945 instead of 1934." For rates already reduced by the full 50 percent, the change permitted a total reduction amounting to 75 percent of the 1934 rate.

The president appealed for bipartisan support, saying "this is no longer a question on which Republicans and Democrats should divide," and that "we must all come to see that what is good for the United States is good for each of us." As in 1934 (and again in 1937 and 1940), however, Republicans argued for protection against "cheap" imports and opposed extension of the president's authority. Hearings before the House Ways and Means Committee, lasting four weeks, revealed a clash of economic interests over trade policy that was to be repeated, with little variation, throughout the first two decades following World War II. Spokesmen for the leading farm organizations, the CIO (Congress of

Industrial Organizations), the Chamber of Commerce and importers supported the bill; opponents included wool growers, watch makers, independent oil producers and manufacturers of glass, pottery and textiles. With Democrats in firm control, however, Congress passed the administration's bill extending the Trade Agreements Act for three years — to June 12, 1948 — and authorizing the president to modify, by not more than 50 percent, the rate of duty existing on any commodity on Jan. 1, 1945.

Truman Proposals for Tariff Cuts

With new tariff-cutting authority assured, the Truman administration moved simultaneously on two fronts to spur the liberalization of world trade. On Dec. 6, 1945, Washington announced its agreement to lend Britain $3.75 billion — a credit, the president said Jan. 14, 1946, that would enable the British "to avoid discriminatory trade arrangements of the type which destroyed freedom of trade during the 1930s."

Also on Dec. 6, the administration published its "Proposals for Consideration by an International Conference on Trade and Employment," to be held in mid-1946 under United Nations' auspices. The proposals called for the progressive reduction of tariffs, quotas and other restrictive devices through periodic multilateral negotiations, in which the concessions granted by one country would be extended to all ("most-favored-nation" treatment). An international trade organization would supervise the agreements.

The task of organizing the conference was turned over to a preparatory committee consisting of the United States and 18 other nations: Canada, Brazil, Chile and Cuba in the Western Hemisphere; Belgium, the Netherlands, Luxembourg, France, Britain, Norway, Czechoslovakia and the Soviet Union in Europe; and Australia, New Zealand, China, India, Lebanon and South Africa. The committee convened on Oct. 15, in London, when it began drafting a charter for the International Trade Organization (ITO) and agreed to sponsor a trade conference in Geneva the next April. The Soviets did not participate in the London meeting.

'Escape Clauses' and 'Peril Points'

Election of the Republican-controlled 80th Congress in 1946 encouraged protectionists to call for repeal of the Trade Agreements Act and postponement of the trade conference. But on Feb. 7, 1947, the

GATT's Role in World Trade . . .

The General Agreement on Tariffs and Trade (GATT), initially signed by 23 countries on Oct. 30, 1947, had, as of the end of 1983, 88 members that together accounted for 80 percent of world trade. In addition to these "contracting parties," many other countries complied informally with GATT regulations. The agreement contains rules on both tariff and nontariff barriers to trade among individual nations. These have been modified in seven successive rounds of negotiations aimed at reducing barriers on a reciprocal basis. The best known of these were the Kennedy Round (1964-67) and the Tokyo Round (1973-79), which resulted in an overall 39 percent reduction in tariffs on manufactured goods.

The main provisions of GATT rules can be summarized as follows:

● Member nations must confer "most-favored-nation" (MFN) status to all other members, allowing equal access to all on their domestic markets. This general rule had been a cornerstone of U.S. policy since 1923. Excepted were certain import tariff preferences of long standing, such as those of the British Commonwealth and between the United States and the Philippines.

● Once tariffs have been removed or reduced by negotiation, they must not be reimposed in the form of compensatory domestic taxes, as by

new chairmen of the Senate Foreign Relations and Finance committees, Arthur H. Vandenberg, R-Mich. (1928-51), and Eugene D. Millikin, R-Colo. (1941-57), issued a statement recommending that the conference proceed and that changes in the trade act be deferred until 1948. Meanwhile, they urged the president to take the following steps:

● Order the Tariff Commission to review all contemplated tariff concessions and recommend the points below which cuts could not be made without injury to the domestic economy ("peril points").

● Include an "escape clause" in all future trade agreements, to permit withdrawal of concessions found to imperil any domestic interest.

● Order the Tariff Commission to hold public hearings — on its own motion or on the request of the president, Congress, or any aggrieved party — to determine whether an escape clause should be invoked.

...Major Force in Cutting Tariffs

levying a higher excise tax on imported products than on the same domestic products.

● Where imports are shown to threaten domestic industries producing similar items, member nations may impose anti-dumping or countervailing duties to offset this damage. Similarly, an "escape clause" permits the suspension or modification of tariff concessions when a surge in imports threatens domestic industries. GATT rules do not, however, prohibit competing nations from retaliating against those invoking the escape clause if consultations do not produce compensatory action on the part of the nation invoking the clause.

● Import quotas are permitted only for agricultural or fishery products when necessary to protect domestic production-control programs and to avoid balance-of-payments crises.

GATT lacks power to enforce its rules because Congress refused to allow the U.S. government to participate in its proposed administrative bodies, which consequently never came into being. The 300-member GATT Secretariat, based in Geneva, provides a forum for the airing of disputes among contracting nations, allowing GATT to perform a mediating role in world trade.

President Truman, by executive order Feb. 25, substantially approved two of the recommendations — inclusion of an escape clause in all agreements (a commitment actually made in 1945) and investigation by the Tariff Commission of complaints of injury in the wake of tariff concessions. Vandenberg and Millikin called the order "a substantial advance," and although both Senate Finance and House Ways and Means committees launched trade hearings in March, no further action was taken in 1947. But the escape clause and peril points became the focus of controversy in 1948.

The General Agreement on Tariffs and Trade

In Geneva, meanwhile, the trade conference ended Oct. 30, 1947, with the signing of a General Agreement on Tariffs and Trade by the

United States and 22 other nations. Consisting of a code of trade practices, together with "schedules" of tariff concessions on more than 45,000 items accounting for more than one-half of world trade, GATT was a multilateral undertaking in behalf of lowered trade barriers, effectively replacing the bilateral agreements that had preceded it. Parallel negotiations on a draft charter for the proposed ITO were moved to Havana in November and concluded in 1948.

President Truman committed the United States to the General Agreement under the authority of the Trade Agreements Act, and GATT was never submitted to Congress, a fact that many legislators found distasteful and probably contributed to growing support for restrictive amendments to the act with each extension. Restrictions first were enacted in 1948 and continued through 1962, as an increasing number of Democrats from coal, oil and textile districts joined persistently protectionist Republicans in voting for restrictions.

Cuts in U.S. tariffs agreed to at Geneva took effect Jan. 1, 1948, adding to pressures for major revisions in the expiring Trade Agreements Act. President Truman asked Congress March 1 to extend the law for three years, linking it with the pending European Recovery Program (ERP) as "essential" to world economic recovery. But the bipartisan support given to ERP broke down on the trade issue, and the Republican majority, with one eye on the presidential election that November, insisted on a one-year extension and the addition of an amendment directing the Tariff Commission to establish the minimum rates necessary to protect domestic producers against imports of similar articles, in advance of tariff negotiations. While the president was authorized to offer concessions below those peril points, he was required to tell Congress why.

The Democratic Party platform of 1948 promised to "restore" the program "crippled by the Republican 80th Congress." President Truman, with his own eyes on the election, deferred until 1949 submitting to Congress the charter for the ITO signed at Havana on March 24, 1948, by the United States and 52 other countries.

Liberal Trade Policy Weakened

With Truman's election, and having gained control of the 81st Congress, Democrats set out to undo the work of the Republicans in revising the Trade Agreements Act in 1948. Action was spurred both by the act's impending lapse and by the approach of a second round of GATT negotiations at Annecy, France. Voting largely along party lines, Congress repealed the 1948 act (thus scrapping its peril point provisions) and extended the original act, as amended in 1945, for three years from the 1948 expiration date. But the 1949 debate reflected the intensity of protectionist sentiment among producers fearful of import competition. Congress took no action on the ITO charter, which had aroused strong opposition in the business community because it went beyond GATT in certain respects.

Although Democrats retained their majority in the 82nd Congress at the 1950 mid-term elections, Republicans enlisted enough Democratic defectors from the liberal trade policies of the Truman administration to enact several restrictive amendments in 1951. In extending the expiring Trade Agreements Act for two years, Congress reinstated the peril points procedures of 1948-49 and required Tariff Commission review of petitions for escape-clause relief, as had been proposed by Sens. Vandenberg and Millikin in 1947.

No major modifications in trade policy were proposed or enacted in the final year of the Truman administration.

U.S. Trade Policy in Eisenhower Years

President Eisenhower entered office in 1953 at a time of increasing concern, in Europe and the United States, over trade relations and the role of U.S. foreign aid. The new Republican administration, anxious to cut federal spending, welcomed the concept of "trade, not aid" put forward by British Chancellor of the Exchequer R. A. Butler in 1952. In his Feb. 2, 1953, State of the Union message Eisenhower asked the GOP-controlled 83rd Congress to renew the Trade Agreements Act and to simplify U.S. customs procedures. But while the president and Secretary of State John Foster Dulles saw the wisdom of enabling the British and others to earn more dollars in the American market, many congressional Republicans were reluctant to abandon their traditionally protectionist views.

Randall Commission Recommendations

In the end, Congress agreed to a one-year extension of the trade act, with some minor but restrictive amendments. The law also established a Commission on Foreign Economic Policy to recommend a long-range program. Congress approved a new International Wheat Agreement and a customs simplification bill, and, in extending the Defense Production

Numerous U.S. Trade Laws . . .

Protectionist measures generally are designed to shelter specific products from import competition. Legislative measures include aid to domestic industries hurt by sudden increases in imports (the "escape clause" in the 1934 Trade Agreements Act) and the establishment of "peril points" fixing the minimum rates necessary to protect domestic producers against imports of similar articles. Other measures include the following:

"Buy American." The Buy American Act of 1933 and its successive amendments gave preference to American bidders for federal business. It did not set the amount of preference American producers were to enjoy, but in practice foreign bidders had to submit prices 25 percent or more below American quotations to get orders. In December 1954 President Dwight D. Eisenhower issued an executive order that the government could buy abroad if the foreign bid was 6 percent or more below the U.S. bid. An exception up to 12 percent was made for domestic bidders in areas of high unemployment even if their bids were higher than the new standards. However, individual agencies, such as the Defense Department, might review proposed foreign purchases in high amounts and require them to be made in the United States, even if the differential was as high as 50 percent.

"Ship American" clauses governed some shipping of goods authorized by federal legislation.

Anti-Dumping. The Anti-Dumping Act of 1921 provided the mechanism under which domestic firms could bring complaints that foreign firms were selling their products in the United States at prices less than fair value, as determined by their domestic or third-country price schedules. Anti-dumping cases originated in the Treasury Department. If the Treasury found that a foreign exporter was dumping on the U.S.

Act, agreed to drop a controversial amendment enacted in 1951 that had placed import quotas on cheese.

On Aug. 14, 1953, Eisenhower named Clarence B. Randall, chairman of the board of Inland Steel Co., to head the Commission on Foreign Economic Policy. The Randall commission's report, filed Jan. 23, 1954, contained 36 dissents by individual members to its 60-odd

... Protect Domestic Firms

market, the case was sent to the Tariff Commission, which had to decide whether U.S. businesses were being injured and should be aided by assessing a penalty added to the price of the imports. In only a small percentage of the cases brought did the Tariff Commission make a finding of injury. In the late 1970s anti-dumping duties were applied against European steel imports. The 1979 trade bill speeded investigations under the anti-dumping law. *(1979 bill, p. 89)*

Countervailing Duties. Contained in the 1930 Tariff Act, countervailing duties are imposed on imports when the Treasury Department determines that foreign governments are offering "bounties or grants" to exporters, enabling them to sell their goods in the United States at reduced prices. Foreign assistance to exporters may be in the form of grants, loans, tax exemptions or rebates, government-financed export insurance or any of a wide variety of other direct and indirect subsidies.

Additional tariffs, or countervailing duties, are levied against the subsidized exports in the amount of the subsidy. However, the 1974 Trade Act authorized the president to waive such additional tariffs while negotiations were under way with foreign governments for the elimination of the subsidies, or when there were pressing foreign policy considerations at stake. The 1979 trade bill overhauled the law. Domestic industries for the first time were required to show they had been seriously injured by subsidized imports before an offsetting duty would be imposed.

Almost all governments — the United States included — offer subsidies to a variety of exports. There is disagreement among the world's trading nations, however, as to which subsidies are necessary or permissible, and which are properly subject to retaliatory action by trading partners.

recommendations but showed a solid majority in favor of a liberal trade policy.

The commission recommended a three-year extension of the Trade Agreements Act, plus authority to reduce existing tariff rates by 5 percent a year and to cut to 50 percent of value all rates in excess of that. Other major recommendations included further simplification of customs regulations and procedures, an amendment to the Buy American Act of 1933 to give the president greater discretion, repeal of statutes requiring that foreign aid shipments be transported in U.S. vessels, and renegotiation of a charter for an organization to supervise GATT. *(Buy American and other restrictive trade measures, box pp. 40-41)*

The commission rejected a proposal for federal assistance to communities, companies and workers injured by tariff changes, submitted by David J. McDonald, president of the United Steelworkers and a member of the commission. The "trade adjustment assistance" proposal later was incorporated in the 1962 Trade Expansion Act. *(See p. 52.)*

Despite a vigorous general dissent by two key members of the commission — Daniel A. Reed, R-N.Y. (1919-59), chairman of the House Ways and Means Committee, and Rep. Richard M. Simpson, R-Pa. (1937-60) — Eisenhower March 30, 1954, asked Congress for a three-year extension along the lines recommended by the commission. But on May 20, in a letter to Charles H. Percy, then chairman of Bell & Howell Co. (an Illinois Republican, Percy was elected to the Senate in 1967), Eisenhower indicated that he would be satisfied with a one-year extension, pending hearings on his proposals. Relieved of White House pressure in a recession year that also was an election year, Congress in 1954 complied readily with the postponement.

Gains and Losses in 1955

With Democrats in control of the 84th Congress, Eisenhower renewed his request for additional negotiating authority that had been put aside by congressional Republicans in 1954. In a Jan. 10, 1955, message, he asked for a three-year extension of the Trade Agreements Act with authority to reduce tariffs by 5 percent a year, or a total of 15 percent.

Following agreement March 21 in Geneva on changes in GATT trading rules and establishment of an Organization for Trade Cooperation (OTC) to administer GATT, the president April 14 asked Congress to approve U.S. membership in OTC but, like President Truman, did not submit the revised General Agreement for congressional action.

In the year that had elapsed since the Randall commission submitted its report, both supporters and opponents of a liberal trade policy had gathered strength. As hearings on the trade bill opened Jan. 17 before the House Ways and Means Committee, both sides launched major lobbying campaigns. The bill enacted five months later combined gains with losses for both camps. New tariff-cutting authority — the first to be added since 1945 — enabled the president to enter a fourth round of GATT tariff negotiations in Geneva, concluded in 1956. (A third round had taken place in Torquay, England, in 1950-51.) But several new restrictions written into the law by Congress gave it an increasingly protectionist flavor. Indeed, the 1955 extension of the act "marked a major turning point in the history of trade agreements legislation," wrote a group of economists at the American Enterprise Institute in Washington, D.C., in 1970. "The increasing emphasis on the avoidance of injury to domestic producing interests by the escape clause and peril-point provisions finally began to overshadow the emphasis on presidential authority to reduce tariffs."

Congress took no action in 1955 on the OTC request, and the administration bowed to protectionist pressures in other respects as well. For example, the president Aug. 19 ordered a 50 percent increase in the tariff on imported bicycles, as proposed by the Tariff Commission. Also in August the Defense Department rejected low bids by the English Electric Co. to supply generators for the Chief Joseph Dam in the Columbia River Basin, despite an executive order issued in December 1954 reducing to 6 to 10 percent (from 25 percent) the price differential required under the Buy American Act of 1933. And on Oct. 31, Arthur S. Flemming, head of defense mobilization efforts, told oil importers to cut their imports or face mandatory quotas.

Failure to Approve OTC Membership

President Eisenhower pressed in vain in 1956 for approval of U.S. membership in the proposed Organization for Trade Cooperation. Membership in OTC, he said Jan. 5, would "provide the most effective and expeditious means for removing discriminations and restrictions against American exports." Since OTC was "strictly an administrative entity," he said, it "cannot, of course, alter the control by Congress of the tariff, import and customs policies" of the nation.

But protectionists, who were convinced that Congress already had surrendered too much of its power to regulate tariffs, saw OTC as a devious project for gaining de facto endorsement of GATT, which never had been submitted to Congress, but had become the major vehicle for tariff reduction since 1947. Indeed, on June 7 the State Department announced that, at the conclusion of the fourth round of GATT negotiations, the United States had agreed to cut tariffs up to 15 percent on imports valued at $677 million annually, in return for concessions on $400 million worth of exports.

The Ways and Means Committee approved an OTC-membership bill after writing in several safeguards, but no further action was taken. Without the participation of the United States (which accounted for 20 percent of total GATT trade in 1956), the project collapsed. But Congress did complete action in 1956 on another customs simplification law and approved a new wheat agreement.

Eisenhower renewed his request for OTC membership in 1957, but the Democratic-controlled 85th Congress ignored it and turned down an administration proposal to aid lead and zinc mining companies with sliding scale import fees.

The major trade policy issue for both Congress and the administration in 1957 concerned the kind of bill that should be enacted upon expiration of the Trade Agreements Act in 1958. The case for a liberal trade policy received substantial support in testimony and studies gathered by a Ways and Means subcommittee headed by Rep. Hale Boggs, D-La. (1941-43, 1947-73).

International Economic Developments

Accompanying the expansion of U.S. trade after the war were some profound political as well as economic developments abroad whose net effect was to reinforce the case for liberalization in the late 1950s and early 1960s. Those developments, in the main, concerned the integration of Western Europe, the recovery of Japan, the problems of new and less developed countries (LDCs) and the role of trade in the worldwide struggle with the communist bloc.

Creation of the European Economic Community

The economic integration of Europe was an explicit objective of American policy as embodied in the European Recovery Program of 1948 and subsequent legislation. Soviet policy foreclosed the linking of Eastern to Western Europe, while Britain's ties with the Commonwealth limited her participation. But integration got under way in earnest when "the Six" — France, West Germany, Italy, Belgium, the Netherlands and Luxembourg — agreed in 1951 to set up the European Coal and Steel Community, creating a common continental market for those commodities by abolishing internal quotas and tariffs. In 1957 the Six went much further, agreeing in the Treaty of Rome, signed March 25, to do away with all restraints on trade among them and to replace their individual tariff structures with a common wall against imports from the rest of the world.

Britain, having refused to join the EEC, or Common Market, then persuaded Denmark, Norway, Sweden, Austria, Switzerland and Portugal to join her in a European Free Trade Association (EFTA), created Nov. 20, 1959, designed like the Common Market to eliminate trade barriers among the members but not to erect a common external tariff. By 1961, however, Britain concluded that EFTA could not compete with the EEC and applied for membership in the Common Market. In 1963 French President Charles de Gaulle vetoed British entry into the EEC, and it was not until Dec. 19, 1973, that Britain joined the original Six (as did Denmark and Ireland, followed by Greece in 1981). *(Further discussion, p. 51)*

For the United States, even these halting steps toward European integration raised serious problems of trade policy because a common external tariff around the large European market could place American exports (particularly of farm commodities) under a severe handicap.

To meet these potential threats, the departments of State and Commerce announced Dec. 9, 1958, that Congress would be asked to extend the Trade Agreements Act for five years and authorize the president to cut existing tariff rates by another 25 percent. Both the unprecedented term and the amount sought were justified as being needed to permit negotiations with the Common Market aimed, in major part, at preserving American access to the new community. The request, coming in the midst of the nation's third postwar recession, prompted Speaker Sam Rayburn, D-Texas (1913-61), to predict it would take "blood, sweat, and tears" to get the program through Congress in 1958.

Japan's Growing Economic Strength

Postwar policy toward Japan, designed to encourage the growth of democracy and of strong economic and political links with the West, was complicated by China's turn to communism in 1949 and extension of the Cold War to the Far East. Deficient in food and raw materials, Japan was heavily dependent on exports to finance economic recovery and growth; at the same time, her markets were restricted by political developments in the Far East and by extensive discrimination against Japanese goods in Europe and elsewhere. The United States, with its special concern for the strength and stability of Japan, encouraged the entry of more Japanese goods by its tariff reductions, and the United States became Japan's largest customer.

But rising Japanese exports of highly competitive manufactures to the United States generated strong protectionist pressures from American textile, electronic and other industries. To ward off restrictions, the Japanese in 1957 imposed quotas on certain textile exports to the United States. By 1961, however, rising textile imports from Hong Kong and other areas led the United States to seek an international agreement by textile-exporting countries to limit their exports in return for freer access to European and other restricted markets. Agreements negotiated in 1961 and 1962 did not represent a permanent solution to the problem, however, and the equalization of export opportunities for Japan in particular remained an urgent American objective.

Special Problems of Developing Nations

After World War II the predominantly agricultural less developed countries (LDCs) of Asia, Africa and Latin America experienced special difficulties in their trading relationships with the industrialized nations. Dependent in many cases on the export of one or two commodities (such as coffee, sugar or oil) for their foreign exchange, they suffered from the general failure of commodity prices to keep pace with those of manufactured goods. At the same time, the rise of nationalism, accompanied by the overthrow of colonial rule in Africa and Asia, accentuated the efforts of those areas to industrialize their economies. After 1953 the United States found itself in increasing competition with the communist bloc in responding to the trade and aid needs of the LDCs.

The formation of the EEC posed a special problem for Latin America in this respect, for the former colonial holdings of France and Belgium in Africa were to receive preferential treatment under the common external tariff, while the proposed addition of Britain held the prospect of a similar relationship with former British possessions. Potentially, therefore, Latin American exports of raw materials to Europe could suffer in much the same way as U.S. exports of manufactured goods. Yet the growth of Latin American exports was a major corollary of the "Alliance for Progress" development program launched by the Kennedy administration in 1961. As part of this, an international coffee agreement was negotiated in 1962 (though Congress did not approve implementation procedures until 1965). On the other side of the coin, however, Congress in 1964 ordered that quotas be imposed on beef imports, thus damaging some Alliance partners.

Impact on U.S. Trade

As noted at the beginning of the chapter, American exports more than doubled from 1945 to 1964 while imports quadrupled. Successive rounds of tariff reductions unquestionably contributed to these increases, although it was difficult to measure that impact precisely. Nor was it possible, except in some very specific instances, to measure the restraining influence of restrictions on trade imposed by the United States and other countries. In all probability, rising trade owed as much to the quick economic recovery of Western Europe and Japan (in which American assistance was a major factor) and the continuing economic prosperity of the United States as to any other influence. These developments were abetted, however, by the general relaxation of restraints on trade that occurred.

One indication of the declining level of U.S. tariff rates was the change in the ratio of duties to the value of dutiable imports. The ratio dropped from a high of 59 percent in 1932 to 36 percent in 1940, to 28 percent in 1945, to 13 percent in 1950, then to between 11 and 12 percent over the next decade. While these figures indicated that the bulk of tariff reduction took place prior to 1950, they also reflected the impact of inflation between 1940 and 1950 when prices rose on many imports subject to specific, or fixed, duties — for example, a duty of 2 cents per pound, whatever the value of the item. Most estimates have ascribed about one-half of the decline in the ratio of duties after 1945 to tariff reductions, the other half to inflation.

Another trend, accompanying the rise in U.S. imports after 1945, was the decline in the proportion of duty-free to total imports, from 67 percent in 1945 to 37 percent in 1963. In absolute terms, dutiable imports increased in value from $1.4 billion to $10.7 billion, duty-free imports from $2.7 billion to $6.3 billion. This reflected a relatively greater increase in demand over the period for dutiable commodities (such as most manufactured goods) than for duty-free items. For example, imports of finished manufactures rose in value from $832 million in 1945 to $6.4 billion in 1963, whereas imports of crude foodstuffs and animal products (85 percent duty-free) only increased from $693 million to $1.7 billion. Some of this discrepancy could be traced to a relatively greater rise in prices of manufactured goods, but tariff reductions also played an

International Monetary System 1945-71 . . .

The United States emerged from World War II as the dominant economic power in the world. Consequently the dollar assumed pre-eminence in monetary relations. Monetary authorities of the Western nations assigned it the central role in restructuring the international monetary system after the war.

Bretton Woods System. The postwar international monetary system was shaped by the representatives of 44 nations at a 1944 conference in Bretton Woods, N.H. The conference produced agreement to set up the International Monetary Fund (IMF) and a new system that was to foster stability without restoring an international gold standard (abolished in 1934) or impinging on national monetary and fiscal independence.

Going into operation in 1947, the IMF provided international drawing rights to help member nations overcome temporary exchange deficits. A member nation's right to draw on the fund was determined by its quota — its contribution to the fund. As a general rule, each nation contributed 25 percent of its quota in gold or U.S. dollars and the rest in its own currency.

Each IMF member was required to declare a par value of its currency in relation to the gold content of the U.S. dollar in 1944. Transactions between the fund and a member nation were based on the official par value; each member also pledged that transactions within its territory involving currencies of member nations would be allowed only at exchange rates not more than 1 percent above or below parity.

Thus, the IMF gave form to an international agreement setting fixed exchange rates in both government and private transactions. A member nation was allowed to propose a change in its currency's par value only as needed to correct a "fundamental disequilibrium" in its balance of payments.

Dollar's Role. As the currency most widely used in international transactions, the dollar provided a convenient base on which to set international exchange rates. The United States in 1949 pledged to maintain the international value of the dollar by buying and selling gold at the established price of $35 an ounce. Other countries agreed to maintain their currencies' IMF-agreed-upon values by buying or selling dollars on international exchange markets. In effect, the dollar's value was pegged to gold, and other currencies were pegged to the dollar. Under these arrangements, the dollar was used by other nations as an intervention currency and, along with gold, as a reserve for their own currencies.

... Growing U.S. Payments Crisis

In 1968 the IMF created Special Drawing Rights (SDRs) to supplement gold and dollars as currency reserves. Popularly, SDRs have been referred to as "paper gold."

U.S. Balance of Payments. The Bretton Woods system functioned well in the immediate postwar period but ran into difficulty as economic realities changed. Dependent on the dollar, the Bretton Woods arrangements were strained when the dollar's strength waned.

For two decades, the outflow of dollars had not been matched by dollars returning from abroad, prodding persistent deficits in the U.S. balance of payments. As other nations presented surplus dollars for redemption, the U.S. gold stock dwindled. In 1949 the U.S. gold supply totaled $23.4 billion. By 1971 it had fallen to $10.1 billion.

Volatile dollars held abroad contributed significantly to instability in the international monetary system. Beginning in the late 1950s the U.S. government adopted a variety of measures to control the balance-of-payments deficit. These included tying foreign aid to purchases of U.S. goods and services; sale of notes and bonds to foreign monetary authorities to absorb dollar balances; negotiated prepayment of foreign debts; voluntary and later mandatory controls in foreign investments abroad by U.S. corporations; and creation of a gold pool with the central banks of other industrial nations to intervene in the London gold market to keep the price of gold substantially equal to the official price.

Despite such measures, Congress twice during the Lyndon B. Johnson administration was called upon to respond to gold crises by enacting major changes in the U.S. monetary structure. In an action taken to free gold to meet claims for redemption of dollars from abroad, Congress in 1965 passed legislation eliminating a 1913 requirement that each Federal Reserve bank keep a reserve of gold certificates worth not less than 25 percent of its holdings in commercial bank deposits.

Congress was called on to meet another gold crisis in 1968 by freeing more of the gold supply from currency reserves by adopting legislation removing the remaining gold backing from the dollar.

The measures bought time, but the deficit grew. In 1971, despite slow recovery from a recession that should have reduced imports, the United States faced its first trade deficit since 1893 and a payments deficit of $4 billion to $5 billion. *(Monetary developments in the 1970s, p. 73)* important part.

American exports experienced a similar growth and change in composition in the postwar era. Exports of crude materials increased in value from $1.4 billion in 1946 to $2.6 billion in 1963; those of finished manufactures, however, rose from $5 billion to $13.3 billion. Foreign aid, increased purchasing power abroad, lower tariffs and some growth in American industry's interest in foreign markets contributed to the rise in exports.

Rising Balance-of-Payments Deficit

Despite a consistently favorable balance of trade (or surplus of exports over imports) after 1945, the United States began in 1949 to run a deficit in its overall balance of payments with other countries. This was because total expenditures abroad (covering payments for imports, costs of maintaining large military forces in Europe and other areas, dollars invested abroad by American business, foreign-aid dollars given or lent by the government to other countries and dollars spent by American tourists) exceeded total receipts from abroad (composed of payments for exports and services, returns on foreign investments, repayments of government loans and foreign long-term investments in the United States).

From 1949 through 1956, the U.S. payments deficit fluctuated but averaged about $1 billion a year, and was "balanced" by a commensurate increase in foreign holdings of dollars — the strongest reserve currency of the postwar period. By thus helping to bridge the "dollar gap" of the early 1950s, the United States contributed to its objective of strengthening the free world. U.S. exports in 1957 jumped by $2 billion, producing an actual surplus of payments. Exports slumped the next year, and other receipts fell while payments rose, resulting in a $3.5 billion deficit.

Unlike the earlier and smaller deficits, moreover, those of 1958 and later years were accompanied by a steady outflow of gold, as the increasing strength of other currencies persuaded foreigners to cash in their dollar claims for gold, readily available from the Treasury at $35 an ounce.

International economic policy took on new complexities in 1959, under the impact of major developments at home and abroad. Despite a substantial export surplus, the United States ran a total payments deficit of $3.8 billion in 1959. Much of this represented the transfer of dollar assets to Western Europe, whose economic resurgence was marked late in

1958 when most of the remaining restrictions on the convertibility of currencies were dropped. At the same time, the threat to U.S. exports implicit in the emergence of the Common Market was compounded by creation of the European Free Trade Association in 1959. This rival grouping raised the spectre of a trade war between the two blocs that could shut out American exports to Europe. *(See above, p. 45.)*

Membership in OECD

The administration continued in 1960 to seek means of redressing the payments deficit and expanding the market for U.S. exports. At a special meeting of the 18-nation Organization for European Economic Cooperation (OEEC) in January, Under Secretary of State Douglas Dillon proposed that OEEC be reorganized and expanded to include the United States and Canada, as a forum for coordinating the trade, aid and general economic policies of the Atlantic Community. Dillon's proposal led to a treaty creating the Organization for Economic Cooperation and Development (OECD), signed in December and ratified by the United States in 1961. Although the organization was a consultative body whose decisions would not be binding on any member, protectionists objected, nevertheless, that OECD made further inroads on the power of Congress to regulate trade.

Meanwhile, President Eisenhower March 17, 1960, sent Congress a special message on the need to expand exports. Noting that "world markets have recently become highly competitive," he announced a series of executive actions to promote increased exports. Following hearings on the president's program (which called for additional appropriations but no new legislative authority), the Senate Commerce Committee May 27 reported a bill authorizing $5 million to set up an Office of International Travel to encourage tourists from abroad to visit the United States. The Senate passed the bill, but the House took no action.

With no visible improvement in the payments deficit in 1960, the president Nov. 16 ordered a series of actions designed to reduce spending overseas by about $1 billion a year. Most controversial was an order to reduce the number of U.S. military dependents abroad from 484,000 to 200,000. In a mission to Bonn Nov. 23, Treasury Secretary Robert B. Anderson asked West Germany to contribute $600 million in 1961 to the cost of maintaining American troops there. The government of Chancellor Konrad Adenauer refused, but agreed to increase its contributions to foreign aid and Western defense efforts.

By the end of 1960, a year in which the United States ran another payments deficit of $3.8 billion, the cumulative three-year deficit of $11.1 billion had resulted in an increase of $6.4 billion in foreign dollar holdings and a transfer abroad of $4.7 billion in gold, reducing the U.S. gold reserve to $17.5 billion. To cut the deficit without reducing U.S. commitments abroad, the newly elected Democratic president, John F. Kennedy, Feb. 6, 1961, sent Congress an 18-point program of legislative and administrative actions. Congress was asked — and subsequently agreed — to approve U.S. membership in OECD, to cut the duty-free allowance for returning American tourists and to set up a program to encourage foreigners to travel in the United States.

1962 Trade Expansion Act and Kennedy Round

Like his predecessor, Kennedy emphasized the need to expand exports and to reduce remaining barriers to world trade. The tariff cuts authorized by Congress in 1958 were the subject of negotiations that began in September 1960 and continued through 1961, first with the Common Market, then with all GATT signatories. Results of the so-called "Dillon Round" of GATT negotiations were announced March 7, 1961. Using the authority of the 1958 law, U.S. negotiators had agreed to cuts averaging 20 percent in tariffs on a wide range of industrial and manufactured goods, in return for comparable concessions by others. Collectively, the items involved accounted for $4.3 billion in U.S. exports and $2.9 billion in U.S. imports in 1960. The White House announcement disclosed that U.S. negotiators, finding themselves "grievously short of bargaining power," had been authorized by the president to cut tariffs below the "peril point" on 61 items accounting for $76 million worth of imports in 1958.

Faced with the problem of winning a new authorization in 1962, when the Trade Agreements Act again would expire, the president set out to placate the strongly protectionist textile industry with a program of assistance, announced May 2, 1961. A principal result of this program was a one-year agreement by 17 nations, signed July 26, designed to redirect from the United States to Western Europe some of the flow of cotton textile exports coming from Japan, Hong Kong and other areas. On Nov. 21 the president asked the Tariff Commission to consider placing a fee on the cotton content of textile imports equal to the export subsidy on raw cotton, on grounds that imports were interfering with the domestic price support program.

Kennedy Seeks New Tariff-Cutting Authority

Some members of the administration advised the president to ask for a simple one-year extension of the 1958 act and to put off until 1963, after the mid-term election, a request for enlarged authority, as Eisenhower had done in 1954. But Kennedy concluded that the momentum of developments in the EEC precluded delay in reformulating U.S. trade policy. "The hour of decision has arrived," he told the National Association of Manufacturers Dec. 6, 1961. "We cannot afford to 'wait and see what happens' while the tide of events sweeps over and beyond us." In a special message Jan. 25, 1962, he asked Congress for unprecedented authority to negotiate with the Common Market for reciprocal tariff concessions. With the help of strong bipartisan support in the business community and concessions to potentially obstructive interests, Kennedy finally got substantially all that he wanted in the Trade Expansion Act of 1962.

In justifying his request, the president cited the problems raised by the emergence of the EEC, the U.S. payments deficit, the lag in economic growth, the communist trade offensive and the needs of Japan and the less developed nations. For American export interests, however, it was clearly the hope of retaining access to the large and growing European market that mattered.

Of $21 billion worth of U.S. exports realized in 1961, $6.4 billion or almost one-third went to Europe, of which $4.7 billion went to Britain and the six Common Market countries. Not only was continuing access to this market of great importance to U.S. commercial interests and to the goal of export expansion as a means of reducing the payments deficit. The Kennedy administration also was vitally interested in strengthening the concept of the Atlantic Community at a time when France, under the direction of President Charles de Gaulle, was actively seeking to capture the leadership of a continental Europe at the expense of American and British influence. So a key element of the president's trade proposals was a provision designed to encourage Britain's entry into the Common Market and to facilitate negotiations with the enlarged EEC.

Major Features of the Proposal

Kennedy asked for special authority to reduce or even eliminate tariffs on imports in cases where the United States and the EEC together accounted for 80 percent or more of total free world trade. This formula would have applied to aircraft only, as matters stood, but to 25 other categories of goods as well if Britain were to join the EEC. In addition to this "dominant supplier authority," the president requested power to cut tariffs generally by up to 50 percent over five years, cut or eliminate tariffs on agricultural products not meeting the 80 percent rule if necessary to maintain or expand U.S. farm exports and eliminate tariffs of 5 percent or less.

In return for such enlarged authority, Kennedy pledged that "ample safeguards against injury to American industry and agriculture will be retained." The administration's trade bill included provisions for "peril point," "escape clause," and "national security" procedures, although revised to make proof of injury more difficult, and for raising tariffs up to 50 percent above the 1934 rates as a measure of "extraordinary relief." But major emphasis was placed on using a new program of "trade adjustment assistance" to accord relief, rather than the traditional and self-defeating methods of raising tariffs or imposing quotas.

The trade adjustment concept had been proposed to the Randall commission in 1954 and was favored by the AFL-CIO as a more constructive way of meeting the injury issue. It encompassed readjustment allowances, retraining and relocation assistance for workers and technical aid, tax benefits and loans or loan guarantees for business firms certified by the Tariff Commission as having been injured by tariff cuts.

Passage, Provisions of the Trade Expansion Act

Hearings on the trade bill were held March 12-April 11, 1962, by the House Ways and Means Committee; 245 witnesses appeared, producing 4,233 pages of testimony in six volumes. As the committee began closed sessions to draft the legislation, the administration continued to stress publicly that the bill was "the most important piece of legislation before the country this year." On June 12 the committee reported a measure that left intact the basic elements of the administration proposals, and the bill was passed by the House June 28. The Senate passed its version Sept. 19.

House-Senate conferees on the measure agreed to the House provisions suspending most-favored-nation treatment for Poland and Yugoslavia, despite administration pleas to the contrary. The final version of the extension was agreed to Oct. 4 by the House, 256-91, and by the Senate by voice vote. Signing the bill one week later, Kennedy hailed it as the most important initiative in foreign economic policy "since the passage of the Marshall Plan" of massive postwar aid to rebuild Western Europe.

Escape Clause Provision of the Trade Act

The 1947 General Agreement on Tariffs and Trade (GATT), although binding the signatories to the concept of trade liberalization, nevertheless contained many loopholes, including an "escape clause" inserted at U.S. insistence and permitting a country to withdraw concessions in the face of threatened injury from imports.

Under Republican pressure, Democratic President Harry S Truman in 1947 had agreed to include an escape clause in all future trade agreements and directed the Tariff Commission to investigate complaints of injury arising from U.S. concessions. But in 1951 Congress put a legislative stamp on the escape clause by amending the 1934 Trade Agreements Act to require the commission to look into any case of alleged "serious injury" caused by tariff concessions and to recommend withdrawal or modification of the concessions. The president could reject its recommendations but was required to tell Congress his reasons for doing so.

Originally, the commission was given 12 months to complete an escape clause investigation. This was reduced to nine months in 1953, then to six months in 1958. Also in 1953 Congress directed that, in the event of a tie vote of the six-member commission, both sets of recommendations be sent to the president. Then, in 1955, the commission was required to consider complaints of a segment of an industry and to recommend relief if satisfied that imports "contributed substantially toward causing or threatening serious injury" to domestic producers.

In 1958 Congress reacted to long frustration over the president's rejection of numerous commission recommendations by providing for a congressional veto in such instances by a two-thirds majority of both houses. President John F. Kennedy in 1962 asked Congress to scrap most of the escape clause procedures, including the veto. Congress wrote most of the old procedures, including the veto, into the Trade Expansion Act. however, although criteria for tariff relief were tightened. (The legislative veto was struck down by the Supreme Court's June 23, 1983, ruling that such provisions were unconstitutional.)

The 1962 act, as requested, also contained an alternative to tariff relief — the new concept of "trade adjustment assistance" under which injured American industries might be helped through loans and other adjustment assistance, rather than through higher tariffs.

Major provisions of the Trade Expansion Act of 1962 (PL 88-794):

● Authorized the president, in the conduct of trade negotiations between July 1, 1962, and June 30, 1967, to reduce duties by 50 percent of the 1962 levels; to remove duties on entire categories of goods when the United States and members of the EEC (at the time of negotiations) together accounted for 80 percent or more of total free world trade; to cut or remove tariffs on agricultural products not meeting the 80 percent rule if necessary to maintain or expand U.S. farm exports; and to eliminate tariffs on products currently dutiable at a rate of 5 percent or less.

● Authorized the president to withdraw concessions to any country maintaining "unreasonable" restrictions against U.S. exports; to impose duties or other restrictions on imports from countries with burdensome restrictions against U.S. agricultural exports; to restrict imports if they threatened national security; and directed him to suspend "as soon as practicable" any trade benefits granted since 1930 under most-favored-nation treatment to "any country or area dominated or controlled by communism" (meaning in effect Poland and Yugoslavia). (Kennedy withheld action to implement this and got Congress to repeal it in 1963.)

● Required the president to submit to the Tariff Commission a list of articles on which he planned to negotiate, the commission to hold hearings and to advise him on the probable economic effect, internationally and domestically, of any tariff cut; to appoint a special representative for trade negotiations as the chief U.S. spokesman in trade talks; and to establish a Cabinet-level Interagency Trade Organization.

● Authorized the president — in case of injury to domestic workers or businesses through earlier or subsequent tariff cuts — to raise tariffs, negotiate an international quota system, provide federal assistance to those injured, or take any of these steps in combination, following investigation and a finding of injury by the Tariff Commission; and authorized aid to firms in the form of technical assistance, loans, loan guarantees or permission to carry back a net operating loss for tax purposes for five years instead of the usual three, and to workers in the form of unemployment compensation, counseling and retraining, travel and relocation allowances.

New Developments Raise Problems

For all the great store the Kennedy administration put in the Trade Expansion Act as a means to strengthen the U.S. bargaining position in

Europe, developments abroad robbed the law of any immediate significance. Barely three months after its enactment, President de Gaulle personally vetoed Britain's application for Common Market membership. He also rejected participation in a multilateral nuclear force proposed by the United States and made clear his continuing opposition to an Anglo-Saxon role in Europe. Preparations went forward for another round of tariff bargaining under GATT, but de Gaulle's veto was a severe setback for the U.S. trade initiative of 1962.

Actual tariff negotiations with the EEC and other GATT members finally got under way in May 1964, but the year ended without a resolution of the most controversial issues; the United States still faced major hurdles to its goal of freer access to the Common Market.

Meanwhile, the trade policies of both the United States and the EEC as well as the other industrialized nations came under concerted attack from the developing nations. Although politically independent, most of them remained at a disadvantage in trade with the developed nations and wanted new rules to ease their plight.

Pressing their case in the United Nations, the LDCs won agreement to a United Nations Conference on Trade and Development, which opened in Geneva March 23 with 119 nations represented. It closed June 16 with agreement to create a 55-member U.N. Trade and Development Board to recommend means of assisting developing nations through trade concessions, commodity agreements and financial aid. The same day, however, 75 of these countries declared themselves a "third force" and pledged to seek a "new and just economic order" that was bound to bring them into continuing conflict with the "have" nations of the world.

Results of the Kennedy Round

The celebrated "Kennedy Round" of negotiations under GATT was concluded in 1967. Specific accomplishments included a reduction of tariffs on industrial products, a joint undertaking to supply 4.5 million tons of wheat per year as food aid to developing nations and the drafting of an international code to help standardize anti-dumping practices. "The negotiation, in short, was an event of major importance in post-World War II efforts to lower barriers to trade and promote closer economic cooperation among nations," wrote Ernest H. Preeg, author of *Traders and Diplomats* (1970). Under the agreement, 53 nations accounting for 80 percent of world trade agreed to tariff cuts averaging 35 percent. More than $40 billion of trade was subject to some form of concession by participating nations. The agreement also established the procedure of across-the-board, or linear, tariff cuts and made the first serious, though largely unsuccessful, attempt to reduce nontariff barriers to trade.

Negotiations on farm products also were largely unsuccessful. France and West Germany wanted to protect their small farmers from an influx of cheaper American food commodities, especially wheat. Moreover, a dispute between France and West Germany on the price of wheat sold within the Common Market countries threatened to wreck the trading bloc and divided the member countries in the Kennedy Round talks.

Rising Protectionist Sentiment

As had been expected, many American industries reacted with horror to the prospect of increased competition from foreign goods and, accordingly, began a vigorous campaign in Congress to enact protectionist bills. The most active groups included textiles, oil, steel and chemicals. This drive in 1967 and 1968 was successfully blocked by the Johnson administration through lobbying and through the president's threat to veto any such bill that was passed. On the other hand, the president did not win congressional approval of a prime request he made — dealing with tariffs on chemicals — that grew out of the Kennedy Round agreements. He also failed to have his tariff-cutting authority, granted under the 1962 Trade Act, extended to permit even further agreements with other nations on expanding trade.

U.S. participation in the International Antidumping Code, which was negotiated as part of the Kennedy Round, was challenged in Congress. Opponents of participation said that domestic industries would find it impossible to obtain relief against foreign dumping under provisions of a 1921 law. That law was designed to prevent injury to American industry from unfair pricing practices involving goods produced abroad and sold in the United States at prices lower than those charged in the producer's country. Relief under the 1921 law involved special tariffs on the imported goods. The Senate in 1968 adopted a rider to an unrelated bill to block U.S. participation in the international code. The administration opposed the move, and a compromise was agreed upon providing that the 1921 law would have supremacy in any case where it and the code were in conflict.

In his book, *The Kennedy Round in American Trade Policy* (1971), John W. Evans, a member of the U.S. negotiating team, noted that "The euphoria generated by the successful conclusion of the Kennedy Round in the summer of 1967 was short lived, and it was soon replaced by serious doubts that the agreement could withstand the forces being mobilized against it." Although the United States, the EEC and EFTA put their tariff reductions into effect on schedule, a number of events threatened to jeopardize the multilateral trade agreements. Foremost among these was a growing international monetary crisis facing the dollar in particular but also sterling (Britain was forced to devalue the pound in late 1967) and the franc. Protectionist sentiment in the United States began to rise, evidenced by the dozens of bills introduced in Congress in 1967-68 to impose import quotas to protect specific products (such as steel, textiles, mink pelts and strawberries) or institute broader, across-the-board protective measures.

By the late 1970s U.S. automakers were facing vigorous competition from foreign automakers, who made substantial inroads into the U.S. market.

Chapter 3

COMPETITION AND PROTECTION IN THE 1970s

By the late 1960s and early 1970s competition for world markets was on the rise. But by this time the winds of free trade after 35 years appeared to be blowing out. The leading international trade organization, the General Agreement on Tariffs and Trade (GATT), reported in mid-1970 that protectionist influences were being felt throughout much of the world more strongly than at any time since the early 1930s. Protectionism arose especially in the United States as a growing tide of imports contributed to the woes of domestic industries already hurt by inflation and as the government became increasingly concerned about the nation's general imbalance of international payments. *(GATT background, p. 36)*

The threat of protectionist action in Congress brought on talk of retaliation from abroad against American exports. The possibility of a trade war involving the United States, Japan and the European Economic Community (EEC, or Common Market) hung over congressional consideration of a bill to impose quotas on foreign-made textiles and shoes. A quota on textiles would hurt Japan primarily, and a quota on shoes would hurt several European countries, Italy especially. The implications of a trade war involving America, Japan and the Common Market were enormous. They dominated world markets, together accounting for one-half of all exports by non-communist countries.

Despite yearly gains in the volume and value of its exports, the U.S. share of world trade had been in persistent decline. By 1969 the EEC (then consisting of six members) was exporting twice as much as the United States — some $76 billion in comparison to $38 billion. (The original Common Market members were France, West Germany, Italy, Belgium, the Netherlands and Luxembourg; Britain, Denmark and Ireland joined in January 1973 and Greece became a member in January 1981.)

America's ability to compete in international markets had an obvious effect on its balance of trade and, therefore, on the U.S. balance of payments — the difference between total dollar income and outgo. Although U.S. exports had increased, imports had grown faster. A cooling off of the American economy would hold down the rise in imports, the First National City Bank of New York said in its *Monthly Economic Letter* of April 1970, "but the damage inflicted by inflation to the competitiveness of U.S. products in both foreign and domestic markets will not be easily remedied." Foreign industrial productivity was developing rapidly, the bank publication noted, and stood ready to challenge the American dominance in sales of technologically advanced products.

The few increases in American exports had been due largely to sales of "big ticket" items — computers, jet aircraft and precision control instruments. But U.S. manufacturers were finding it increasingly advantageous to establish subsidiaries in foreign countries to circumvent national tariff walls. This activity not only removed exports from the U.S. trade balance ledger but often resulted in additional imports to the United States.

U.S. Complaints Against Major Trading Partners

Writing in the August 1970 issue, Lawrence A. Mayer of *Fortune* magazine commented, "The U.S., to be sure, has grievances: Japanese restrictions on imports and on investments from abroad, Common Market agricultural policies that have cut sales of U.S. farm products to Europe, and the preferential trade agreements between the Common Market and countries in the Middle East and Africa. . . . But to turn to a system of quotas as a remedy for U.S. trade troubles," he added, "would probably mark the end of the successful and generous crusade for free trade that the U.S. has led for thirty-five years." More than that, "it would invite retaliation from other nations and perhaps set off trade wars."

Nonetheless, the conviction was growing in Washington that both Japan and the Common Market had to allow U.S. products to compete more readily in their countries. As assistant secretary of commerce, Kenneth N. Davis Jr. voiced that thought in a speech in March 1970 before the Electronic Industries Association. "For the benefit of all the world's trade," he said, "it is time for Japan and Europe to respond more fairly than heretofore to 20 years of U.S. leadership in expansionist world trade policies." His views were more extreme — or outspoken — than those of many others in the administration. Davis resigned his post three months later after charging publicly that President Richard Nixon had been misled by those of his advisers who opposed protectionist legislation.

The EEC, Trade Barriers and Preferences

Political and economic unification of Europe and the economic recovery of a democratic Japan had been among the goals of American foreign policy ever since the end of World War II. When Congress authorized the Marshall Plan to promote European recovery, it declared that the "policy of the people of the United States [is] to encourage the unification of Europe." Paul G. Hoffmann, first head of the European Cooperation Administration, repeatedly urged the countries receiving Marshall Plan aid to integrate their economies into a single, large market free of all internal trade barriers. As commander of the North Atlantic Treaty Organization (NATO), Gen. Dwight D. Eisenhower declared in London on July 3, 1951, that "Europe cannot obtain the towering material stature possible to its people's skills and spirit so long as it is divided by patchwork territorial fences." Later, as president, Eisenhower gave full backing to the 1957 Treaty of Rome establishing the EEC.

President John F. Kennedy likewise spoke of a strong, united Europe. At an Independence Day address in Philadelphia in 1962, Kennedy said, "We do not regard a strong and united Europe as a rival but a partner ... capable of playing a greater role in the common defense, of responding more generously to the needs of poorer nations, of joining with the United States and others in lowering trade barriers, resolving problems of commerce and commodities and currency and developing coordinated policies in all economic and diplomatic areas."

President Nixon in his Feb. 25, 1971, State of the World message affirmed that America's policy of supporting the expansion of the EEC had not changed. "We welcome cohesion in Europe because it makes Europe a sturdier pillar of the structure of peace," he said.

Apprehension Over EEC Policies. But fears began to grow in Washington that a unified Europe might become an inward-looking rival. Some Americans by 1971 were contending that the Common Market was reverting to economic nationalism. They charged the EEC was erecting trade barriers against U.S. products and was luring other nations into special arrangements that discriminated against U.S. products.

Trade officials in Washington looked upon the EEC's preferential trade agreements with other nations as a violation of the spirit, if not the letter, of the 1947 GATT agreement, which held that the principles of free trade should be extended to all member countries. Sen. Hubert H. Humphrey, Jr., D-Minn. (1949-64, 1971-78), the Democratic presidential candidate in 1968, addressed this issue in a July 30, 1971, speech at the Trade Policy Research Center in London. He accused the EEC of "taking a series of steps which add up to a shift from multilateral trade . . . to regional and bilateral special arrangements and the formation of a preferential trading bloc."

European Resentments. Europeans, on the other hand, tended to regard the United States as a superpower trying to dominate them economically. There was growing resentment, particularly in France, at the way gigantic U.S. corporations used the dollar to gain control of European industries. At the same time, members of the European Community contended that the United States had erected barriers to protect its own industries whenever foreign competition appeared on its home markets. Europeans pointed out that while the EEC had eliminated 11 quotas on imported goods between 1963 and 1971, the United States had added 60 during the same period. It also was recalled that during the GATT multilateral trade negotiations in 1960, the Common Market offered to reduce its tariffs by 20 percent. Those reductions were made despite the fact that the U.S. negotiators did not have the legislative authority to reciprocate.

Ralf Dahrendorf, the EEC commissioner responsible for foreign trade matters, contended in the spring 1971 issue of *The Atlantic Community Quarterly* that the Common Market supported "the rules of free international trade out of conviction, not just necessity." Dahrendorf added, "We do not want a trade war, for we have other instruments to settle our differences." Dahrendorf was outspoken in his criticism of the 10 percent surcharge on U.S. imports that President Nixon imposed Aug. 15, 1971, as part of his economic plan to stop inflation, speed recovery from the 1970 recession, reduce unemployment, bring American foreign trade back into balance and force revaluation of several foreign currencies in relation to the dollar. *(See below, p. 75.)*

Conflict With Japan Over Reciprocity and Quotas

Quotas were one of the major trade issues confronting the United States and Japan during the Nixon administration (1969-74). Unlike tariffs, quotas limit the amount of goods allowed to enter a country. Except in special circumstances, they are contrary to the international trading rules established by GATT in 1947, but many countries, including the United States and Japan, set quotas on some imports.

By 1970 Japan had become America's second largest trading partner, after Canada, and one of its chief competitors in Asia. And while Japan's share of the American market was growing, U.S. exporters found it difficult to get their products through Japan's trade barriers.

"How pleasant it is to dream that 100 million Japanese consumers are standing on the piers of Yokohama and waiting for our shiploads of goods to sail into harbor," wrote Robert J. Ballon, an American at Sophia University in Tokyo, in the June 1970 issue of *Business Horizons*. "The reality, from the Western point of view, is far less agreeable; too many consumers are standing on the piers of Hamburg, London and New York waiting for ships laden with Japanese goods."

"Throughout Southeast Asia, Japanese businessmen are so numerous that Bangkok hotel clerks find it essential to speak Japanese, and residents of a half-dozen countries are paying their Japanese visitors what in a perverse commercial sense is the ultimate compliment: They call them 'yellow Yankees,' " wrote E. J. Kahn Jr., in a "Letter from Osaka," in the June 6, 1970, *New Yorker*.

The Japanese argued that their economy was not capable of withstanding an invasion of foreign goods. Significantly, Japan faced textile competition in its home market while it was negotiating with the United States over limiting its textile exports to America. Cheap imports from even lower-wage nations in Asia — such as Taiwan and the Philippines — threatened to cut into the home sales of Japanese producers.

The Textile Quota Battle. The growing protectionist mood in Washington was reflected in a statement by Nixon's secretary of commerce, Maurice H. Stans, who declared that "in many respects we have been Uncle Sucker to the rest of the world." The remark, made in 1969, grew out of frustration over the inability of the Nixon administration to persuade Japan to impose "voluntary" quotas on its textile exports to the United States. During 18 months of fruitless negotiations between the two countries, Japan pointed out that in 1964 it had accepted voluntary quotas on a "temporary" basis for cotton exports and that these still were in effect. It also insisted that no U.S. textile company had been able to prove that Japanese imports were a primary cause of its falling sales, a procedure required by GATT before quotas could be applied. The voluntary agreement did not cover wool and synthetic fabrics or any textiles whose cotton content was less than 50 percent. Consumption of synthetic fabrics was rising dramatically in the United States and by 1970 accounted for more than one-half of the market. Moreover, the gap between the domestic textile industry's wage scale and that existing in Japan was steadily widening.

American negotiators said the United States had incurred progressively larger imbalances year by year in its textile trade with Japan, reaching $504 million in 1969. U.S. officials also put the textile question in the larger context of total Japanese-American trade. In an $8 billion exchange of goods in 1969, the United States ran up a $1.4 billion deficit.

Throughout the textile talks, Japanese negotiators retorted that their country was being asked to pay a Nixon political debt to the South. Nixon had promised help to the suffering textile industry during the 1968 presidential campaign. Upon receiving the Republican nomination, Nixon sent telegrams to Sen. Strom Thurmond, R-S.C., and other Republicans from southern textile-producing states criticizing his predecessor, Lyndon B. Johnson, for ineffective action on textiles and promising that, "as President, my policy will be to rectify this unfair development." Specifically, Nixon pledged to administer effectively the existing agreement on cotton and negotiate one for wool and synthetics.

Congressional Challenge. Japanese negotiators remained adamant throughout 1969, and the Japanese Diet (parliament), in a rare show of unanimity, voted in May 1970 to resist American pressure for quotas on non-cotton textiles. The next month, Stans announced the administration's "reluctant" support for provisions of a trade bill imposing quotas on textile imports. The bill, sponsored by Rep. Wilbur D. Mills, D-Ark. (1939-77), chairman of the House Ways and Means Committee, also extended quotas to footwear imports. Furthermore, Mills appeared receptive to the clamor of congressional colleagues for adding quotas on a variety of other items to the list.

By the summer of 1970 there were indications that the Japanese government and textile industry had become alarmed about the possibility that Washington might be forced to impose quotas. Japanese newspapers reported that their country's negotiators had miscalculated the American mood. An article in the July 13, 1970, *U. S. News & World Report* observed that the impasse on textiles had resulted in "fresh talk, surprisingly, of Japan's dropping more of its own trade barriers, such as removing high duties on American cars. . . .

"Not to be ruled out," the magazine added, "is a bid to resume negotiations — before any new U.S. protectionist bills may be signed into law."

Nixon Administration's Position on Trade Issues

In his 1969 Economic Report to Congress, President Nixon dedicated his administration to the expansion of foreign trade and the removal of nontariff barriers. "While we work to reduce trade barriers, we must not drop our guard against the advocates of protectionism at home and abroad," the report said. "But the only real solutions are ones that improve our economy — not ones that erect new barriers that could provoke retaliation, or insulate producers from the invigorating force of world competition." At a news conference held soon afterward, on Feb. 6, 1969, Nixon said he believed in free trade, but added that the textile situation was "a special problem."

Mixed Feelings About Free Trade

Some observers saw cracks in the president's commitment to trade liberalization when, a year later, he continued duties of about 20 percent on sheet glass imports. The U.S. Tariff Commission had recommended an increased duty on this product to shelter the domestic industry. But the European Common Market countries, led by Belgium, warned that any increases would result in retaliation against American exports. Nixon took a middle course in maintaining the duty at its existing level. Any reduction was deferred until 1972. *The Wall Street Journal* March 2, 1970, quoted White House aides as saying they had been under pressure from members of Congress who wanted the president to increase glass duties further.

Indeed, administration signals on trade policy were conflicting during the period 1969-72. This was apparently a result of disagreement among high administration officials. In addition, as already noted the president, who had supported freer trade during his election campaign, at the same time was indebted to southern protectionists for substantial help during that campaign.

Nixon sent Congress late in 1969 legislation that would have permitted him to reduce tariffs and increase assistance to U.S. businesses harmed by imports. The president's bill proposed to restore expired presidential authority to make minor adjustments in U.S. tariffs; eliminate the American Selling Price (ASP) system of calculating duties on imports (primarily chemicals); liberalize the 1962 Trade Act's "escape clause" provisions for relief to industries adversely affected by imports; liberalize the 1962 act's adjustment assistance provisions to allow individual firms and workers to receive loans, technical aid, tax relief, relocation and training when increased imports were found to be a "substantial" rather than primary cause of actual or potential serious injury; and strengthen the president's authority to retaliate against unfair trade practices. *(ASP, p. 71; escape clause, p. 55; adjustment assistance, pp. 23, 55)*

Congress Pushes Quotas

At a July 20, 1970, news conference the president threatened to veto any restrictive trade bill that emerged from Congress broadened beyond the scope of the administration's limited support for textile quotas. "I would not be able to sign the bill because it would set off a trade war," he said. But the veto threat had little impact on the protectionist mood on Capitol Hill, and by the end of the year the administration's modest trade bill had been altered almost unrecognizably into a protectionist measure as numerous industries contended that they were as deserving of protection as textiles and had been unfairly excluded by the president.

Lobbying intensified, and even the AFL-CIO, previously an advocate of free trade, pushed for quotas to protect the jobs of American workers. Consumer groups and a number of economists, on the other hand, argued that quotas or other trade restrictions would raise retail prices and cause further inflation.

As passed by the House, the measure contained quotas on textiles (which the administration had agreed to) and other controversial provisions such as shoe and oil import quotas and a trigger system instituting quotas on other products whenever they increased their share of the U.S. market.

The House-passed legislation was bitterly attacked. *The New York Times* called it "the worst piece of trade legislation in 40 years." Representatives of farm, aircraft and electronics groups lobbied against it, feeling that it would invite retaliation against their products. Nevertheless the bill, when reported by the Senate Finance Committee, contained basically the same protectionist amendments as those added by the House. Senate supporters sought to ensure its passage by attaching it to a popular bill increasing Social Security benefits. The strategy failed when a filibuster forced trade bill proponents to strip it from the Social Security

Protecting Industries from Imports

Protectionist measures generally are designed to shelter specific products from import competition. Legislative measures include aid to domestic industries hurt by sudden increases in imports ("escape clause" of the 1974 Trade Act), anti-dumping (1921 Anti-Dumping Act), countervailing duties (1930 Tariff Act) and unfair import practices (1930 Tariff Act).

There are other strategies for easing the pressure of import competition. One is to negotiate with foreign suppliers for quotas, or "orderly marketing arrangements." The U.S. government determines what level of imports can be sustained without damaging domestic producers and then negotiates with the principal foreign suppliers to limit the inflow of their goods to specified amounts. Although in theory "voluntary," there is an element of coercion in these arrangements; foreign suppliers liken the bargaining to "negotiating with a gun at your head." Nonetheless, these arrangements regulate U.S. imports of such items as shoes, textiles and meat.

A second strategy is to offer temporary federal aid, called "adjustment assistance," to industries hard-pressed by import competition. The assistance may be in the form of direct payments to workers whose jobs are displaced by imports or by the transfer overseas of manufacturing operations. Or such assistance may be used to establish retraining facilities to upgrade job skills. Still another form of assistance entails loans and grants to manufacturers so they can modernize their plants. Critics of adjustment assistance have said that it often becomes a subsidy to inefficient industry. But supporters have contended that it is preferable to outright restrictions on imports.

bill and send it back to the Finance Committee, where it died.

It was unclear whether the president would have vetoed the bill if it had reached his desk. He did not resubmit a trade bill during the 92nd Congress, but Treasury Secretary George P. Shultz (who succeeded Nixon's first Treasury secretary, John B. Connally, in June 1972), in a September 1972 speech on international monetary reform called for a system with built-in incentives for trade liberalization.

Global Trade Issues

The appeal of trade liberalization appeared to be waning throughout the world. While all trading nations by 1970 freely admitted the advantages of unrestricted international commerce, they continued to protect weak sectors of their own economies. Nonetheless, restrictions continued to be whittled away, although at a slower pace than during the 1960s. The slowdown was obvious at the February 1970 GATT meeting, when member nations refused to commit themselves to another attack on trade barriers. The failure to take up what was called a "second Kennedy Round" was widely viewed as a setback for GATT Director General Olivier Long, who had proposed such a meeting. Long also failed to get a commitment from member countries that they would refrain from introducing new trade barriers, or enlarging existing ones. GATT members did agree in a mildly worded way that each of them "should refrain from aggravating the problems and obstacles to be dealt with."

Difficulty of Removing Nontariff Barriers

The Kennedy Round (1964-67) generally had been successful in lowering tariffs. Members of GATT had agreed to reduce duties an average of about 35 percent on some 60,000 items affecting more than $40 billion annually in world trade (based on 1964 figures, the base year for the negotiations). *(Kennedy Round, p. 57)*

Types of Barriers. With tariffs having been lowered, nontariff barriers had been growing and had come to be considered the greatest obstacle to the creation of a truly free world economy. Those restrictions are defined generally by GATT as "any government law or practice which is not a tariff which tends to limit the free flow of trade between one country and another."

They fall into five general categories:

● Specific limitations on imports, such as quotas, embargoes and import licenses.

● Government participation in trade in the form of granting export subsidies, setting official procurement policies, engaging in state trading and state monopolies.

● Customs and administrative entry procedures, such as countervailing duties, arbitrary classification of goods, some anti-dumping provisions and various methods of placing a value on imports. *(Box, p. 40)*

• Standards involving imports and domestic goods, including industrial, health, safety or certification procedures, that impede imports.

• Restraints on imports by price mechanisms such as import deposits, surcharges, taxes — port, statistical and excise — and credit restrictions.

Imposition of these barriers represented only part of the picture. President Nixon stated in his 1973 international economic report that "many important nontariff barriers ... elude inventory." As an example, he cited countries where local businesses agreed among themselves not to import certain competitive items, sometimes with their government's acquiescence.

Dealing with these restrictions on trade often involves national sovereignty, which is one reason why they are difficult to remove. Nontariff barriers obviously can be used effectively to block unwanted imports. GATT in 1970 was in the process of determining which of those practices most seriously affected trade.

Case of the ASP. Many foreign suppliers regarded the "American Selling Price," a special method of computing duties on imports, primarily benzenoid chemicals, as this country's most serious impediment to trade and a symbol of its protectionist tendencies. Under the ASP system, duties were computed not on the value of the product when it reached an American port — the traditional way — but on the U.S. sales price of a comparable item made in the United States.

During the Kennedy Round negotiations in 1967, the Johnson administration agreed to seek congressional repeal of the American Selling Price system in return for tariff concessions by Western European nations. But the administration was unable to bring it about. Nixon repeated the request in 1969 but was turned down by the House Ways and Means Committee in 1970. The American Selling Price finally was abolished in 1979.

Trade Problems of Developing Nations

While industrialized nations primarily were concerned about maintaining a favorable balance of trade, it was often overlooked that trade was one of the principal means of extending aid to the less developed countries (LDCs). George W. Ball, a former undersecretary of state (1961-66) and ambassador to the United Nations (1968), wrote in the Aug. 2, 1970, *Washington Post*, "One of the most cherished myths of the 1960s — and particularly in the early years of the Kennedy administration — was that the industrialized countries of the Northern Hemisphere could best meet the capital needs of the developing countries of the Southern Hemisphere by opening markets to the imports of their manufactured goods."

As this theme was elaborated by the Argentine economist Raul Prebisch, manufactured goods from the LDCs would be accepted on a preferential basis. That idea became the central theme of the United Nations Conference on Trade and Development when it first met in Geneva in 1964. Nothing but frustration came of this approach, Ball added, because protectionist interests would not accede to it.

"Regardless of how one assesses the blame," Ball concluded, "the point has been made that the developing countries are unlikely to find wealth and happiness through any dramatic increase in the sale of their industrial products to Northern Hemisphere countries. . . . Textiles are obviously the acid test, since they are the industry through which an emerging new country is most likely to take the first faltering step toward industrialization."

Dissatisfaction With Kennedy Round. For those third world nations of Africa, Asia and Latin America that still depended almost exclusively on agricultural exports, frequently from a one-crop economy, there was more bad news in the making. The so-called Green Revolution, with its "miracle seeds" and heavy fertilization, yielded not just needed food for hungry people but the prospect of enormous gluts on world grain markets in the early 1970s.

The Kennedy Round left the developing nations dissatisfied with their portion of world trade, and they were becoming increasingly vocal in demanding better trade deals from the United States and other industrial countries. The United States offered duty-free entry to nearly all the manufactured and semi-manufactured goods of LDCs except in three categories — textiles, shoes and petroleum. But at a meeting of the United Nations Conference on Trade and Development (UNCTAD) in Geneva in March 1970, the United States succeeded in attaching a general escape clause condition to its trade with developing countries whereby concessions made under a trade agreement could be withdrawn when they were found to be causing harm to a domestic industry.

Criticism of the United States. To some foreign officials, the United States appeared to be reneging on its promised aid to the industries of developing nations. The U.S.-imposed escape clause contrasted to the increasing number of trade privileges offered to African nations by the EEC.

The competition for world markets thus was tempered by the long-range need to bring less affluent nations into the greater global prosperity. But even in this field there seemed to be room for dispute. The Common Market favored a regionalized system of trade and aid in which it would be responsible for Africa, Japan for Asia and the United States for Latin America. The United States refused to accept this concept, decrying it as counter to the large-scale aim of GATT — the liberalization of trade on a worldwide basis and not just between new economic spheres of influence.

Dollar Problems: Payments and Trade Deficits

By the early 1970s there was growing recognition in the world that the U.S. economy was not performing well. After having enjoyed balance-of-payments surpluses of $1.6 billion and $2.7 billion in 1968 and 1969, respectively, the United States recorded a balance-of-payments deficit of $9.8 billion in 1970, a whopping $29.7 billion deficit in 1971 and $10.1 billion in 1972. These balance-of-payments deficits led to major congressional and executive actions affecting international economic policies between 1969 and 1972. For the first time, the United States began to import more than it exported, and this contributed to the worsening balance of payments.

Attempts to control the deficit led ultimately to the first devaluation of the dollar since 1934. Before the devaluation was announced in late 1971, concern about the balance of payments had led to passage of several bills designed to control the outflow of dollars and a presidential order suspending the convertibility of dollars into gold.

Causes of the Dollar's Overvaluation

A 1971 report by the Joint Economic Subcommittee on International Exchange and Payments said the failure of previous efforts to improve the balance of payments "leads to one inescapable conclusion — the dollar is overvalued. It is not really worth as much in international transactions as exchange rates imply, and its foreign currency value is thus overstated."

The overvaluation of the dollar "impedes sales of U.S. exports abroad, stimulates purchases of imports here, encourages American firms to invest abroad, and retards foreign investment in the United States," the subcommittee report said.

The International Monetary Fund (IMF) was founded, in part, to help member nations deal with disequilibrium in their payments balances. But it failed to assume responsibility for recommending exchange rate changes that were needed because of the dollar's overvaluation, the subcommittee said.

Paul W. McCracken, chairman of the Council of Economic Advisers under Nixon, attributed the overvaluation of the dollar to its central role in the world monetary system. Over the years, he said, other nations tended to devalue their currencies against the standard of value — the dollar. "Thus the exchange rate of the dollar was slowly appreciated by the actions of others," McCracken said, "and this — plus our own inflation after 1965 — finally overvalued the dollar to the point of producing a basic imbalance in our external trade and competitive position."

Because of the dollar's international role, however, the United States could not take action to correct its overvaluation without upsetting the world monetary system, and until 1971 the United States was unwilling to do so.

Events Leading to 1971 Devaluation

Events directly leading to the devaluation can be traced to Aug. 15, 1971, when President Nixon announced a broad new economic policy designed to stop inflation, create new jobs and protect the dollar. To achieve the latter goal he suspended the convertibility of the dollar into gold. This repudiated the 26-year-old U.S. commitment to maintain the external value of the dollar by buying and selling gold at $35 an ounce. It allowed the value of the dollar to float on demand in international markets. *(Background on international monetary system, box, p. 48)*

To put pressure on other countries to join in planning more permanent changes in the international monetary system, the president also announced a temporary 10 percent surcharge on all imports into the United States. This was a key bargaining weapon for the United States when finance ministers of the major industrial countries met throughout the fall of 1971 to negotiate a new pattern of exchange rates. The United States pressured West Germany and Japan, among others, to revalue their undervalued currencies to eliminate what it felt was an unfair trade advantage. But those countries insisted that the United States must first devalue the dollar.

European Response. The EEC was at first unable to agree on a unified response to the American "challenge" posed by the imposition of the import surcharge. Finance ministers of the six Common Market nations and Britain, meeting in Brussels four days later, initially could not reconcile French and West German differences over what common monetary policy to adopt in response to the dollar crisis. It was not until Sept. 13 that they reached agreement. Their joint statement, accepting the U.S. contention that it was time to restructure the world monetary system, proposed the following as preconditions: an official devaluation of the dollar by raising the price of gold for intergovernmental transactions; a gradual end to reliance on "national currencies" (the dollar) as reserve units in world trade and monetary relations; retention of gold as the principal common denominator of international monetary relations, with increased emphasis on Special Drawing Rights (so-called "paper gold") issued by the IMF; realignment of the world's major currencies, "including the dollar," to restore equilibrium to the system of international payments; restoration of fixed parities among the major currencies, but with greater flexibility in exchange rates to inhibit future speculation; and revocation of the U.S. import surcharge.

Import Surcharge Issue. Secretary of the Treasury Connally told delegates to the annual meeting of the IMF in Washington Sept. 20 that the United States would remove the surcharge if other leading countries would let their currencies "float" freely upward in relation to the dollar and if some countries took "specific" measures in the coming weeks to reduce barriers to American exports. Testifying the following day before the Senate Finance Committee, Connally stuck by his basic position that the United States would not remove the surcharge "until we can be assured there will be a turnaround in our balance of payments." He added, "We are not going to have a trade war — we don't want it, nobody wants it." The Treasury secretary said that "beyond question we have set the stage for negotiations" on the monetary issues.

Europe was not pacified, however. The Common Market countries formally protested to the United States Oct. 4 — Britain had done so earlier — against other aspects of the Nixon economic plan. Those involved administration requests to Congress for tax credits on new machinery and equipment produced in the United States for export and for a tax deferral on business earnings from export sales. The EEC warned that these measures, if passed, might lead to retaliation. The protest, delivered to the U.S. ambassador to the Common Market, J. Robert Schaetzel, characterized the measures as being in violation of GATT principles.

An agreement eventually was reached, and the import surcharge was rescinded Dec. 18 at a historic meeting of the finance ministers at the Smithsonian Institution in Washington, D.C. The United States agreed to devalue the dollar by 8.57 percent by raising the price of gold to $38 from the $35-an-ounce price in effect since 1934. The effect was to make the value of the dollar less but to make the price of American products more competitive abroad. At the same time several other nations revalued their currencies.

The U.S. devaluation decision won general acceptance among congressional leaders, who were resigned to a reappraisal of the dollar's role in the world economy. In early 1972 Congress gave formal approval to the devaluation, passing the authorization with one dissent in the Senate and by a 342-43 roll call in the House. The change had an immediate effect: the U.S. balance-of-payments deficit began to decline.

Monetary Reform. In September 1972 the Nixon administration, through Treasury Secretary Shultz, put forth proposals for a complete overhaul of the international currency system. The proposals continued the administration's efforts to diminish the importance of gold and find an alternative for the dollar as the standard measure of world monetary relationships. Shultz acknowledged that the proposals were "difficult, complicated and controversial" and would take some time to negotiate. Once negotiated, the new system would have to be approved by each national legislature, including the U.S. Congress.

Under the administration proposal, SDRs would replace the dollar as the standard measure of money relationships among different currencies. However, holdings of dollars and other currencies as reserves by other countries could continue, and the United States would return to exchanging other countries' surplus dollars for gold or some other monetary reserve if a procedure could be worked out.

Under the proposed system, each currency would have a central exchange rate. However, the currency would be allowed to fluctuate by as much as 4.5 percent on either side of the central rate.

Countries that failed to control balance-of-payments surpluses or deficits would be subject to strict penalties. Surplus countries would face import surcharges against their goods. Deficit countries could lose their Special Drawing Rights if they failed to take corrective actions.

Need for Further Action: 1973 Devaluation

Nixon in December 1971 had called the Smithsonian agreement "the most significant monetary agreement in the history of the world."

But little more than a year later, at the end of the president's first term, it was clear that it had been little more than a pause on the way to a second devaluation. The overall improvement in the balance-of-payments deficit in 1972 was disappointing, largely because of a sharp increase in the U.S. trade deficit.

Early in 1973 the dollar began to run into trouble in foreign money markets. On Feb. 12, 1973, the administration announced that Nixon would ask Congress to authorize a 10 percent dollar devaluation. The request was the result of a round of hurried negotiations by Paul A. Volcker, under secretary of the Treasury for monetary affairs, with the finance ministers of Japan, West Germany, France, Italy and Great Britain. The objective was to quell a wave of currency speculation, involving sales of U.S. dollars for West German marks and Japanese yen, on international financial markets by bankers, corporations, some Middle Eastern governments and private individuals. In converting their holdings into stronger currencies, financial experts in effect were betting that the dollar's value would fall relative to those currencies, making the yen and mark worth more in U.S. currency.

Those speculative pressures undercut the realigned currency exchange rate, based on the 8.57 percent dollar devaluation accepted under the Dec. 18, 1971, Smithsonian agreement.

Another factor — although disputed by the Nixon administration — was doubt overseas about the effectiveness of the administration's Phase II voluntary wage and price controls in keeping down inflation.

In the face of upward pressure on their currencies, both West Germany and Japan had resisted revaluation for domestic economic and political reasons. Undervalued currencies gave their export industries substantial advantages in competing in U.S. markets.

In the Feb. 12 agreement, however, West Germany accepted an effective 10 percent increase in the mark's value against the dollar by pledging not to match the U.S. devaluation. Japan accepted a larger increase in the yen's value against the dollar through a combination of the 10 percent dollar devaluation and upward movement of the yen's value as determined by market forces, without Japanese central bank intervention to maintain the official par value.

Shultz acknowleged that the devaluation, along with the Nixon administration trade proposals that followed, was primarily aimed at Japan, which in 1972 enjoyed a $4.2 billion surplus in trade with the United States. The Treasury secretary contended that the currency realignments "are designed, along with appropriate trade liberalization, to correct the major payments imbalance between Japan and the United States which has persisted in the past year."

Congress Sept. 7 approved the dollar devaluation. The adjustment in the dollar's value in terms of other nations' currencies, like the earlier devaluation, tried to peg the U.S. currency at a level that more realistically reflected the nation's underlying economic strength.

International Economic Instability, 1973-76

A series of extraordinary economic shocks — including grain harvest shortfalls, critical commodity shortages and petroleum price increases dictated by a producing nations' cartel — helped set off a worldwide round of inflation in 1972-73. Their effects were compounded by simultaneous stimulative actions by all the major trading nations, which fed a short-lived economic boom in early 1973. The ravages of the resulting rise in prices, along with deflationary actions taken by governments, then helped bring on a recession in 1974-75. An uneven recovery followed, led by the United States, Japan and West Germany, but the pace faltered in mid-1976 even in those relatively strong economies. Recovery lagged behind in other nations, notably Great Britain and Italy, where inflation persisted at high levels, forcing those governments to tighten restraints on demand.

Oil Price Increases

All the Western industrialized nations, and most less developed countries as well, spent 1973-76 making painful adjustments to skyrocketing energy costs. The most deeply felt international economic development of the period was the fourfold crude oil price increase that the Organization of Petroleum Exporting Countries (OPEC) cartel imposed in stages. The OPEC nations' determination to maximize their earnings from production of petroleum — and willingness to use oil as a political weapon, as demonstrated by the 1973 export embargo imposed after war broke out with Israel — produced severe energy shortages and inflation that contributed heavily to the recession. Even as other raw-material-producing nations considered similar cartel tactics, the petroleum crisis made the industrialized nations all too aware of their dependence on dwindling supplies of critical materials.

Rising oil import bills created severe imbalances in the flow of goods, services and capital among nations. High energy consuming countries ran up heavy trade and international payments deficits as oil payments flowed to the OPEC nations. In 1974 alone, OPEC countries accumulated $70.5 billion in payments surpluses. Because the producing nations could absorb relatively few imports and had not begun to reinvest oil earnings in other countries, that wealth was not returned to the industrialized economies.

The payments drain eased in 1975 as the recession curtailed energy demand in the industrialized nations and many OPEC countries stepped up their imports and foreign investments. Nevertheless, high energy costs threatened to exhaust the ability of some nations, such as Great Britain, to borrow foreign funds to cover rising government indebtedness and domestic consumption. The resulting financial squeeze forced retrenchment in domestic economic goals in some countries, while rising oil prices fueled inflation in all nations and discouraged investment.

Floating Exchange Rates

Shortly after the February 1973 devaluation of the dollar, inflationary pressures and volatile monetary fluctuations among the industrialized nations led governments to give up all attempts to maintain fixed exchange rates through market intervention. The Bretton Woods structure was replaced by a *de facto* system of floating exchange rates, in which supply and demand forces on international exchanges were left free to determine the relative values of currencies. The IMF nations meanwhile continued negotiations on devising a new monetary system to replace the Bretton Woods arrangements.

In theory, the floating exchange rate system was supposed to help correct international payments imbalances through largely automatic adjustments. Market judgments would cause the currency of a country with a weak economy, high inflation and persistent payment outflows to float downward in value against other currencies. With its currency costing less in terms of other currencies, and its products therefore cheaper to purchase in other nations, demand for its exports would strengthen. At the same time, more costly imports from other countries would decline in the country with a weak currency, its domestic output would increase and the payments balance would swing back toward equilibrium. A country with a payments surplus, on the other hand, could expect its currency to appreciate, cutting back foreign demand for its exports while making imports more attractively priced.

Problems With Floating Rates. In practice, the system worked much less smoothly. Large currency fluctuations were caused by inflation rate differentials. Countries such as Great Britain and Italy — whose currencies had depreciated — were unable to maintain their export market shares once world trade began to expand after the 1973-74 recession. West Germany and Japan, with much stronger currencies, on the other hand, increased their exports, in part because their lower inflation rates and amicable management-labor relations promised better performance in fulfilling contracts. Critics contended that exchange-rate fluctuations worsened price pressures in inflation-plagued nations because depreciation made imports more costly. Defenders of the system argued that exchange rates could be held steady only if a government took adequate measures to curb underlying inflationary pressures at home.

Regardless of such problems, the floating rate system weathered fluctuating worldwide economic fortunes without disastrous strains. Along with special arrangements by the IMF for directing OPEC surpluses to deficit nations, the system was beginning to accommodate itself to the redistribution of economic power and the mounting assets concentrated in Middle East countries resulting from the oil price increases.

Bretton Woods Amendments. Following a 1975 understanding between France and the United States, the IMF drew up revised international monetary agreements that in effect made permanent the floating system. Congress in 1976 approved U.S. ratification of the agreement, under which IMF nations agreed to avoid exchange rate manipulation except to counter disorderly conditions. The arrangement also provided for possible reinstitution of fixed rates in the future, replaced gold with IMF Special Drawing Rights as the medium of settlement in IMF transactions and authorized sale of some IMF gold reserves to finance a trust fund to help poor nations adjust to higher oil import costs.

Known as the Bretton Woods amendments, other major IMF rule changes endorsed by the arrangement included official confirmation of the practice of allowing currency exchange rates to "float" to varying values according to market forces, reallocation of IMF quotas cutting the U.S. share relative to other countries (but with modified IMF voting procedures that maintained the U.S. veto power) and expanded authority for disposal of the IMF gold stock.Treasury Secretary William E. Simon hailed the measure as "of major importance to the U.S."

1979 Trade Reorganization

Congress in 1979 accepted President Jimmy Carter's plan for consolidating and coordinating U.S. trade policies. The trade reorganization plan went into effect on Jan. 2, 1980, after Congress refused to approve resolutions to block it.

Formally submitted by Carter on Sept. 25, the plan gave the Office of the U.S. Trade Representative (formerly the Office of the Special Trade Representative) overall responsibility for developing U.S. trade policy and coordinating its implementation by federal agencies. It shifted most trade programs to the Commerce Department, including responsibility for determining whether countervailing duties or anti-dumping procedures should be imposed to counter foreign imports.

The Treasury Department had administered the anti-dumping and countervailing duty laws, but business interests complained that the Treasury's enforcement was lax. In its report on the 1979 trade bill, the House Ways and Means Committee noted that "investigations and determinations are often too lengthy, and assessment and collection of duties are often unreasonably delayed." *(Anti-dumping law and countervailing duties, p. 40-41)*

Carter's final trade reorganization plan was close to House proposals but fell short of demands made in the Senate for a separate Cabinet-level trade department. The proposal for a new department, championed by William V. Roth Jr., R-Del., while he was in the House (1967-70) and later in the Senate, was approved by the Senate Governmental Affairs Committee Oct. 4, 1983. *(See p. 21.)*

1973 Trade Proposals and the Tokyo Round

President Nixon's 1973 proposals for new trade negotiating authority were made in response to a deteriorating U.S. position in international commerce that had become painfully evident after 1970. The United States ran a trade deficit of $2.7 billion in 1971, and in 1972 the deficit jumped to $6.8 billion.

In the latter year, the United States had a trade deficit of $4.2 billion with Japan — nearly two-thirds of the entire deficit. Although the United States and Japan had successfully negotiated the removal of some restrictions in previous years, quotas and other barriers to U.S. exports and investments still existed.

The U.S. trade deficit with the Common Market was $600 million in 1972, compared to an annual surplus of $2.5 billion in the 1960-65 period. Particularly irritating to the United States was the EEC's common agricultural policy (CAP) that had hindered the growth of U.S. farm exports through such devices as variable import levies (rather than fixed tariffs) and subsidies for EEC farm exports. U.S. exports to the EEC of commodities covered by the CAP had declined by more than 15 percent since 1966.

The United States also had objected to the EEC's extension of preferential treatment to imports from non-member countries, especially when EEC exports were given reverse preferential treatment. Another major U.S. complaint dealt with obtaining compensation for anticipated losses sustained by exporters of U.S. products, particularly in agriculture, resulting from the expansion of the EEC to include the United Kingdom, Ireland and Denmark. (The CAP and common external tariff thus would be extended to those nations.) Negotiations on the latter question began in Geneva in March 1972, and the three nations joined the group in January 1973.

Passage of the 1974 Trade Act

The major industrial nations began preparing in 1973 for another round of trade negotiations (known as the Tokyo Round) aimed at further reductions in tariffs and other barriers to international commerce. As the U.S. trade position deteriorated, the Nixon administration April 12, 1973, asked Congress for wide-ranging authority to adjust U.S. tariffs and negotiate removal of nontariff barriers at the upcoming trade talks.

Congressional action was required because the presidential authority to enter into trade agreements conferred by the Trade Expansion Act of 1962 had expired in 1967. In the aftermath of the 1967 tariff-cutting agreement produced by the Kennedy Round, moreover, other trade restrictions imposed by other nations had exacerbated U.S. trade problems.

Nixon Proposal. The president urged Congress to act "as expeditiously as possible" on the comprehensive trade legislation. The proposal gave the president authority to enter into negotiations to reduce trade barriers, to grant expanded relief for industries and workers harmed by imports, to retaliate against unfair practices by other nations, to impose temporary import surcharges or quotas to correct balance-of-payments imbalances, to extend most-favored-nation tariff treatment to products from other countries and to allow duty-free imports from developing nations. The measure also included some limited restrictions on U.S. tax preferences for companies that built plants overseas or set up wholly-owned foreign subsidiaries to take greater advantage of those incentives.

After a year's delay, Congress in December 1974 authorized U.S. participation in the Tokyo Round by giving the president authority to negotiate and implement some reductions in trade barriers, ignoring organized labor demands for strong protectionist measures to curb competition from foreign imports. The bill was signed Jan. 3, 1975, by President Gerald R. Ford. (Ford, Nixon's vice president, had succeeded Nixon on Aug. 9, 1974.) Responding to concern in Japan and Europe that the president lacked the flexibility and necessary authority to participate in multilateral negotiations, the Ford administration had pushed hard for final congressional action in the post-election session of the 93rd Congress.

Disputes over Soviet trade and emigration policies had stalled final action on the critical trade legislation. It took one of Secretary of State Henry A. Kissinger's delicate diplomatic compromises, worked out in negotiations with the Soviet government and with Senate opponents of granting trade concessions to Moscow, to break the House-passed trade measure free from a year-long impasse over the Soviet Union's policies on Jewish emigration. The Soviet government soon repudiated the unwritten understanding with Kissinger, but only after Congress had given final approval to the additional trade negotiating authority that the administration desperately needed. *(Details, Chapter 4, p. 111)*

Provisions of the Act. In its final form, the Trade Act of 1974 conferred presidential trade negotiating authorities generally along the lines approved by the House in 1973. The bill extended the president's authority to enter into trade agreements for five years and authorized the president to eliminate tariffs on goods carrying duties of 5 percent or less and to reduce higher tariffs by up to 60 percent. Reductions of more than 20 percent had to be staged in equal installments over 10 years, but annual reductions of up to 3 percent or one-tenth of the total were authorized.

Aside from the trade provisions with the U.S.S.R., Congress gave the president most of the powers he wanted to enter into multilateral trade negotiations. The Senate followed the House lead in insisting upon congressional restrictions on his use of those powers. Perhaps the most significant Senate change, accepted by the House, required the president to notify Congress at least 90 days in advance of a proposed agreement and to consult with the appropriate congressional committees on nontariff barrier agreements, which would be subject to congressional approval.

In deference to protectionist sentiment in Congress and the nation, the act required the president to take measures to aid domestic producers injured by imports. If the U.S. International Trade Commission found that a domestic industry had sustained serious injury, the president had to act to restrain imports or provide other assistance to the industry unless he determined that to do so would be contrary to U.S. economic interests.

The Tokyo Round: Difficult Negotiations

Trade agreements since World War II had emphasized tariff cuts. But the Tokyo Round, launched in the Japanese capital in 1973, concentrated as well on developing new international rules limiting nontariff policies adversely affecting free trade, such as government subsidies for exports, product standards, procurement procedures and customs valuation methods, that gave a country's products an advantage in foreign markets or created barriers to competitive imports.

After five and a half years of tough negotiations, the major trading nations signed the Tokyo Round trade package in Geneva on April 12, 1979. Although the talks failed to produce agreement on several difficult issues — including a wheat convention and a domestic industry protection clause to permit temporary import restrictions — the package included a series of nontariff barrier codes, agricultural agreements, a framework for GATT reform and phased tariff cuts averaging about 33 percent.

The trade talks had been difficult. Several deadlines elapsed and the negotiations at several stages were on the verge of collapse over seemingly intractable issues. Until the 1974 Trade Act became effective in January 1975, the United States had no authority to enter into the negotiations. The following November, Western leaders meeting at an "economic summit" at Rambouillet, France, extended the deadline for agreement for a year to late 1977.

By midsummer 1977, only minimal progress had been made.

Tokyo Round Tariff Cuts

The so-called Tokyo Round multilateral trade negotiations (initiated in Tokyo in 1973 but conducted for the most part in Geneva) were the fifth in a series of major tariff-cutting "rounds" of negotiations among signatories to the 1947 General Agreement on Tariffs and Trade (GATT).

During the Tokyo Round the United States agreed to cut its tariffs on industrial goods by an average of 31 percent — from 8.2 percent to 5.7 percent — over an eight-year period beginning in 1980. On some import-sensitive products such as textiles and steel, tariff reductions were deferred until 1982.

The U.S. tariff reductions, outlined in a summary released by the Carter administration during congressional consideration of the 1979 trade bill implementing U.S. participation in the agreement, covered the following items:

Textiles. Average U.S. tariffs for textiles from the six-nation European Economic Community (EEC) were reduced to 13.7 percent from 19.5 percent; tariffs on Japanese textiles were cut to an average of 16.8 percent from the existing 23.2 percent. Nearly all of the $637 million worth of imports to the United States covered by tariffs that still exceeded 30 percent were in the textile and apparel category.

Iron and Steel. Average U.S. tariffs on EEC iron and steel imports were lowered to 4.3 percent from 6.1 percent; for imports from Japan, tariffs were reduced to 4.6 percent from the existing 6.2 percent.

Leather and Leather Products. Because import-sensitive footwear was left out of the negotiations, tariff cuts were relatively small. U.S. tariffs on EEC leather imports were reduced only to an average of 8.8 percent from 9.2 percent; tariffs on imports from Japan dropped to an average of 11.7 percent from 13 percent.

Drugs and Soaps. The average U.S. tariff dropped to 5.1 percent from 9.1 percent for imports of drugs and soaps from EEC countries.

Industrial Chemicals. U.S. tariffs for chemicals from the EEC countries were cut to an average of 7.3 percent from 11.2 percent.

Aerospace, Automotive Equipment. U.S. tariffs on imports of automobiles and aircraft were completely eliminated.

American and European representatives then agreed to begin detailed, final negotiations by Jan. 15, 1978. But the deadline was extended several times.

The Tokyo Round was more protracted than any of the six previous GATT negotiating rounds. Earlier negotiations focused rather narrowly on tariff cuts in industrial goods. In contrast, the Tokyo Round dealt with tariff reductions on both industrial and agricultural goods, embracing thousands of items, and with nontariff barriers as well. After those negotiations were completed, average tariffs on dutiable industrial products were only 4.4 percent for the United States, 4.7 percent for the EEC, and 2.8 percent for Japan.

1979 Trade Bill Politics

Even before the Tokyo Round negotiations were completed, officials of President Jimmy Carter's administration, which had come to power in January 1977, began meeting behind closed doors with the Ways and Means and Finance committees to shape legislation to implement the nontariff codes.

The White House formally submitted the legislation June 19, 1979. It passed the House July 11 and the Senate July 23. Carter signed the bill three days later, maintaining that its provisions would create jobs, spur U.S. exports and enhance prospects for peace.

Procedural Maneuvers. In the past, trade bills often had bogged down over a barrage of special interest amendments as members tried to protect individual domestic industries against foreign competition. But working through a unique legislative process laid out by the 1974 Trade Act, which barred any amendments to the legislation, members of the tax-writing House and Senate panels short-circuited those amendments. Consulting with U.S. Special Trade Representative Robert S. Strauss committee leaders tailored the bill to head off opposition from troubled industries such as textiles and steel. The bill came to both the House and Senate floor under provisions forbidding floor amendments.

As a result, the House passed the bill with only seven dissenting votes, the Senate with only four dissents. "In a regular process, you might never have had a bill," remarked Rep. James R. Jones, D-Okla., a Ways and Means Trade Subcommittee member. "If everybody had had an open crack at it, you could have that thing amended forever."

And, as Rep. Bill Frenzel, R-Minn., commented, prompt and smooth congressional action on the bill was "an enormous tribute to the collossal skills of Bob Strauss" (who, before becoming special trade representative, had been national chairman of the Democratic Party and was considered one of the canniest political operatives in the Carter administration).

Dividing the Opposition. The politics of the trade bill had dealt with the need to make deals in order to mollify key elements of a potential opposition coalition. Put another way, in the minds of many trade experts the process was less a matter of building a winning coalition than avoiding the formation of a losing one. Most of them agreed that the guiding genius of that strategy had been Strauss.

Harald B. Malmgren, a trade consultant and a former deputy trade representative, noted in 1979 that building a winning coalition was difficult because there was little clear-cut support for the trade package. Traditional supporters of trade liberalization, including farm groups and much of the business community, had become increasingly concerned about rising competition. Industries like electronics, Malmgren said, were split down the middle, with TV companies leaning toward protectionism and other segments of the industry willing to liberalize. Though the AFL-CIO earlier in the 1970s had opposed trade liberalization, organized labor was divided on the issue. "These are microcosms of the national situation," Malmgrem noted. The situation was similar in Congress, where many members had mixed emotions on trade policy.

Challenges at the End of the 1970s

A principal reason for the difficulties, delays and limited success of the Tokyo Round was protectionism. The challenges to the free trade concept were worldwide, but for the United States three factors in particular were responsible for the increasing reluctance of Washington to open the domestic market to foreign competition:

● Sharply higher volume of exports from other industrial countries such as Japan, which was trying to stimulate a sluggish domestic economy by boosting sales overseas. The Japanese effort was so successful that it caused a massive trade surplus having political consequences for U.S.-Japanese relations.

● The emergence of a group of advanced developing countries (Singapore, Taiwan, Hong Kong, South Korea, Brazil, Mexico and Malaysia) that established a dominant position in the export of light manufactures.

● Greater intervention by governments in trade through measures such as export subsidization, price support arrangements, nationalization of major industries and support for research and development, particularly in the field of high technology.

The emergence of multinational corporations also added a new dimension to the trade competition picture. Manufacturing had become far more mobile than in earlier years. Corporate managers more and more frequently made decisions on plant location on the basis of "rationalizing production." Stated simply, this meant that a corporation would close an obsolete, money-losing plant in the United States if it saw a chance to replace it with a modern, low-cost plant in, say, Taiwan, South Korea or Mexico. Moreover, since many multinationals were, by nature, both importers and exporters of goods, the corporation might support free-trade measures in one sector of the economy, while arguing for protectionism in another.

As a result of these and other factors, the U.S. balance of merchandise trade swung sharply into deficit, reaching $26.5 billion by 1978. To counter surging imports, the United States negotiated voluntary quotas on specialty steel imports, on color televisions from Japan and South Korea and on footwear from Korea and Taiwan. In late 1977 the Carter administration imposed a system of trigger prices for steel designed to stop imports from being "dumped," or sold in the United States below the cost of steel from Japan, which was considered to be the most efficient producer. The Common Market imposed similar restrictive measures on textiles, clothing, electronics, chemicals and steel imports.

The European common agricultural policy had been a particularly blatant example of large-scale government intervention in trade. U.S. farm groups contended that sales of the Common Market's heavily subsidized surplus commodities in third country markets had depressed U.S. agricultural exports.

Despite pressure from some members of Congress allied to such industrial interests as steel, chemicals, textiles and shoes, the United States by the end of the 1970s was far from being a protectionist nation. Tariffs were at their lowest levels in more than a century. Like his predecessors, Carter rejected numerous congressional and executive branch attempts to limit imports. Among items denied import relief in 1979 were copper, stainless steel, ferrochromium, shoes, honey and mushrooms.

Major Provisions of 1979 Trade Act

The 1979 trade act made the changes in U.S. law that were "necessary and appropriate" to carry out agreements reached in the Tokyo Round of multilateral trade negotiations. Unlike previous negotiations, which emphasized tariff cuts, the Tokyo Round concentrated on developing new international rules to deal with nontariff barriers to trade, such as government subsidies that affect exports. These nontariff aspects of the agreements required congressional approval.

Those changes, as embodied in the final law:

● Overhauled the U.S. countervailing duty law, which was designed to protect domestic industry against foreign government subsidies on imported goods. Domestic industries for the first time were required to show they had been seriously injured by subsidized imports before an offsetting duty would be imposed. The bill extended existing sanctions on foreign trade practices to include domestic subsidies that indirectly affected exports — such as government-backed loans to export industries — as well as direct government export subsidies.

● Speeded investigations and imposition of penalties under both the countervailing duty law and anti-dumping statutes, which barred imports of goods at prices below home market levels.

● Established a new system of customs valuation that would use the price actually paid for merchandise when it was sold for export to the United States as the primary method of assessing its value for customs purposes.

● Discouraged discrimination against foreign suppliers in bidding for government purchases.

● Directed federal agencies to use product standards in a way that treated imported products "no less favorably" than domestic products.

● Authorized the president to grant least-developed countries full tariff reductions (instead of phased reductions) on products that were not import-sensitive.

The measure also renewed for eight years the president's authority to take part in other multilateral negotiations to remove further nontariff barriers to the free flow of goods.

Controversy Over Jobs and Imports

Nonetheless, protectionist forces argued that rising competition from imports was taking jobs away from Americans. Steel and electronic plant closings and textile industry layoffs were widely reported in the press. An AFL-CIO study prepared for the labor organization's annual convention in December 1977 claimed that more than half a million American jobs had been lost in recent years through plant closings and transfer of operations overseas. Particularly hard hit, according to the AFL-CIO, were electronics and electrical machinery (150,000 jobs), textiles and apparel (300,000 jobs), primary metals (100,000 jobs) and shoes (70,000 jobs).

Opponents of protectionism, however, replied that the AFL-CIO figures were incomplete. While acknowledging that jobs had been lost in the domestic apparel industry, a September 1978 study by the American Exporters Association said that "employment in the industry as a whole has grown by 100,000 in the past three years." The jobs that disappeared tended to be the less productive and lower paying. "Protecting those inefficient economic activities from import competition freezes the status quo, preventing the shift of capital and labor into more productive channels and better-paying jobs," the group asserted.

The pressure for government action to protect domestic industries and preserve jobs was real, not only in the United States but around the world. All the industrial countries faced economic problems similar to those of the United States. The more serious the problems, the more intense the demand for protection. Robert S. McNamara, then president of the World Bank, warned in a September 1978 address that existing economic growth rates could not be sustained "if the protectionist barriers erected by the developed nations against the manufactured exports of the developing countries continue to rise as they have recently." A report by the Organization of American States declared that "an alarming rise of protectionism has occurred in the last several years in the industrialized countries which threatens the development strategies of a number of countries in Latin America and in other regions of the world."

Protectionism Among Developing Nations

While the industrialized countries were most often accused of protectionism, the practice also was widespread in the third world. The World Bank observed in its "World Development Report" for 1978:

Comparison of Pay and Productivity

(average annual percent change)

	1960-1973	1973-1981	1980	1981	Estimate 1982
Output per Hour					
United States	3.0	1.7	0.2	2.8	−1.1
Canada	4.5	1.6	−1.9	0.6	−1.7
Japan	10.7	6.8	6.8	2.9	2.4
West Germany	5.5	4.5	1.1	2.6	2.7
United Kingdom	4.3	2.1	0.5	5.8	5.6
France	6.0	4.6	0.6	2.4	0.6
Italy	6.9	3.6	5.8	2.0	−1.1
Hourly Compensation					
United States	5.0	9.6	11.8	10.2	8.3
Canada	6.4	11.2	10.2	11.1	11.3
Japan	14.6	9.7	6.5	7.4	5.8
West Germany	9.4	9.4	9.0	7.7	4.6
United Kingdom	8.6	19.1	23.6	15.0	11.1
France	9.2	15.1	16.7	16.5	15.3
Italy	12.3	19.6	18.5	20.6	20.6

Source: U.S. Department of Labor, Bureau of Labor Statistics

"Protectionist measures are common in the developing countries as well. For many, particularly those still in the early stages of industrialization, protection can be justified. But for those that are well advanced in the development process, the adverse effects of industrial protection on economic efficiency and growth become increasingly evident."

To promote their own products and build an industrial base, many developing countries turned to high tariffs, import quotas and other protectionist devices. Frequently, such negative actions against imports were accompanied by measures, such as subsidies, to encourage exports. There was evidence that protectionist measures, once adopted, tended to become entrenched. The argument was advanced that high tariffs brought "structural distortions" to a nation's economy. The tariffs could not be lowered without causing distress to domestic industry. Subsidies then became necessary to "correct the distortions."

Loss of U.S. Competitive Advantage?

For most of the century, the United States had been the preeminent industrial nation — "the world's first atomic and technological superpower, a Titan towering over the international economy and politics," in the words of a Nov. 27, 1978, *U.S. News & World Report* article. By the late 1970s chinks had begun to appear in the giant's armor. For a multitude of reasons — ranging from the drain caused by U.S. involvement in the Vietnam War to plant obsolescence, declining productivity growth, high energy costs and many others — American dominance of world trade and finance was eroding steadily.

Some experts attributed the decline in competitiveness to the "mind-set" of American businessmen. They saw American industry as so beguiled by the size and wealth of the domestic market that it was relatively uninterested in overseas sales. To many American corporations, exports were a fringe benefit. Exports were a considerably larger share of GNP of other industrialized nations. *(See also chapter on export subsidies, p. 187.)*

Probably more fundamental to America's declining competitiveness in overseas markets (and, in the case of some industries, at home as well) were the country's decreasing lead in technology and the slump in the productivity of American workers. Output per man-hour grew rapidly for nearly a quarter century following World War II but began to fall off in the late 1960s and early 1970s.

Productivity performance involves a broad range of factors — management skills, worker training and incentives, management-labor relations, government regulations, technological advances and investment in new equipment. Many experts attributed the decline in U.S. productivity to steadily decreasing investment in the research and development of new production techniques and equipment. Data compiled by the National Science Foundation showed, for example, that U.S. spending on research and development shrank from 2.73 percent of the GNP in 1962 to 2.44 percent in 1977, while the corresponding 1977 figures of most other industrial nations, with the exception of Britain, rose. *(For further discussion, see chapter on Industrial Policy.)*

An intriguing argument was offered by Melvyn B. Krauss, a professor of economics at New York University, in his book *The New Protectionism* (1978). Krauss wrote that declines in productivity, as well as the increase in protectionist sentiment, could be attributed to the rise of the modern "welfare state." Krauss defined the goals of the welfare state as 1) providing economic security for its citizens by protecting them from change that would hurt their economic positions, and 2) redistributing income (and economic power in general) from capital to labor.

> Simply stated [Krauss continued], the inherent contradiction of the welfare state is that the welfare state requires a high level of productivity to support it, but that the welfare state interventionist policies necessarily reduce productivity levels. Hence ... the welfare state ... consists of policies that undermine the factors upon which it critically depends.

New Challenges From Developing Countries

Although the principal competition to American industry continued to come from the industrial nations of Western Europe and Japan, a 1978 congressional study suggested that American manufacturers could expect increasing competition from suppliers in developing countries. The Joint Economic Committee study analyzed the export potential of eight "advanced developing nations" — Brazil, Hong Kong, India, Mexico, the Philippines, Singapore, South Korea and Taiwan. The eight countries together accounted for 29 percent of all U.S. imports from the developing world.

The study identified 158 product categories in which American industries might be "vulnerable" to competition from foreign suppliers. These included some traditional imports that had long been competitive in the U.S. market, such as electronics equipment, textiles, ceramics and glass, footwear, hats and gloves, bicycles, toys and leather products. Also included were several that previously had not been regarded as competitive threats. Among these were manufactured wood products, hand tools, agricultural machinery, typewriters and office equipment and cameras and photographic equipment.

The main challenge to U.S. industry from developing countries would not come in the form of a sharp increase in imports, but rather in a rising level of industrial "sophistication" that would permit those countries to compete with American goods in other overseas markets. The study predicted that

> The United States is likely to retain an unchallengeable competitive advantage only in products and techniques that are at the very forefront of technological development or that require a huge integrated market for their creation.
> Examples of these are satellite communications and photogra-

phy, deep-sea mining and the very largest electrical generating and delivery systems. Development of these technologies requires government support for initial research, assistance in the primary stages of marketing and government purchases of a significant share of the final output.

By the end of the 1970s rich and poor nations alike seemed to recognize their stake in maintaining good trade relations. The international trading system had become an interlocking network, inextricably linking all countries' economies.

The world depression of the 1930s had been brought on, in large part, by the "beggar-thy-neighbor" policies of the leading industrial powers. Beset with economic problems at home, and pressed by the competition of imports from abroad, each country tried to erect protective walls around its domestic markets.

Since the 1930s the world's economies had become much more dependent on the international flow of goods and services. The actions of a single country could have a profound effect on all the others. Recession, inflation and high unemployment in the United States also hurt America's trading partners. Similarly, economic distress in foreign countries could damage the U.S. economy. The challenge to the administration and Congress in the 1980s was to breathe new life into ailing domestic industries without disrupting the liberal patterns of world trade on which all depended.

Soviet pipeline construction. Using the foreign policy controls authorized by the Export Administration Act, President Reagan blocked the export of U.S. pipelaying equipment to the Soviet Union in 1981.

Chapter 4

TRADE WITH COMMUNIST NATIONS

The United States' trade relations with the communist world evolved separately from its dealings with the industrialized nations of the West and the developing countries of Asia, Latin America and Africa.

U.S. policy makers for the most part have viewed trade with the West in basically economic terms, unlike their perception of trade with communist nations. America's general approach to free world trade has been to pursue policies that served U.S. interests foremost but also the economic well being of all concerned (although protectionism has encroached on this objective from time to time).

When the issue is trade with communist nations, however, U.S. decision makers have tended to follow a "carrot and stick" approach, with the result that economic policy frequently has been subordinated to broader political goals and viewed almost exclusively as a tool to further those more sweeping objectives.

There have been similarities, and paradoxes, in the U.S. approach to the two sets of relations. Initially, the desire to liberalize trade with America's postwar allies and the less developed nations was founded on the foreign policy goals of fostering democratic political systems and free market economies. But it also was grounded in basic economic self-interest for the United States. Fortunately for America, the two coincided nicely in the immediate postwar period.

In the first two decades of the postwar era, America's trade policy with the communist bloc nations (the Soviet Union and the Eastern European states of Albania, Bulgaria, Czechoslovakia, the German Democratic Republic, Hungary, Poland and Romania) was, for a short time, focused on attempts to draw those countries into the free world, and then, when that failed, to isolate and weaken them.

In the late 1960s and 1970s U.S. foreign policy makers again came to believe that communist nations could be persuaded to alter their character through increased contact with the West; hence, they pursued a policy of détente. Trade was seen as a way to further that objective.

Strains in East-West Relations

The balance sheet on that policy was mixed. By the early 1980s there was considerable pessimism as to whether trade incentives could fundamentally alter the domestic and foreign policies of communist nations. The economic advantages of East-West trade increasingly became paramount in U.S. trade relations with the communist world. Even so, East-West balance of power considerations (political, military and economic) remained the decisive factors in determining trade relations with the Soviet bloc. Nowhere was this more evident than in the opening of trade relations with the People's Republic of China (PRC), beginning in 1971-72, during the presidency of Richard Nixon, and culminating six years later in the formal recognition of the PRC by President Jimmy Carter. China was viewed as a counterweight to (and even a potential U.S. ally against) Soviet military expansionism. Opening trade with the vast Chinese market was viewed not only as a spur to U.S. business, but also as a means of cementing good relations between the two nations.

The controversy over exports to communist countries of so-called high-technology items, which also could be used for military purposes, was another example of the continuing interconnection between economic and foreign policy objectives. The communist nations held out the potential of a lucrative market for the export of American technical know-how. Yet foreign policy and national security considerations directed at the use to which that technology might be put militated against broadening that market.

The growth of East-West trade during the 1970s seemed beneficial to both sides. The Soviet Union and its satellites needed the food, particularly grain, and technology that they were unable to produce. To some extent, trade with the West made improvements in Soviet living standards possible.

In the 1970s many of the industrialized nations on which the Soviets depended for imports were experiencing trade deficits and balance of payments problems, and they were grateful for the fact that the Russians paid promptly for what they bought. Moreover, some U.S. officials believed that trade links with Moscow would force the Soviet Union to act with restraint in the whole range of East-West dealings or risk losing

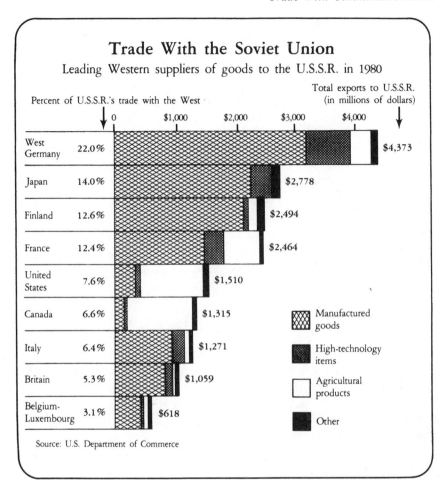

Trade With the Soviet Union
Leading Western suppliers of goods to the U.S.S.R. in 1980

Percent of U.S.S.R.'s trade with the West

Total exports to U.S.S.R. (in millions of dollars)

West Germany	22.0%	$4,373
Japan	14.0%	$2,778
Finland	12.6%	$2,494
France	12.4%	$2,464
United States	7.6%	$1,510
Canada	6.6%	$1,315
Italy	6.4%	$1,271
Britain	5.3%	$1,059
Belgium-Luxembourg	3.1%	$618

Manufactured goods

High-technology items

Agricultural products

Other

Source: U.S. Department of Commerce

the goods and services it so desperately needed (a view that came to be known as "linkage").

U.S. Policy Questioned

By the 1980s this view was increasingly being challenged as a series of crises strained East-West relations and put an end to détente. One of the principal architects of linkage and détente, former Secretay of State Henry A. Kissinger (1973-77), described his disillusionment with the way the policy he had once espoused had worked out. Writing in *The New York Times* Jan. 16, 1982, Kissinger commented:

99

A decade or so ago, when East-West trade, technology transfer and financial relations began to develop, many believed that economic ties could become an instrument — among others — for moderating Soviet behavior. In a crisis, we thought, the fear of losing markets or access to raw materials, Western technical innovations or bank credits would produce Soviet caution. But this assumption presupposed a Western willingness to use its economic strength in the service of overall strategy. This clearly has not happened. On the contrary, so many Western nations have let themselves become dependent on Soviet trade that a trade cutoff is more likely to turn into a Soviet weapon against the West.

This chapter traces the evolution of America's trade policy with the communist world, beginning with the Cold War era of confrontation, followed by the policy of détente and the subsequent cooling of relations after the Soviet invasion of Afghanistan in December 1979, the imposition of martial law in Poland in December 1981 and other events that strained U.S. ties with the Soviet Union.

From Cold War to Détente

The U.S. postwar commitment to liberal trade policies was sharply modified respecting commerce with most of the communist countries. Beginning in 1947, President Harry S Truman placed tight restrictions on American exports to the Soviet Union under provisions of the Export Control Act of 1940. The Commerce Department announced Jan. 15, 1948, that all shipments to Europe would be subject to individual export licensing. And the following year Congress enacted a new Export Control Act, which was renewed and revised in subsequent years.

Embargo on Trade With Communist Bloc

All commercial trade between the United States and the People's Republic of China (PRC) was halted on Dec. 16, 1950, after the Chinese intervened in the Korean War. That embargo, together with previous controls, virtually eliminated trade with the communist world.

Although the United States initially persuaded most of its North Atlantic Treaty Organization (NATO) allies to impose tight controls on trade with communist governments, by 1953 both East and West Europeans had begun to press for resumption of economic contacts. U.S. policy underwent some changes, but remained essentially restrictive into the 1960s.

After the North Atlantic Treaty was signed in 1949, the United States and its allies set up a Coordinating Committee (COCOM) to seek common policies on exports to communist nations. There was general agreement from the outset to bar shipments of arms and munitions. But the allies soon differed on what other items should be considered "strategic" and included in COCOM's list of embargoed goods. The United States consistently argued for a more extensive listing than did the Europeans. With the death of Soviet dictator Joseph Stalin and the achievement of truce in Korea in 1953, pressure mounted in Europe for reduced restrictions on trade with communist nations, and COCOM's list was cut sharply in 1954 and again in 1958.

The United States continued to maintain tighter restrictions on its own exports to the Soviet bloc. There were two notable exceptions on the countries affected: Yugoslavia was given substantial military and economic aid after its break with Moscow in 1948, while Poland was assisted after a lesser rupture in 1956 by "sales" of surplus wheat for local currency (which remained frozen under terms of the Battle Act, however). *(Battle Act, p. 102)*

Commercial exchanges with both countries were encouraged. These two exceptions encountered much criticism in Congress, where continuing efforts were made to curtail executive discretion in dealing with all communist nations.

The administration of John F. Kennedy, more anxious than the Eisenhower administration to encourage a "détente" with the Soviet Union, began to reassess U.S. policy on communist trade in 1961, but it initiated only limited changes. (The PRC was excluded from the reappraisal.) When the Export Control Act was extended in 1962 for three years, Congress directed the president to bar shipments that would make "a significant contribution to the military or economic potential" of nations threatening U.S. security. Kennedy nevertheless overrode strong opposition in Congress to approve credit guarantees for large sales of wheat to the Soviet bloc in 1963 and 1964.

Legislative Controls on Trade

During World War II, the United States conducted full-scale economic warfare against the Axis powers (Germany, Italy and Japan), cutting off U.S. exports and blacklisting those companies in neutral countries doing business with the enemy. Exports of commodities in short supply continued to be controlled after 1945, when inflation became a major concern. The deterioration in East-West relations following the establishment of communist regimes in Eastern Europe and China led to additional legislative controls on trade, ostensibly for security purposes. Three major laws were involved:

Export Control Act. Passed in 1940 and rewritten in 1949, the Export Control Act empowered the president to bar or limit exports to further the foreign policy or national security interests of the United States or to cope with domestic shortages and inflation. Administered by the Commerce Department through a licensing system, the act was extended periodically through the 1950s and 1960s. It was extensively rewritten again in 1969 and renamed the Export Administration Act.

Trading With the Enemy Act. The 1917 Trading With the Enemy Act permanently empowered the president to regulate all transactions between Americans and foreigners in time of war or a declared national emergency involving the transfer of funds. Administered by the Treasury Department, this authority was invoked in 1950 to prohibit all trade with Communist China and North Korea after the Chinese sent troops into Korea and President Harry S Truman declared a national emergency Dec. 16.

Mutual Defense Assistance Control Act. Enacted in 1951, the Mutual Defense Assistance Control Act, dubbed the Battle Act after its sponsor, Rep. Laurie C. Battle, D-Ala. (1947-55), flatly prohibited U.S. aid to any third country shipping arms to communist nations and directed the president to suspend aid to nations shipping specified "strategic" goods to these countries unless he thought it contrary to the national interest to do so. Presidents Eisenhower and Kennedy urged Congress to allow them more discretion, but to no avail.

U.S. policy on trading with communist nations, as reflected in the foregoing laws, remained virtually unchanged until the late 1960s. Such laws affected all trade with China, North Korea, Mongolia, North Vietnam and Cuba, except that food and medicines could be sent to Cuba. The embargo was applied in 1950 to the first three countries, in 1954 to North Vietnam and in 1960 to Cuba.

In addition, there was a ban on the export of U.S. arms and strategic and critical materials from the United States to the Soviet Union and its European satellites (however, restrictions were somewhat lighter for exports to Poland and Romania). Trade in other items was not forbidden, but exporters whose products received subsidies, such as wheat farmers, had to get special permission. Generally, no restrictions were placed on trade with non-communist countries or with Yugoslavia.

Various foreign aid bills as well as amendments to the Agricultural Trade Development and Assistance Act of 1954 imposed still other restrictions. For example, they barred the government from providing foreign economic or military aid, credit guarantees or similar benefits to communist countries. Legislation enacted in the early 1950s reflected a feeling in Congress that America's allies should enforce equally restrictive export regulations. Several amendments to foreign aid bills in the 1950s authorized the president to withhold assistance from any country that allowed shipments to communist countries of goods the United States had embargoed for export to those nations. The strongest expression of this policy was embodied in the Battle Act.

Categories of Strategic Controls

Under the Battle Act the United States drew up three lists of items subject to security controls. They were:

● Category A: 21 classes of war materials, including "arms, ammunition, implements of war, and atomic energy materials," deemed to be of such strategic importance as to require complete embargo.

● Category B: 260 items of "primary strategic significance," including petroleum, transportation equipment, and types of equipment used in the production of war materials, also subject to total embargo.

● Category C: some machine tools, raw materials, construction and electrical equipment of secondary strategic importance, subject to lighter controls than imposed on the other two categories.

Fifteen Western nations agreed to establish three international control lists in 1952: 1) an embargo list corresponding to Categories A and B of the Battle Act lists; 2) a quantitative list covering goods of secondary strategic importance subject to lesser controls; and 3) a "watch list" of items to be kept under constant surveillance. Differences among the 15 nations cropped up almost immediately over the extent of the controls and the items to be placed under embargo.

Soviet Overtures to Reopen Trade

Feeling the economic pinch because of its heavy responsibilities and commitments to its satellites, Moscow made overtures to Western nations as early as 1951 for a restoration of trade. Kremlin spokesmen asserted that normal trade relations were the key to an enduring peace. The Soviets, pushing the development of their heavy industry, were anxious to ease Western restrictions on machinery as well as on joint ventures for the construction of entire factories.

With the easing of tensions after Stalin's death in 1953, Western Europe was eager to respond, urging a thorough review of the embargoes. A general revision of the international embargo lists was carried out in the following year. It went further than the United States desired, according to a 1954 report to Congress made by Harold Stassen, director of the Foreign Operations Administration and administrator of the Battle Act. The number of items subject to total embargo was reduced to 170 from 260, and materials subject to quantitative controls were reduced to 20 from 90. Trade between communist countries and Western Europe took a pronounced jump, helping to raise the value of total East-West trade to $4.4 billion in 1955, some 20 percent above the 1954 figure and more than 40 percent above the 1953 total.

The United States did not participate appreciably in the East-West trade expansion until 1957, when it eased some restrictions on exports to Poland. Trade with other East European nations and the Soviet Union remained small, however. Soviet Premier Nikita S. Khrushchev suggested to President Eisenhower in 1958 that a large-scale exchange of goods would be "of great mutual benefit to both countries" and would further "the cause of peace", but little came of that overture.

Khrushchev and First Deputy Premier Anastas I. Mikoyan pressed the Soviet drive for relaxation of trade controls during a visit to the United States in 1959. Prospects of several billion dollars' worth of orders were dangled before American businessmen. But in return the Soviets demanded favorable credit arrangements, most-favored-nation (nondiscriminatory) tariff treatment for Soviet exports and the removal of export controls, all of which were rejected by the Eisenhower administration.

Communist efforts to increase trade with the outside world in the 1950s were viewed in the West as evidence of Moscow's failure to achieve a "division of labor" among the Soviet bloc countries of Eastern Europe. That goal was set at a summit conference of communist nations held in Moscow in 1958. The economies of the bloc countries had been developed along parallel lines, with the emphasis on heavy industry and economic self-sufficiency in each nation. But eventually they found themselves competing for a limited supply of raw materials and transportation facilities. Their supply and distribution system collapsed in

1956, causing an economic crisis throughout Eastern Europe that led to unrest in several communist countries.

At the summit the bloc revamped the system of cooperation within the Soviet-directed Council for Mutual Economic Assistance (COMECON). (The group had been formed in 1949 as a counterpart to NATO. In 1983 it was composed of the Soviet Union, East Germany, Poland, Bulgaria, Romania, Hungary, Czechoslovakia, Mongolia, Vietnam and Cuba.) Afterward, the U.S.S.R. and the East European nations attempted to form a single, centrally planned and coordinated economy. Had the integration gone according to plan, the need for outside trade would have been greatly reduced. But cracks began to appear in the plan almost immediately as the allocations of production for export and designated imports played havoc with existing national economies.

U.S. Opposition to Trade Relaxation

Throughout the 1950s the topic of expanding East-West trade was debated frequently in the United States. But the existing policy of severely restricting economic relations remained essentially unchanged. When the Export Control Act was extended for three years in 1962, Congress directed the president to bar shipments that would make "a significant contribution to the military or economic potential" of nations threatening U.S. security.

Nonetheless, some changes were made. Despite strong opposition in Congress, Kennedy in 1963 negotiated large sales of wheat to the Soviet bloc. Deliveries were made in 1963 and 1964. Opponents of the move tried to insert a provision in a foreign aid funding bill to prohibit Export-Import Bank guarantees of private credits to communist countries for the purchase of U.S. commodities. (Established in 1934, the bank provides low-interest loans for the purchase of U.S. goods by foreign nations and businesses.) After four days of partisan wrangling in late December 1963, opponents agreed to give the president discretion to authorize the Ex-Im Bank to provide guarantees if he considered it to be in the national interest.

East-West trade relations were the subject of extensive study by the Senate Foreign Relations Committee in 1964. While most administration officials who testified were cautiously favorable toward a resumption of trade with the Soviet Union, some lawmakers were adamantly opposed. Sen. Karl E. Mundt, R-S.D. (1948-73), a senior committee member, reflected the feelings of a number of members when he said that opening up trade "even to the extent of perhaps giving the communist bloc lower shipping rates, longer-term credits, and low-interest rates — we are going to expand the power of communist countries. At the same time," he added, "we are going to continue to ask the American taxpayer ... to supply money for an aid program to strengthen the free world against the attack of the communists...."

Moves Under Johnson to Increase Trade

By 1965 there was considerable support among administration officials and those outside the government for expanding trade with communist nations. President Lyndon B. Johnson in his 1965 State of the Union Message said the government was exploring ways of increasing trade with the Soviet bloc. Various groups in government, business and agriculture released studies and reports supporting the idea that expanded trade with the communist nations was in America's interest. Organized labor, however, held to a hard-line anti-communist position and denounced all efforts to expand East-West trade. (Labor's position was to see-saw, however, depending not only on Soviet policies and actions but also on the U.S. economy and employment situation; moveover, there were divisions within organized labor.)

Congress in 1966 rebuffed proposals to expand American trade with the Soviet Union and Eastern Europe. The administration's major legislative proposal, the East-West Trade Relations Act, would have given the president authority to extend most-favored-nation (MFN) status to European communist nations (except East Germany) if he thought it would be in the national interest. The proposal was virtually ignored on Capitol Hill. This came as no surprise to administration officials who knew that few members of Congress would vote in an election year to improve trade with communist countries while the United States was fighting a communist enemy in Southeast Asia. The administration hoped only for a full discussion of the legislation, but even that was not forthcoming.

Nonetheless, in a major foreign policy speech in New York City Oct. 7. 1966, Johnson announced several actions taken to ease East-West trade restrictions. "Our task," the president said, "is to achieve a reconciliation with the East — a shift from the narrow concept of coexistence to the broader vision of peaceful engagement.... We seek healthy economic and cultural relations with the communist states." Johnson announced that the United States was negotiating a civil air agreement with the Soviet Union to establish direct air service between Moscow and New York and that the administration would reduce East-West trade controls on hundreds of items.

Ex-Im Bank Restrictions and FIAT Agreement

As it had in 1963, the Ex-Im Bank in 1967 again became embroiled in congressional controversy over East-West trade. Taking a routine administration proposal to extend the life of the bank for five years, the Senate added a provision barring Ex-Im Bank credits to non-communist nations for the purchase of U.S. goods that were intended to be exported to communist countries. The provision, contained in the final version of the bill approved Feb. 27, 1968, also blocked Ex-Im Bank credits for purchase of U.S. goods by nations at war with the United States or by nations that aided such belligerents, a move related to the growing U.S. war effort against North Vietnam. The president could waive the ban if he found it to be in the national interest. (The provision was repealed in 1971.)

The Senate amendment was provoked by an Ex-Im Bank plan to participate in the financing of a joint Italian-Soviet FIAT automobile plant to be built in the Soviet Union. The issue arose Oct. 7, 1966, when Johnson announced that the Ex-Im Bank was prepared to guarantee Italian credits for the purchase of American machine tools to be used in the plant. In what was the largest East-West trade deal ever undertaken, the FIAT motor company had agreed to build an $800 million automobile plant that would produce 600,000 automobiles a year. Of that sum, about $350 million was to be spent to buy machinery in the West. About $50 million was planned for direct purchases of automotive machine tools from the United States, and an additional sum was to be spent on purchases from European firms operating under license arrangements with U.S. companies.

The plans had called for the Ex-Im Bank to make loans to the Instituto Mobiliare Italiano, an Italian financial institution, and for FIAT then to use the funds to buy the U.S. equipment. Administration witnesses testifying against the amendment said it would neither block financing by other nations of the FIAT plant nor affect trading by other nations with North Vietnam. On the other hand, they charged that it would severely cut U.S. exports to European nations that had only minor contact with North Vietnam and further damage the shaky U.S. balance-of-payments position.

1969 Export Administration Act Eases Controls

Restrictions on trade with communist countries were relaxed somewhat with passage of the Export Administration Act of 1969. President Nixon had asked for a simple four-year extension of the 1949 act. But supporters of loosening the restrictions on trade with the Soviet bloc argued that Cold War hostilities had quieted and that the main effect of the controls in the old act was to deny U.S. exporters access to a growing East European market.

The 1969 act included a provision enabling the United States to sell items to communist nations if the same goods were freely available from other areas or countries, such as Western Europe and Japan. The provision reflected the fact that all but 200 of the 1,200 items subject to controls at the end of 1968 could be obtained from European nations. The bill also recognized that "the unwarranted restrictions of exports from the United States has a serious adverse effect on our balance of payments."

The 1969 version still permitted the president to prohibit all trade for reasons of national security regardless of foreign availability. But it required him to explain in detail reasons for restricting trade in non-military goods and items that could be obtained from other nations.

In the 1970s, Congress continued to relax U.S. restrictions on trade with the communist bloc. In 1972 Congress passed a bill requiring prompt removal of unilateral export controls except where it was determined that such action would be detrimental to the national security. At the same time, the bill also extended, until June 30, 1974, the president's authority to control exports under the Export Administration Act of 1969.

Volume of U.S. Trade With Communist Bloc

U.S. trade with Eastern Europe never amounted to more than a small portion of total exports. American exports to the U.S.S.R. reached a pre-war peak of $114 million in 1930 and imports a high of $31 million in 1937. Lend-lease shipments to Russia during the war amounted to about $10 billion, but by 1949 U.S. commercial transactions with the Soviet Union had dropped to $6.6 million. In 1952 U.S. exports to all communist countries (excluding Yugoslavia) were valued at $1.1 million, an all-time low.

Meanwhile, the volume of trade between America's allies and the communist world grew rapidly. The countries of Western Europe,

Canada and Japan together exported $2.5 billion to the Sino-Soviet bloc in 1962. The same year U.S. exports to the bloc came to $125 million (of which $94 million worth went to Poland), plus $154 million to Yugoslavia. Imports from the bloc (excluding $54 million from Yugoslavia) totaled $82 million, half of it from Poland. These levels were somewhat higher in 1963, but still constituted a minute fraction of total U.S. exports ($23.2 billion) and imports ($17.2 billion).

Apart from the question of security, U.S. trade policy toward the communist states was shaped by political and technical factors. Unlike Britain, France or West Germany, the United States was poorly equipped to negotiate with the state-trading bodies of the bloc. But as East-West tensions subsided, American firms pressed for policy changes that would permit them to compete for new business with communist nations.

Trade and Détente in the 1970s

The foreign affairs achievement most prominently identified with Nixon's first term in office was the general improvement in relations with the communist bloc. Success in that direction was made possible in part by the president's past reputation as a strong anti-communist, according to some political observers, which undercut any criticism that he was "soft" on communism.

The tone was set by Nixon's first inaugural address, Jan. 20, 1969, when he said that "after a period of confrontation, we are entering an era of negotiation." Nixon was the first American president to visit Romania (August 1969), Yugoslavia (September 1970), the People's Republic of China (February 1972) and the Soviet Union (May 1972). The China trip opened communications between the two countries, while the trip to Moscow resulted in pledges of better trade relations. *(U. S.-China relations, see p. 123.)*

Nixon's Trip to the U.S.S.R.

The most dramatic product of Nixon's visit to the Soviet Union was agreement on a strategic arms limitation treaty (SALT I). A milestone in U.S.-Soviet relations, the agreement overshadowed somewhat another noteworthy achievement of the summit meeting between Nixon and Soviet leader Leonid T. Brezhnev — a pledge by both nations to improve and expand trade relations.

The statement on basic principles released at the end of the summit noted that both sides viewed commercial ties "as an important and necessary element in the strengthening of their bilateral relations." In concrete terms, this meant the establishment of a Joint United States-U.S.S.R. Commercial Commission on May 26, 1972, and the announcement on July 8, 1972, that the United States had advanced to Moscow a $500 million line of credit in return for a Soviet pledge to buy $750 million worth of U.S. grain (8.7 million metric tons) over a three-year period. The agreement was announced on July 5 after a delegation of U.S. officials, led by Secretary of Commerce Peter G. Peterson, traveled to Moscow to discuss further trade accommodations. The discussions were the first formal meeting of the U.S.-Soviet commercial commission.

A major stumbling block in the bargaining was settlement of the Soviet Union's World War II lend-lease debts to the United States, which amounted to $722 million. Administration officials insisted on settlement of the debts as part of any broad trade agreement. Negotiations culminated Oct. 18 with the signing of a three-year trade pact and an agreement on repayment of the lend-lease debts.

Implementation of the trade agreement also hinged on congressional approval of most-favored-nation (MFN) status for Soviet products. If the nondiscriminatory tariff status were not granted by Congress, the pact would not enter into force and the Soviet Union, in accordance with the second agreement, would not have to repay the balance of its lend-lease debt. According to the agreement, the Soviets would remit $48 million by July 1975, but the remaining debt would be deferred until MFN treatment was granted.

Controversy Over 1972 Wheat Sale

Nixon's negotiation of the 1972 grain deal with Moscow proved to be controversial. As arranged by the U.S. Agriculture Department, the bulk of the transaction was to consist of feed grains, such as corn, which would be used by the Soviets to bolster their poultry and livestock production. By late summer, however, it became apparent that Soviet interest had shifted to wheat. Agriculture Secretary Earl L. Butz said in September that Soviet purchases of wheat alone under the agreement could reach 400 million bushels in 1972 — more than one-fourth the total U.S. crop. Butz added that total U.S. grain sales to the Soviets had approached $1 billion for the year, far more than the total value originally contemplated over the entire three-year life of the agreement. The Soviets, in fact, bought more than 700 million bushels of grain, including nearly 440 million bushels of wheat. As a result, the U.S. government paid more than $300 million in export subsidies to American grain traders. Worldwide prices for grains rose steeply in the wake of the Soviet purchases, which, some critics of the sale said, pushed up food costs to consumers in the United States.

There was speculation that the large grain traders were aware that the Russians were planning to buy an unprecedented amount of grain — which would hike prices — but negelcted to share that information with farmers before they sold their goods.

The Senate Government Operations Permanent Subcommittee on Investigations, in a report issued July 29, 1974, had harsh words for the Agriculture Department's handling of the 1972 grain sales. While the subcommittee lauded the Nixon administration's goals — easing tensions between the United States and Soviet Union, improving America's balance-of-payments deficit and allowing U.S. farmers to profitably and usefully dispose of crop surpluses — it concluded that due to inept management and poor judgment in the Department of Agriculture the grain sale resulted in a domestic shortage of farm products, a snarled U.S. transportation system, waste of taxpayers' dollars, "unprecedented" rises in the cost of food and added inflation.

Memories of the 1972 sale led to an "informal" administration embargo on grain sales to the Soviet Union in 1975 after Moscow again began buying large amounts (9.8 million tons by late July). The embargo was lifted Oct. 20 when a five-year Soviet-American grain agreement was signed in Moscow. The Soviets pledged to buy between 6 million and 8 million tons of grain each year. It was hoped that planned Soviet purchases would cause less disruption of U.S. markets.

The Soviet Union and the 1974 Trade Act

Despite the public criticism of the wheat sale and the administration's promotion of expanded U.S.-Soviet trade, President Nixon followed up his commitment made to Kremlin leaders at the May 1972 Moscow summit by submitting to Congress April 10, 1973, a measure that included a provision empowering the president to extend most-favored-nation (MFN) status to the Soviet Union.

When the General Agreement on Tariffs and Trade (GATT) was concluded in Geneva in 1947, the contracting parties agreed to extend MFN treatment to each other. In submitting his trade bill to Congress, Nixon requested authority to allow the United States to enter into bilateral commercial arrangements to extend MFN treatment to countries that did not receive such treatment.

As already noted, implementation of the October 1972 U.S.-Soviet trade agreement hinged on congressional approval of MFN treatment for the Soviet Union. If it was not granted, the pact would not enter into force and the Soviets, in accordance with the other agreement signed in October, would not be obliged to repay the balance of their World War II lend-lease debt.

Extension of MFN treatment was said to be of both material and psychological importance. According to administration officials, it was estimated that MFN status for Soviet products would result in additional imports from the U.S.S.R. worth between $10 million and $25 million.

Jackson-Vanik Amendment. The bill ran into trouble on Capitol Hill. Anti-Soviet sentiment increased during 1973 as a result of the Kremlin's role in the Middle East war and the imposition of a tax on Soviet citizens wishing to leave the country.

In August 1972 Moscow began to levy an exit fee — reportedly up to $30,000 — on holders of advanced academic degrees. The Kremlin justified the fees as reimbursement to the state for its investment in education, the benefits of which would be lost through emigration. But the general effect of the fee was to block the emigration of Soviet Jews to Israel because Jews were among the most highly educated in the Soviet Union and formed the bulk of those wishing to leave.

In response, pressure increased in Congress to withhold MFN treatment from the Soviets. By the end of March 1973, 76 senators and 273 representatives had joined in sponsoring an amendment that barred MFN status and the extension of credits, credit guarantees or investment credits to any non-market economy country denying its citizens the right to emigrate or taxing emigration. The amendment initiative was led in the Senate by Henry M. Jackson, D-Wash. (1953-83), and in the House by Charles A. Vanik, D-Ohio (1955-81).

Over administration opposition, the House Dec. 11 passed the trade bill containing the restrictive Vanik amendment. During hearings on the bill, held by the House Ways and Means Committee, Secretary of State William P. Rogers argued that better treatment of Soviet Jews "will come not from the confrontation formal legislation would now bring about, but from a steady improvement in our overall relations." The measure endorsed by the House allowed the president to give MFN status to Soviet imports, but only if he certified to Congress that the Soviet government's restrictive emigration policies had been eased. It also gave either the

House or the Senate power to overrule the president's action.

Compromise Reached. Consideration of the bill in the House was delayed three times in October and November at the request of President Nixon and Kissinger, who by then had succeeded Rogers as secretary of state. Faced with strong anti-Soviet sentiment, officials feared that House debate on the trade bill at that time would only increase U.S.-Soviet tensions.

The Senate did not act on the trade bill until late in 1974. Throughout the year, the Soviets took the position that emigration was an internal matter unrelated to U.S.-Soviet commercial affairs. The administration was forced into negotiating with both the Kremlin and the Senate in an attempt to fashion a compromise that would not alienate the Soviets yet satisfy Congress.

Agreement between the White House and Congress was announced Oct. 18. An exchange of letters between Jackson and Kissinger released that day outlined the conditions the Soviets would have to meet in their emigration policies before the president would certify to Congress that their practices were leading substantially to a free emigration policy. Jackson said the agreement, based on assurances of Soviet leaders, assumed that the annual rate of emigration from the Soviet Union would rise from the 1973 level of about 35,000 and would in the future correspond to the number of applicants, which Jackson said exceeded 130,000. A benchmark of 60,000 annually would be considered a "minimum standard" of compliance, he said.

In Dec. 3 testimony before the Senate Finance Committee, Kissinger said the compromise did not reflect "formal government commitments" between the two countries, but was based on "clarifications of Soviet ... practices from Soviet leaders." He cautioned the committee that any attempt "to nail down publicly" additional details or commitments was "likely to backfire." "If I were to assert here that a formal agreement on emigration from the U.S.S.R. exists between our governments, that statement would immediately be repudiated by the Soviet government," Kissinger said. He added that no commitments had been made by Soviet leaders on specific numbers of emigrés. The Jackson letter, he said, contained interpretations and elaborations "which were never stated to us by Soviet officials."

Soviet Objections. The Soviet Union Dec. 18 issued a statement denying that it had given any specific assurances that emigration policies would be eased in return for American trade concessions and replying in particular to Jackson's claim that emigration would increase. It also released the text of an October letter to Kissinger from Foreign Minister Andrei A. Gromyko, criticizing the Jackson-Kissinger letters as a "distorted picture of our position as well as of what we told the American side on that matter." Gromyko called the issue a wholly domestic one and said the Soviet Union expected a decrease, rather than an increase, in the number of persons wishing to emigrate.

Despite the confusion over what exactly had been worked out, Congress passed the bill — the Trade Act of 1974 — Dec. 20, thereby allowing the United States to participate in the multilateral trade negotiations scheduled to begin in February 1975. Soviet reaction to the legislation came quickly. Kissinger announced Jan. 14, 1975, that the Kremlin had rejected the terms for trade contained in the Jackson-Vanik amendment and accordingly would not put into force the 1972 trade agreement. *(Provisions of 1974 Trade Act, p. 83)*

Export-Import Bank Credits

Congress had another opportunity to register disapproval of the Soviet Union when, on Dec. 19, 1974, it approved a measure satisfying senators' demands for closer congressional oversight of the Ex-Im Bank's operations, particularly its support for exports to the Soviet Union. The Senate twice rejected conference reports on the measure before the House accepted the Soviet trade restrictions. Specifically, the legislation included provisions that:

● Set a $300 million ceiling on total Ex-Im Bank loans and guarantees to finance exports to the Soviet Union. The president could set a higher limit if he determined that an increase was in the U.S. national interest, but Congress would have to approve any higher ceiling by concurrent resolution.

● Prohibited use of more than $40 million of that amount to finance exports to the Soviet Union of fossil fuel research or exploration equipment and services, and prohibited any financing of exports intended to develop Soviet fossil fuel resources.

● Required the bank to notify Congress at least 25 days before approving any transaction with any country involving loans, credits or a combination of financing arrangements that totaled $60 million or more, or any transaction of $25 million or more for fossil fuel projects in the Soviet Union.

Export Control Act Extended

Congress in 1977 extended the 1969 Export Administration Act for two years. The 1977 measure modified existing law to base export control policy on existing and potential U.S. relations with foreign nations, rather than on whether they had communist systems. The 1977 measure also prohibited export restrictions on U.S. goods that could be obtained from other nations, unless potential damage to national security could be demonstrated.

The law was again extended in September 1979, this time for four years. Congress made few major changes in the act. The 1979 law, however, spelled out criteria for the president to follow if he sought to limit exports for foreign policy reasons. It also streamlined export licensing procedures and ordered officials to prune the number of items subject to controls. Business lobbyists said the bill met many exporters' complaints about the way controls were administered. Raymond Garcia, vice president of a business coalition called the Emergency Committee for American Trade, said that the measure "for the first time, puts significant restraints on the president's use of controls for foreign policy reasons, sets timetables for action on license applications, and it opens up the entire process for public participation."

A further extension of the act was the subject of heated controversy in 1983. While some members of Congress wanted to loosen the controls, others expressed concern that easing restrictions would make available American technology for Soviet military modernization. *(Details, see high technology chapter.)*

Strains in U.S.-Soviet Trade Relations

President Jimmy Carter entered office having pledged to base America's dealings with its allies and foes on a heightened concern for human justice. Carter also pledged to get the stalled U.S.-Soviet strategic arms limitation talks (SALT II) moving again. By the time he left office, the use of human rights as a guide to the conduct of foreign relations largely had been discarded, and the SALT II agreement that Carter had pressed for so zealously had been shelved. The Carter team was replaced by Republican Ronald Reagan, who took a harder line toward the Soviets.

Carter's hopes for a revival of détente with the Soviet Union were destroyed on Dec. 25-26, 1979, when, in a dramatic military operation, several thousand Russian troops and military equipment were airlifted into Kabul, the capital of Afghanistan. Two days later, on Dec. 27, Hafizullah Amin, the Afghan president who himself had been placed in power in a Soviet-backed coup, was ousted and executed.

The invasion ended more than a decade of détente. Exchanges between Carter and Brezhnev contained some of the harshest accusations directed at each other's country since the Cold War of the 1950s. On NBC-TV's "Meet the Press" Jan. 20, 1980, Carter said that the invasion "in my opinion, is the most serious threat to peace since the second world war."

Imposition of Partial Grain Embargo

On Jan. 4, 1980, Carter had announced a series of nonmilitary retaliatory measures against the Soviet Union, including a grain embargo. The embargo against Soviet grain sales affected all transactions above the 8 million metric tons authorized under the 1975 U.S.-Soviet grain agreement, thus blocking a previously approved sale of 14.7 million metric tons of corn, wheat and soybeans. It was the first major use by the United States of food sales as a foreign policy weapon. The president also imposed an embargo on the sale of items incorporating "high technology," such as large computers and advanced machine tools, and tightened restrictions on certain oil and gas production equipment. (Previously, Carter in 1978 had imposed export controls on oil and gas equipment in response to the jailing of Anatoly B. Shcharansky and Aleksandr Ginzberg, two Soviet dissidents.)

Embargo Ended. In the first congressional votes on Carter's controversial grain embargo action, the House by wide margins July 23, 1980, rejected a series of amendments intended to shut off funds for administering the embargo. However, the Senate reversed that action Sept. 26, voting 43-39 to overturn the embargo.

By the spring of 1981 farmers had become increasingly vocal in their opposition to the embargo. In part to placate farmers, and to fulfill a campaign pledge, President Reagan on April 24 announced he was discontinuing the "curb on sales because American farmers had been unfairly singled out to bear the burden of this ineffective national policy." Reagan attributed the delay in announcing the embargo's end to his fear that the Soviets might misinterpret his action as a weakening of the U.S. condemnation of the Soviet occupation of Afghanistan.

New Grain Agreement. As of mid-1983 the Soviets had purchased only 6.2 million tons of grain, the minimum amount they were committed to buy under the existing agreement, which Reagan had renewed twice in one-year extensions. However, in an unexpected conciliatory gesture to Reagan, Moscow in July agreed to a new grain agreement providing for higher purchases of American grain over a five-year period. Under the new agreement, signed Aug. 25, the Soviet Union committed itself to buy at least 9 million tons of wheat and corn annually and could purchase up to 12 million without additional negotiations. The deal also permitted the Soviet Union to substitute a purchase of 500,000 metric tons of soybeans or soy meal for one million metric tons of wheat or corn.

Observers speculated that Moscow might use the grain trade as leverage on Reagan, who was under pressure from U.S. farmers to permit the expansion of grain sales in the lucrative Soviet market. U.S. officials said the agreement was worth a minimum of $7 billion to $8 billion in grain sales over its five-year life.

In agreeing to the pact, U.S. and Soviet negotiators dropped language in the previous agreement that had permitted the United States to cut off sales in times of short supply. *(For a further discussion of grain sales, see agriculture trade chapter.)*

1982 Pipeline Controversy

Although Carter's 1980 imposition of the grain embargo, using the authority of the Export Administration Act, was hotly debated, by far the most controversial application of that law in recent years was taken by President Reagan in response to the imposition of martial law in Poland in December 1981 following the crackdown on the Solidarity trade union. On Oct. 28, three weeks after the Polish government disbanded Solidarity, Reagan suspended indefinitely Poland's most-favored-nation trading status, which the country had enjoyed for 22 years. To justify his suspension of MFN, Reagan declared that Poland had failed since 1978 to meet its obligations under the General Agreement on Tariffs and Trade (GATT) to increase the total value of its imports from other GATT member nations by at least 7 percent each year.

More important than the sanctions against Poland was a prohibition on sales to the Soviet Union of equipment or technology needed for the transmission or refining of oil and natural gas. A principal goal of the sanctions was to prevent the Soviets from using U.S. technology to build a 2,600-mile natural gas pipeline linking the vast natural gas reserves east of the Ural Mountains with markets in energy-poor Western Europe. The sanctions first were imposed in December 1981 and were expanded in June 1982.

Among other things, the Dec. 29 sanctions required U.S. firms to obtain government licenses for sales to the Soviet Union of equipment or technology that could be used in conjunction with the construction of the pipeline. The sanctions also applied to equipment and technical data for two Soviet truck plants. To put teeth in the sanctions, Reagan ordered the Commerce Department to stop processing all applications for the licenses.

Reagan argued that the natural gas pipeline would make Western Europe overly dependent on the Soviet Union for energy supplies and would provide billions of dollars in hard currency to prop up the ailing Soviet economy.

The president raised the international political stakes June 22 by also prohibiting foreign subsidiaries of U.S. firms from selling pipeline equipment and technology to the Soviets and prohibiting foreign companies from selling the Soviet Union those products made under U.S. licenses.

Protests From Europe and Congress. Administration efforts to enforce the June 22 sanctions brought bitter protests from European leaders, who complained that Reagan was attempting to use U.S. law to force non-American companies to break valid contracts. Great Britain, France and Italy ordered their firms to proceed with their Soviet contracts, and West Germany encouraged its firms to do the same.

The president's action came only a few weeks after a Western summit meeting at Versailles, France, in which European leaders reportedly left with an understanding that the United States would take no further unilateral actions affecting European-Soviet relations.

Meanwhile, in Congress a bipartisan move to force the president to lift the sanctions was gaining strength. In an unusually bold demonstration of its willingness to challenge the president on foreign policy, the House Foreign Affairs Committee Aug. 10, 1982, approved a measure to lift the sanctions. However, the full chamber essentially gutted the bill Sept. 29. By a 206-203 vote, the House inserted a clause in the bill saying the sanctions would be repealed only if Reagan certified to Congress that the Soviet Union was not using slave labor on the natural gas pipeline project. Because Reagan realistically could not make such a certification, the sanctions would remain in effect.

Jobs vs. Foreign Policy. Throughout the House debate on the bill (the Senate never considered the legislation), it was evident that two political factors were in conflict: American jobs and the president's freedom to conduct foreign policy. The morning before the Foreign Affairs Committee voted on the bill, Secretary of State George P. Shultz sent all members of the panel a letter saying passage "would severely cripple the president's ability" to carry out foreign policy. The letter admitted that the sanctions had hurt American firms, but it argued that "unfortunate sacrifice" was needed to continue pressure on the Soviet Union.

The sanctions issue was particularly difficult for House Republicans, many of whom had to choose between supporting their president and voting for a measure that seemed to promise new job opportunities for Americans, or retention of existing jobs during a recessionary period. One of those who broke with the administration was Minority Leader Robert H. Michel, R-Ill., whose central Illinois district was among those hardest hit by the sanctions. The sanctions overturned a contract that Caterpillar Tractor Co., based in Peoria, had with the Soviet Union to provide 200 pipe-laying machines. "I have to say, frankly, that it is a matter of parochial interest for me," Michel said in opening debate on the bill. *(Caterpillar tractor problems, box, p. 203)*

Others noted that the sanctions had strained the ties between the United States and its European allies. Jonathan B. Bingham, D-N.Y. (1965-81), said the outcry caused by Reagan's attempt to enforce the sanctions in Europe was the strongest argument for lifting them. The allies had decided to fulfill their contracts with the Soviet Union, Bingham said, "and now we are telling them, as if they were children, that they are wrong, and we are going to try to punish their companies that hold U.S. licenses."

Reagan Lifts Some Sanctions. Reagan himself lifted the pipeline-related sanctions on Nov. 13, saying they had accomplished the purpose of demonstrating U.S. concern about Soviet pressure on Poland. Reagan also said the United States and its Western allies had agreed to conduct a study of ways to limit future trade that bolstered the Soviet economy.

Reagan's Nov. 13 decision left in place a 1980 licensing requirement for exports to the Soviet Union of oil and gas exploration and production equipment. Administration officials said those licenses would be processed on a "case-by-case basis." The government also continued the requirement for licenses for exports to the Soviet Union of "high technology" items, such as computers, that could be used for military purposes. Also left intact were licensing requirements for exports of parts and equipment for two Soviet truck plants.

Reagan's action did not affect a companion series of moves that he took late in 1981 to protest Soviet pressure on Poland. Those actions, which were to remain in effect, were the suspension of service to the United States by Aeroflot, the Soviet airline; imposition of a new series of controls on access to U.S. ports by all Soviet ships; closing of the Soviet Purchasing Commission office in New York City, and postponement of negotiations for a new U.S.-Soviet maritime agreement. Similar sanctions against Poland also remained in effect.

Agreement With Allies. Reagan said he was able to lift the sanctions because the United States and its key allies had agreed not to "engage in trade arrangements which contribute to the military or strategic advantage of the U.S.S.R. or serve to preferentially aid the heavily militarized Soviet economy." As examples of such trade, he cited "high technology products, including those used in oil and gas production."

Reagan also said the allies would conduct an "urgent study" of alternate sources of energy, including the questions of Western dependence on Soviet energy supplies and East-West trade and its implications for Western security.

Effectiveness of Sanctions Questioned

A number of analysts questioned the effectiveness of the 1980 grain embargo. Although some farm experts believed the embargo contributed to consumer food shortages in the Soviet Union, others felt it had little impact. The 1980 Republican platform had called it "ineffective." In any case, Moscow was able to find other sources of grain, notably Argentina and Canada.

A study by the congressional Office of Technology Assessment (OTA), released May 9, 1983, questioned the effectiveness of U.S. efforts to punish Soviet actions through trade sanctions. The report concluded that embargoes had no major effect on the Soviet economy and in fact created divisions within the Western alliance, fostered a perception of the United States as an unreliable supplier in industrial and farm trade, caused problems for American companies attempting to deal with Moscow and added to U.S. farm surpluses. *(Further details, p. 212)*

"The aftermath of U.S. attempts to embargo grain and energy equipment exports to the U.S.S.R. dramatically demonstrate the limitations on U.S. power to successfully conduct a trade leverage policy," the

Eastern Europe's Net Hard-Currency Debt to the West**

(in billions of U.S. dollars)

	1970	1975	1980	1981*	1985*
Bulgaria	0.7	2.1	2.7	2.6	4.0-5.0
Czechoslovakia	0.6	1.2	3.4	3.5	5.0-6.0
Hungary	0.6	2.3	7.0	7.7	10.0-11.0
Poland	1.1	7.7	21.9	22.0	31.0-35.0
Romania	1.6	3.1	9.0	10.8	19.0-21.0
East Germany	1.4	4.8	11.8	13.0	18.0-20.0
U.S.S.R.	1.0	7.8	9.6	14.0	30.0-35.0
COMECON banks***	0.3	2.2	4.1	3.9	6.0-7.0
Yugoslavia	1.9	5.7	16.8	18.0	25.0-28.0
Eastern Europe and U.S.S.R. total	9.2	36.9	86.3	95.5	148.0-168.0

* Forecast

** Net hard-currency debt to the West is defined as gross hard-currency debt to Western banks (including most of the debt owed to Middle Eastern and LDC banks whenever data are available), Western governments, and international financial organizations (IMF and the World Bank, in the case of Romania) minus COMECON deposits in Western banks.

*** Two multinational banks owned by the Council for Mutual Economic Assistance, which includes Russia and all Eastern European countries except Yugoslavia.

Source: Centrally Planned Economics Service, Wharton Econometric Forecasting Associates.

OTA report said. The "chilling effect" of sanctions "may lead to long-term adverse impacts on East-West trade, far more important to the U.S. economy than trade [solely] with the Soviet Union," the OTA study warned.

The study also questioned whether export controls were effective in preventing Moscow from acquiring Western technology to boost its military power. That issue had prompted heated debate in Congress, which was considering extension and revision of the Export Administration Act at the time the OTA report was released. *(Details, see high technology chapter.)*

Impact of Korean Plane Incident. U.S.-Soviet trade relations took a turn for the worse in the aftermath of the Sept. 1, 1983, shooting down of a Korean civilian airliner by a Soviet warplane. A number of members of Congress suggested canceling the grain agreement in retaliation, but Reagan, who had repeatedly opposed the use of grain embargoes to punish the Soviet Union, refused to do so.

Although there was widespread outrage at the incident, reprisals were limited. The president disappointed hard-liners by failing to halt arms talks with the Soviets, nullify the grain deal or ban technology transfers to the U.S.S.R. The president, in a Sept. 5 televised address, announced only that the United States was suspending certain cultural, scientific and diplomatic exchanges with the Soviets and would work with other nations to curb Soviet civil aviation in the West. (The administration subsequently closed Aeroflot's two U.S. offices.)

Future of U.S.-Soviet Trade

In the early 1980s East-West tension over Afghanistan, Poland and the conflicts in Central America and the Middle East exacerbated the slump in U.S.-Soviet trade, which had peaked in 1979 when American non-farm exports to the U.S.S.R. totaled $749 million. By 1980 those exports had slipped to $363 million. "I think the heady days of the early 1970s when we had talk of détente, and businessmen were talking of [the Soviet Union] as a great new market, are gone and won't return soon," said a staff member of the House International Economic Policy and Trade Subcommittee in early 1981.

Soviet Economic Problems. International and internal events, including the crisis in Poland, a succession of poor harvests in Russia and the shakiness and interdependence of world financial institutions, had a damaging impact on the Soviet economy. By the 1980s it was widely acknowledged, even by Soviet leaders, that the country's economy had performed poorly. There was some debate, however, about how serious the problems were, even among U.S. intelligence agencies. A study of the Soviet economy published in August 1981 by the CIA noted that "shoddy goods and services, queues and shortages have become characteristic features of everyday life, along with endemic black markets and corruption. . . . In the 1980s, overall economic growth probably will slow markedly under the impact of sharply declining increments to the labor force, energy shortages and sluggish productivity advance."

The Soviet and Eastern-bloc hard currency debt to the West grew enormously between 1970 and 1980 and was expected to further increase during the 1980s. If the hard-currency debt continued to grow, it would become increasingly difficult for Moscow and its satellites to continue to borrow from the West. *(Box, p. 121)*

About half of Soviet foreign trade in 1982 was with Eastern Europe and roughly 35 percent was with the West. Prices for Soviet goods sold in Eastern Europe were highly subsidized and generally were not paid for in hard currency. Estimates compiled by the Bank for International Settlements found that Moscow borrowed more than $15 billion in 1981, largely to pay for the grain and technology it imported from the West. For the Soviet Union and Eastern Europe, the debt was well over $70 billion.

Expanding U.S.-China Trade

President Nixon's "era of negotiation" was directed at Communist China as well as the Soviet Union. American attitudes toward the People's Republic of China already had begun to soften during the mid-1960s. In 1966 Washington eased restrictions on travel of scholars to communist countries, including China, and President Johnson said in a televised speech that, eventually, reconciliation with the PCR was necessary.

But it was under Nixon that the United States actively pursued improved relations with the Chinese. In a speech July 6, 1971, the president noted that China was potentially "one of the five great economic superpowers" that would determine the course of world events in the remainder of the 20th century. An end to two decades of Chinese isolation, he said, would remove a threat to world peace but would mean "an immense escalation of their economic challenge."

Nixon in July 1969 had begun to ease travel and trade restrictions with China. (A total embargo had been in effect since President Truman invoked the 1917 trading with the Enemy Act against Peking in 1950.) And in June 1971 he lifted curbs on exports of a wide variety of non-strategic goods to China and on commercial imports from the mainland.

The thaw in U.S.-Chinese relations took a dramatic turn July 15, 1971, when Nixon announced he would visit Peking in early 1972 "to seek the normalization of relations between the two countries." A trade pact was signed and liaison offices were established several months after the Nixon visit (which took place in late February 1972), followed by a resumption of trade.

Modest Trade Growth in the 1970s

Despite Nixon's initiative, trade between the United States and China remained relatively modest until 1978. Although Chinese exports to the United States grew steadily, reaching $203 million in 1977, they remained a small fraction of China's total exports of $8 billion. Exports to the United States consisted largely of textiles and apparel, antiques and handicrafts, bristles and feathers, fireworks and non-ferrous metals.

U.S. exports to China fluctuated wildly, largely in response to Chinese demands for agricultural commodities such as wheat and soybeans. Large food shipments in 1974 boosted U.S. exports to $819 million, but improved Chinese harvests in subsequent years caused a substantial decline. China in this period also bought 10 Boeing aircraft, eight ammonia plants and substantial amounts of equipment for the exploration and drilling of oil.

In 1978 trade between the two nations more than doubled from the previous year, exceeding $1 billion, primarily because of a resumption of U.S. food exports. Of total exports to China of $824 million, three-fourths ($614 million) were agricultural commodities, primarily wheat ($291 million), cotton ($157 million) and corn ($118 million).

Chinese exports to the United States also jumped substantially, rising from $203 million in 1977 to $324 million in 1978, with the pattern of exports remaining generally the same.

By 1979 the United States ranked third as a major Western supplier of goods to the People's Republic (behind Japan and West Germany) and third as a major market for Chinese exports (behind Hong Kong and Japan). Trade for the first six months of 1979 equaled that for all of 1978. Sino-American trade in 1979 amounted to $2.3 billion, twice the 1978 figure. This represented 7.8 percent of China's total imports and exports of $29.4 billion. By 1979 the United States had become China's second largest non-communist trading partner, after Japan, whose trade with China totaled $6.6 billion.

In 1979 crude oil was exported for the first time, quickly becoming China's leading export to the United States (valued at $71.8 million). And with vast estimated oil deposits, especially in the Bohai Gulf off the northern coast of China, some observers thought oil would become an even more central factor in future U.S.-China trade. The United States actively sought new foreign sources of oil — especially after the Iranian crisis of 1979 and concomitant oil price increases by the Organization of Petroleum Exporting Countries (OPEC) — while the Chinese were

U.S.-China Trade, 1971-82

(millions of dollars)

Year	U.S. Exports	U.S. Imports	Total Trade	U.S. Balance*
1971	–	4.9	4.9	−4.9
1972	63.5	32.4	95.9	31.1
1973	740.2	64.9	805.1	675.3
1974	819.1	114.7	933.8	704.4
1975	303.6	158.4	462.0	145.2
1976	135.4	201.0	336.4	−65.6
1977	171.3	202.7	374.0	−31.4
1978	823.6	324.1	1,147.7	499.5
1979	1,716.5	592.3	2,308.8	1,124.2
1980	3,749.0	1,058.3	4,807.3	2,690.7
1981	3,598.6	1,895.3	5,493.9	1,703.3
1982	2,904.5	2,283.7	5,188.2	620.8
Total	**$15,024.5**	**$6,932.7**	**$21,958.0**	**$8,092.6**

* The difference between exports to the People's Republic of China (PRC) and imports from the PRC.

Source: National Council for U.S.-China Trade

expected to need American help in developing their oil resources through more sophisticated exploration and drilling techniques and equipment.

Other leading U.S. imports from China in 1979 included fireworks, antiques, white cotton shirting, shrimp, carpets, crude or processed bristles, bamboo baskets and bags and feathers. Leading U.S. exports to China included corn, cotton, wheat, soybeans and soybean oil, polyester fibers, oil and gas drilling machines and parts, and chemicals.

1978 Breakthrough in Trade Relations

Two factors added a dramatic new dimension to U.S.-China trade relations in 1978. One was President Jimmy Carter's Dec. 15 announcement that the United States and China would formally restore full diplomatic relations, beginning Jan. 1, 1979. The second development was a significant new emphasis by the Chinese government, led by Vice Premier Deng Xiaoping, on international trade and foreign investment as a vital instrument in China's modernization plans.

The retreat from economic self-reliance was signaled by an explosion of new trade deals by Peking, which made commitments to buy roughly $8 billion in technology from Western Europe, Japan and the United States in 1978.

The Chinese imports almost exclusively consisted of capital goods rather than consumer goods. The U.S. Steel Corp. agreed to build an iron ore processing plant worth about $1 billion; another U.S. firm, the Fluor Corp., signed a $10 million agreement heralding construction of a proposed $800 million complex to mine and process copper; and Pan American Airways, through its subsidiary Intercontinental Hotels, negotiated a $500 million agreement to build luxury hotels. Other contracts included purchase of three Boeing 747s with an option to buy two more, worth $250 million, and an agreement to sell and later bottle Coca-Cola.

1979 China Trade Agreement

With U.S. business eager to get a toehold in a vast new market, support grew in Congress to end trade discrimination against the PRC. Under an agreement signed in Peking July 7, 1979, the United States proposed to grant China most-favored-nation status. The three-year trade pact had two major parts: It reduced tariffs on Chinese imports to the same level as that enjoyed by most other nations and it made China eligible for Export-Import Bank financing. It also promoted the establishment of business and government trade offices in the two countries.

Both the Senate and House had to approve the agreement before it could go into effect. Once it was submitted, Congress had 60 legislative days to act under the expedited procedures of the 1974 Trade Act.

The Carter administration hesitated, however, and Chinese leaders showed signs of impatience about delays in finalizing the pact. The administration had withheld submission of the treaty while it tried to work out three essential problems: protectionist sentiment against imports of Chinese textiles, opposition to granting MFN status to China without simultaneously awarding the Soviet Union the same privileges and a dispute over whether China's emigration policies qualified it for MFN status under the Jackson-Vanik amendment.

The administration reportedly forestalled the opposition of U.S. textile interests by unilaterally imposing non-preferential textile import quotas on the Chinese on Oct. 30, 1979. But the other issues — Chinese emigration and MFN status for Russia — remained a problem.

Simultaneous Concessions to the U.S.S.R. The administration had been split over how to deal with the Soviet Union in the light of normalization of U.S.-China relations. One camp, reportedly led by Secretary of State Cyrus R. Vance, favored providing roughly simultaneous trade concessions to both China and the U.S.S.R., while national security adviser Zbigniew Brzezinski reportedly favored "playing the China card" and capitalizing on the opening to Peking to extract concessions from the Russians.

Another complication was a split between two key members of Congress, Rep. Vanik and Sen. Jackson. Their amendment to the 1974 Trade Act barred MFN and Export-Import Bank credits to communist countries that did not allow freedom of emigration. Congress could waive the ban for 12 months if the president received "assurances" that a country's future emigration policies would be liberalized.

Jackson said he wanted immediate action on granting MFN status to China. He said the PRC had complied with requirements linking MFN to improved emigration policies, while the Soviet Union had not. Vanik, on the other hand, preferred providing trade concessions to both nations at about the same time. Instead of demanding assurances from the Soviet government about future emigration practices, Vanik said existing emigration levels were a sufficient indication of Soviet intentions.

Amid growing Chinese impatience over the delay in implementing the treaty, Vice President Walter F. Mondale, during his visit to China in August 1979, reaffirmed the administration's promise to submit the agreement to Congress. On Oct. 23 President Carter finally sent the Sino-American trade agreement to Congress for approval, nearly four months after it was signed. On the same day, Carter signed a proclamation waiving the requirements of the Jackson-Vanik amendment as they applied to the PRC.

Lobbying for the Trade Pact. Perhaps the most widespread support in the United States for closer relations with China came from the business community. In statements accompanying the 1979 normalization initiatives, President Carter emphasized the importance of the trade issue, saying the establishment of diplomatic relations opened "a new vista for prosperous trade relationships with almost a billion people in the People's Republic of China."

Support for closer U.S.-China ties by the U.S. business community also helped to soften the opposition of conservative politicians to recognition of the People's Republic and the termination of diplomatic relations with the Chinese Nationalist government on Taiwan. With business anticipating potentially big gains in the large, virtually untapped communist market, the customary alliance of American business interests and the political right was all but absent.

Thus, the White House looked to American business for help in getting the Chinese trade agreement approved on Capitol Hill. Large U.S. businesses were early entrants in the sweepstakes for trade with the mainland. One group lobbying in Washington for the agreement was the National Council for U.S.-China Trade, which represented banking, construction, transportation and other firms anxious to do business with the Chinese. Its president, Christopher H. Phillips, said lower tariffs on Chinese goods would boost U.S.-Chinese commerce by about $540 million over the next three years and give the United States a wider variety of imports from China at prices comparable to those from other Asian nations. "In other words," Phillips said in November 1979, "at a time when inflation is moving at 13 percent a year, this will be one means of helping keep prices down — a welcome prospect for American consumers."

The National Foreign Trade Council also endorsed the pact. "In our opinion," said council official Cord Hansen-Sturm, vice president of the American Express Company, "this agreement will open up a substantial new market for exports of U.S. goods and services at a time when continued trade deficits have made export expansion a necessity."

Evidence of a relaxed attitude toward emigration on the part of the

Chinese was vividly evident during Vice Premier Deng Xiaoping's trip to Washington in February 1979. When President Carter broached the subject of emigration, Deng replied, "I'll send you 10 million emigrants right away." Whatever objections remained over granting MFN status to China without simultaneously bestowing the same benefits on the Soviet Union all but disappeared after the Soviet invasion of Afghanistan on Dec. 27, 1979. Although the 96th Congress was in adjournment at the time of the Afghan developments, it had become apparent before the legislature reconvened in January 1980 that it was likely to approve the China Trade Agreement as a means of punishing the Soviets for their action.

Two days into its 1980 session, Congress without further ado overwhelmingly passed a joint resolution approving the trade agreement. There was no question that the lopsidedness of the vote — 294-88 in the House and 74-8 in the Senate — reflected Congress' eagerness for a vehicle by which to "get tough" with Moscow.

Terms of the Treaty. The principal provisions of the Sino-U.S. trade agreement were similar to the understandings between the United States and Hungary and Romania that had been approved in the 1970s. As summarized by the Senate Finance Committee the pact included the following major provisions:

● The United States and the People's Republic of China would provide non-discriminatory (most-favored-nation) tariff treatment to imports from each other's country.

● Safeguards were to be provided to remedy market disruption in the event of rapidly increasing imports, and to permit the taking of unilateral action following consultations between the two countries.

● Arrangements for the promotion of business and financial dealings would be provided, including the establishment of business representation offices and provisions encouraging visits by economic, trade and industrial groups.

● The People's Republic of China would provide copyright, patent and trademark protection equivalent to the protection afforded the Chinese by the United States.

Other Pacts on Trade, Cooperation

China and the United States signed four agreements on Sept. 17, 1980, completing the normalization of relations between the two

129

countries. The agreements were:

● A civil aviation pact allowing direct flights between the United States and China.

● A maritime agreement granting the two countries mutual access to each other's ports.

● A consular convention spelling out the duties of consular officers in providing services to citizens of both countries. In addition to the U.S. consulates in Canton and Shanghai, three more would be opened — in Wuhan, Chengtu and Shenyang — to promote trade, travel, cultural and education exchange.

● A textile agreement limiting the import of six categories of Chinese textiles to the United States through 1983. U.S. protectionism had been a sore point for the Chinese. Negotiations on import restrictions broke down in 1979 and the United States clamped restraints on seven categories of textile products from China. The textile trade pact, though a dampener on Chinese textile exports, tied up one of the loose ends of U.S.-China trade.

In addition, the Export-Import Bank extended a $2 billion line of credit in the form of low-interest loans to be used for a five-year period. The bank approved an $80 million loan for the sale to China of steel-making equipment.

China's Trade Potential

American investment in China is certain to continue, even without a new Sino-U.S. trade agreement, though the upper limits of Chinese investment in Western technology can only be roughly estimated. The National Council for U.S.-China Trade predicted in 1978 that Peking would spend $40 billion on foreign capital investment between 1978 and 1985, while Commerce Department experts estimated spending in the $60 billion to $80 billion range.

At the same time, a Commerce Department study cautioned against unrealistically high forecasts of China's trade potential. The study predicted that in the 1978-85 period Chinese imports would probably not exceed $136 billion, while exports would be unlikely to surpass $103 billion. The U.S. share of the Chinese import market in this period was estimated at $12 billion to $15 billion, or about 10 percent of total Chinese imports.

In 1980 the United States exported almost $3.8 billion of merchandise to China; the figure had fallen off slightly to about $3.6 billion in 1981. Merchandise imported from China totaled almost $1.1 billion in 1980 and rose to $1.9 billion in 1982, according to the Commerce Department.

Visions of a lucrative China market were dimmed by the fact that American businessmen were discovering that doing business with the PRC required much time and patience, while the Chinese appeared apprehensive about the policies of a staunchly anti-communist Republican president.

Indeed, during the first two years of the Reagan administration, U.S.-Chinese relations cooled. But by 1983 there were signs of an increasing rapport. In May Reagan said the administration was exploring ways of expediting sales of advanced technology to China. The guidelines were submitted formally to the Chinese by Defense Secretary Caspar W. Weinberger during a visit to Peking in late September. The regulations shifted the PRC to the category of "friendly, non-aligned" nations that were permitted to receive technology transfers. Technology sales to China grew to about $800 million in 1983 from $300 million in 1982; it was estimated that they would pass $1 billion in 1984. The high-tech items included computers, semiconductors, telecommunications equipment and electronics, all with military potential.

Meanwhile, in July 1983 the two governments reached an accord in textile trade that allowed an increase in imports from China of 2 to 3 percent annually (China had sought a 6 percent rise). U.S. Trade Representative William E. Brock III said the five-year accord was the result of "very good, hard, tough negotiations" and that both sides "left the bargaining table respecting each other." Textiles accounted for about 40 percent of the PRC's trade with the United States in 1982, amounting to $800 million. (China was the fourth largest supplier of textiles to the United States, after Taiwan, South Korea and Hong Kong.) The agreement ended a bitter, year-long trade dispute during which the Chinese boycotted U.S. farm products, at an estimated cost to American farmers of $600 million in lost sales. On Sept. 26, 1983, it was announced that the PRC had agreed to buy 200,000 metric tons of grain, the largest Chinese purchase of U.S. grain in nearly a year.

Testifying before the House Foreign Affairs Committee Feb. 28, 1983, Paul Wolfowitz, assistant secretary of state for East Asian and Pacific Affairs, said, "Given the progress made thus far and the undeniable benefits to both sides, it is clear that there will be no turning back. Some difficult problems lie ahead in U.S.-China relations. We intend to deal with them fairly and openly and not take the relationship for granted. . . . The stable and enduring relationship we seek is important to the healthy economic growth we all desire. . . ."

Oil refinery in Alberta, Canada. Foreign interests, primary among them the United States, own 65 percent of the oil and gas industries in Canada. This has been a source of friction in U.S.-Canadian relations.

Chapter 5

CANADA: LARGEST U.S. TRADING PARTNER

For Canadians, the 1979 East Coast fishery agreement marked a turning point in their relations with the United States. That treaty, the product of 18 long months of complex negotiations with officials in the Jimmy Carter administration, divided the rich store of fish and scallops in the Georges Bank area, off the coast of Maine. When the treaty was signed March 29, 1979, the Canadians assumed the matter was settled. They knew the U.S. Senate had to ratify the treaty but considered the process to be pro forma, as was ratification by the Canadian Cabinet.

"We didn't really believe that the president couldn't deliver" on the treaty, said Allan Gotlieb, Canada's ambassador to the United States in 1983. "As far as we could ascertain, the opposition was limited to two senators." But those two senators — Claiborne Pell, D-R.I., and Edward M. Kennedy, D-Mass. — successfully blocked the treaty's approval. Other senators viewed the matter as a parochial New England concern and bowed to the wishes of the two influential Democrats.

To the Canadians, the defeat of the treaty was a shock. They were used to working in a parliamentary system, where legislatures neither initiate legislation nor make foreign policy. And they had long believed that their diplomacy with the United States should consist solely of dealings with the executive branch. Like many other nations, they had not grasped, in Gotlieb's words, "the full implications of the doctrine of separation of powers" in U.S. government and the need to deal with Congress as well as the White House.

After the fishery fiasco, however, Canadians became aware of congressional activism. As Congress stepped up its involvement in foreign policy issues, particularly those related to trade, it repeatedly threw itself, often inadvertently, into the vortex of U.S.-Canadian relations. As a result, the U.S.-Canadian relationship had become three-sided by the early 1980s. On trade and economic issues, Canada often found itself battling Congress, with the administration as an ally. On other matters, Canadians discovered themselves working with Congress in opposition to the administration. A prime example of a Canadian-congressional alliance was that formed over the sticky acid rain controversy. Despite the mounting evidence that acid rain falling in Canada originated from U.S. sources, notably Midwest coal-burning industries, the Reagan administration refused to implement a program to reduce emissions causing acid rain. But the Canadians found allies in Congress and were often invited to Capitol Hill by concerned members.

Close U.S.-Canada Trade Relations

Canada has been by far the United States' major trading partner, outstripping Japan and all the European countries. Indeed, the economic exchange between the two North American nations represents the largest bilateral relationship in the world. The total amount traded in 1981 between the two countries was approximately $110 billion, an increase of 14 percent over 1980. The importance of this trade relationship, especially to Canada, is evident in the import/export figures. The United States absorbed 66 percent of Canadian exports in 1981 and furnished Canada with 69 percent of its imports. Canada, as the leading U.S. trading partner, accounted for 17 percent of America's exports and almost 18 percent of its imports. Between 1973 and 1983 the total volume of U.S. trade with Canada grew by more than 50 percent. With such vast quantities of goods and services flowing between the two nations, it is little wonder that trade disputes have proliferated.

U.S. Regional Interests Complain. Potato farmers in Aroostook County, Maine, for example, voiced their own particular complaints against the Canadians. They once considered their region the "Potato Capital of the World," but beginning in the late 1970s they were forced to relinquish that title as their share of the Northeastern potato market slipped and the volume of imported Canadian potatoes increased sevenfold.

Three thousand miles away, in the state of Washington, lumbermen also complained they were unfairly hit by Canadian trade. During the recession of the early 1980s, inexpensive wood from British Columbia was shipped freely across the border, adding a painful extra kick to the depressed local economy.

U.S. truckers were yet another group that had their ax to grind with

U.S.-Canada Trade, 1975-81

	U.S. Exports to Canada*	Percent of Total U.S. Exports	U.S. Imports from Canada*	Percent of Total U.S. Imports
1975	$21,785	20.1%	$21,913	22.2%
1976	24,130	20.9	26,439	21.4
1977	25,788	21.2	29,598	19.6
1978	28,374	19.7	33,527	19.1
1979	33,096	18.1	38,049	18.1
1980	35,395	16.0	41,459	16.9
1981	39,564	16.9	46,414	17.7

* Millions of dollars

Source: U.S. Department of Commerce, International Trade Administration, "United States Foreign Trade Annual 1975-81," July 1983.

the Canadians. So, too, did oil companies, airlines, uranium miners, border television stations, gas companies, magazine publishers and a host of other industries. While no single trade issue posed a serious threat to the relations of the United States with its northern neighbor, the sheer number and frequency of disputes has made those relations increasingly difficult. "We have hundreds of issues, any one of which could create a problem if it is not addressed openly, candidly and quickly," said Democratic Rep. Dante B. Fascell of Florida. Fascell was co-chairman in the 98th Congress of the Canada-United States Interparliamentary Group, a congressional panel that meets annually with members of the Canadian Parliament.

Like the fishery dispute, many U.S.-Canadian trade problems have tended to be regional in nature. The groups involved, while not large enough or broad enough to cause the administration to act, often have swayed members of Congress. Republican Sen. William S. Cohen of Maine, for instance, championed the Aroostook County farmers in the Senate by introducing legislation to curb potato imports; Democratic

Sen. Daniel Patrick Moynihan of New York led an unsuccessful campaign to retaliate against the Canadians for tax discrimination against U.S. border television stations; and Sen. Pete V. Domenici, R-N.M., whose state was the center of the financially ailing U.S. uranium industry, tried to curb Canadian uranium imports in a fiscal 1982-83 funding bill for the Nuclear Regulatory Commission, but had to settle for a congressional resolution to study the problems confronting the industry.

Canada's Economic Role Overlooked. In spite of these disputes, Canada still was not subjected to the general criticism in Congress that plagued other U.S. trading partners in the early 1980s. Members frequently dragged Japan, France, Taiwan or South Korea through the mud, but Canada stayed relatively clean. Indeed, Capitol Hill sometimes has seemed simply to ignore Canada.

"There is almost zilch congressional interest in Canadian issues," said Allan Nanes of the Congressional Research Service in 1983. "For most members, U.S.-Canadian relations is a big bore." To the Canadians, congressional indifference has been considered as harmful, and far more infuriating, than congressional hostility. Canadians have resented being taken for granted by their powerful southern neighbor. Their nation boasts the seventh largest economy in the industrialized world, and located elsewhere on the globe it would play the role of a major regional power. Next to the United States, however, it is easily overlooked.

"You don't even think of us as foreign," Ambassador Gotlieb told a group of Washingtonians in April 1983. "That's a very great compliment, but it is also part of the problem." Gotlieb's wife, Sondra, put the point more bluntly in a 1983 interview with *The New York Times*. "For some reason a glaze passes over people's faces when you say Canada," she said. "Maybe we should invade South Dakota or something."

Sideswipes: Auto Trade Curbs, 'Buy American'

Because Congress has given little heed to Canadian concerns, the Canadians often have found themselves stung inadvertently by actions not intended to harm them. Prime Minister Pierre Trudeau has likened Canada to a mouse in bed with an elephant: Every twitch of the elephant, whatever its intention, threatens the mouse.

The United States' controversial automobile domestic content legislation, for instance, was clearly aimed to affect Japanese imports. Initially proposed at the height of the 1982 recession in an attempt to protect the faltering American auto industry, it would have forced automakers to use a high percentage of U.S. labor and parts in cars sold in the United States. Although the measure did not pass in 1982, it was revived in 1983 and passed by the House Nov. 3. If approved as written, the bill made no distinction between Canadian and other foreign manufacturers and thus would have a disastrous effect on the multi-billion-dollar auto trade with Canada. Fortunately for the Canadians, it was doubtful at the end of 1983 that the measure would become law. The Senate had not yet acted, and the U.S. auto industry appeared to be recovering, thereby reducing the pressure for action.

The Canadians were also disturbed with "Buy American" provisions slipped into a bill that passed during the hectic lame-duck session of the 97th Congress in December 1982. Included in the gas tax and highway construction bill were requirements that cement, steel and manufactured products used in federally funded highway and certain transit projects, such as rail tracks and bus garages, be American-made if they cost no more than 25 percent more than foreign products. Previously, the preference for domestic products had been limited to a 10 percent cost difference. The change was a heavy blow to Ontario cement makers, who had been selling $15 million worth of cement in New York state each year. While the administration sympathized with the Canadian protests, the strong steel caucus in Congress prevailed.

In the fall of 1983, the Canadians also were keeping an eye on a number of emergency public works and infrastructure improvement proposals that contained "Buy American" provisions.

To help prevent these sideswipes, the Canadians decided to step up their lobbying efforts on Capitol Hill. "It is obvious to us that we have to communicate our views to Congress for reasons of effectiveness," said Gotlieb. His embassy staff learned to keep in touch with congressional staff members, and the ambassador himself found it useful to write letters, make phone calls and meet personally with members of Congress. The Canadian Embassy also began to use other methods to garner support. It contracted with Washington law firms to provide lobbying help on certain issues and began to work with other U.S. interest groups that shared its concerns on some subjects. The embassy planned to expand those efforts.

Gotlieb was unabashed about these activities. He rejected the opinions of those who viewed foreign lobbying as offensive meddling in U.S. domestic affairs. "We should not and we cannot be criticized for promoting our interest," he argued. "Certainly the United States when it acts abroad is not prepared to see its interests ignored." *(Japanese lobbying, p. 154)*

Philosophical Differences Between Neighbors

For a few months in 1980 the Canadians were national heroes in the United States. They helped six U.S. diplomats escape from Iran, where the U.S. Embassy had been seized and its occupants held hostage. Across the nation, Canadian maple-leaf flags were raised next to the Stars and Stripes. Telephone calls, telegrams, bouquets, champagne and even chocolate chip cookies were sent by grateful U.S. citizens to Canadian embassies and consulates. Banners saying "Thank you, Canada" draped Washington, D.C., buildings, and a West Virginia service station even offered free tows to stranded Canadian tourists. In Congress, both the House and the Senate unanimously approved resolutions praising Canada for its courageous actions.

But the love affair was short-lived. Elections during that same year returned Prime Minister Pierre Trudeau to power and brought in President Ronald Reagan. The contrast between the leaders underlined the differences that traditionally have made relations between the two nations difficult. Trudeau, a liberal, ran his 1980 campaign on a platform built in part of economic nationalism and government intervention. Reagan, on the other hand, espoused a free-market ideology abhorring the kind of government involvement that Trudeau embraced.

"There is a tendency here to believe the Canadian viewpoint is similar to our own, and their interests are identical to ours, but in fact they are not," said Charles F. Doran, director of the Center of Canadian Studies at Johns Hopkins School of Advanced International Studies in Washington, D.C. Canadians, Doran said, tend to have a deep respect for order, responsibility and deference to authority. That attitude is a far cry from the American brand of individualistic conservatism, which traditionally harbors deep suspicions of government intervention. "The Canadian attitude toward government accepts authority with much more equanimity than the U.S.," said Doran. "The degree of government involvement in Canadian economic matters is far greater than here. And more importantly, it is accepted."

The government presence in Canada's economy is extensive. The government runs the major airline, railroad and telephone services, owns a number of other utilities and a major oil company and provides all Canadians with virtually free medical care. Canadians have said that their government's role in the economy is not the result of an ideological commitment to socialism; rather, it is a reflection of Canadian pragmatism. A large country with relatively few people, Canada always has had difficulty raising the capital to finance its development. Its industry has had to rely heavily on investment either from the government or from foreign sources, particularly the United States. That fact has been at the root of many of the disputes between the two nations.

In sectors where the Canadian government has provided aid and investment, U.S. businesses have tended to cry foul play. They have complained that government support has given their Canadian competition unfair advantages, and they sometimes have sought retaliatory sanctions from Washington.

On the other hand, in those sectors where U.S. investment in Canada has been extremely high, the Canadians sometimes have worried that their sovereignty might be threatened. Unwilling to be the subjects of economic colonialism, they have been fearful of being swallowed up whole by their southern neighbor. As a result, they have placed some conditions on investment that have raised complaints from U.S. investors.

U.S. Investment in the Canadian Market

For the United States, Canadian restrictions on foreign investment have presented the most troubling economic problem. The U.S. economy has become heavily dependent on the export of services to obtain a favorable balance of trade. Services exports involve such industries as banking, accounting, advertising, insurance, telecommunications and engineering and design. In 1982 the nation suffered a deficit in merchandise trade of $43 billion but boasted a surplus in services trade of $36 billion. Services trade, in turn, has been heavily dependent on American investment abroad. A large portion of the export of such services has gone to foreign subsidiaries or affiliates of U.S. firms.

If foreign investment in a major market like Canada were to be restricted, or if foreign investors were required by the Canadian government to purchase services in Canada, U.S. services trade would suffer. In contrast, the Canadians have come to consider foreign investment in their country as a potential threat to their independence and their economic health.

Foreign Ownership Issue. Canada has the highest rate of foreign ownership of any industrialized country in the world. Some 45 percent of its manufacturing industry in 1983 was owned by foreigners; and in some sectors, such as energy, foreign ownership was as high as 65 percent. By contrast, less than 5 percent of manufacturing industry was foreign-owned in the United States. The Canadians have argued that foreign ownership could damage their economy. Foreign-owned companies, they said, might favor foreign suppliers, or they might forfeit opportunities to export in order to avoid competing with their parent company.

Canadians also have grown wary of U.S. government efforts to exert "extraterritorial" jurisdiction over the Canadian subsidiaries and affiliates of U.S. companies. The problem became an issue in 1982 when the Reagan administration extended to U.S. subsidiaries and affiliates overseas its restrictions on exports of materials to be used in the Soviet natural gas pipeline project.

Canada has long been aware of foreign ownership problems. In 1974 the government established a Foreign Investment Review Agency (FIRA) to screen plans by outside interests to acquire Canadian companies or to establish new businesses in Canada. The agency is responsible for negotiating with foreign investors to ensure sufficient benefits for Canadian interests. During his 1980 election campaign Prime Minister Trudeau promoted a program of "Canadianization" that involved strengthening FIRA and establishing a National Energy Policy designed to reduce to 50 percent, from 65 percent, the share of foreign ownership allowed for Canadian oil and gas companies.

'Canadianization' Criticized. The Reagan administration and Congress were harshly critical of this program of "Canadianization," which they viewed as a euphemism for economic nationalism. When Apple Computer Inc. applied for permission to open a Canadian subsidiary, for example, FIRA granted the request. Although eager to promote high-technology industries in Canada, the agency made Apple agree to a long list of restrictions. According to the U.S. Embassy in Ottawa, the company had to guarantee that Canadian labor and parts would account for at least 30 percent of the value of the products it sold in Canada; that it would establish a Canadian software and research group; that all the Canadian company's officers, except the chairman and secretary, and all operating management would be Canadians; that at least 80 percent of its products would be sold through independent retailers; and that it would operate a manufacturing unit in Canada.

Canadians did not see the FIRA's actions as unjust. "Just how unreasonable can a country be when it sets up a mechanism to ensure that new investment from outside the country will create significant benefit for Canadians?" Minister of Finance Marc Lalonde asked in a October 1982 speech. "That is hardly a radical notion." Lalonde also suggested that the Canadian system was much more simple and much less time consuming to deal with than the web of laws, regulations, state approval systems and antitrust requirements that governed investment in the United States.

Lalonde's contention that the Canadian system was not restrictive was supported by a November 1982 report comparing investment policies in 73 countries published by the U.S. accounting firm, Price Waterhouse. "As the Canadian economy matures there has been an increasing tendency for the federal and provincial governments to impose some restrictions on new foreign investment, particularly in certain sensitive sectors of the economy," the report said. "In spite of this, there are still relatively few restrictions in Canada compared to other industrial countries."

Reciprocity Measures. Faced with a recession more severe than that in the United States, the Canadian government realized that it could not offend foreign investors. In June of 1982 the government announced plans to "streamline" FIRA and to slow down efforts to "Canadianize" the energy industry. And in October of that year Prime Minister Trudeau invited 21 senior U.S. business executives to Ottawa in an attempt to erase perceptions that the nation was reluctant to accept foreign investors.

Despite those assurances, Congress was considering in late 1983 a "reciprocity" bill that would expand the president's authority to deny licenses to, or otherwise restrict, foreign services companies based in nations that had barriers to U.S. services exports. Besides preventing such companies from establishing businesses in the United States, the bill also would allow the president to retaliate against nations that blocked trade-related foreign investment, or refused to protect U.S. intellectual property rights, such as patents, copyrights and trademarks. The Canadians viewed the proposal as a threat to their national economic policy and an attempt to unilaterally assert U.S. investment rights in foreign countries. Ambassador Gotlieb, speaking in Washington, D.C., in February 1983, explained the conflict. "In an area where U.S. competitiveness has eroded relative to some other countries, the call is for protection. Where U.S. products are competitive, the call is for expanded access to foreign markets. But a foreign country sees it in just the opposite way. Where its products are competitive, the U.S. is ready to restrict access; but in areas where it suffers a competitive disadvantage, the U.S. is demanding increased access."

Tough Economic Issues Ahead

The list of economic problems facing the United States and Canada was lengthy but the following highlights some of the more critical ones.

Regulation. The deregulation movement in the United States has created some difficult problems between the two countries. A dispute over trucking is typical. Before 1980 the United States and Canada had roughly similar truck licensing procedures that restricted the entry of foreign truckers. As a result, U.S. and Canadian trucking companies reached "interlining" agreements: U.S. truckers would drive to the border and transfer their goods to Canadian trucks, and the Canadian truckers would transfer their loads to U.S. trucks. In 1980, however, the United States deregulated the trucking industry. That raised the possibility of Canadian truckers providing cross-border service while U.S. truckers still were restricted entry into Canada.

To prevent that from happening, Sen. John C. Danforth, R-Mo., in 1982 offered an amendment to a bill placing a two-year moratorium on U.S. truck licenses for Canadians and Mexicans. The Canadians were enraged, but a last-minute compromise in Congress gave President Reagan the power to suspend the moratorium if he found it in the national interest. To the Canadians' relief, the president used that authority to suspend the moratorium the same day that he signed the bill. Using the implicit threat of reimposition of the moratorium, the administration was able to work out an agreement with the Canadian government assuring reciprocal access to the Canadian market by U.S. truckers.

U.S. airline deregulation gave rise to similar problems, as demonstrated early in 1983 when the U.S. Civil Aeronautics Board briefly threatened to block entry to some 56,000 Canadians who had purchased cut-rate air fares to the United States on Air Canada.

Energy. Since the early 1970s energy trade has been a source of friction between the two nations, as both have attempted to shelter their domestic markets from the effects of the sharp rise in prices following the 1973 Arab oil embargo. By the early 1980s natural gas prices had become the most controversial U.S.-Canadian energy issue.

One of Canada's principal exports to the United States has been natural gas, which provided almost 10 percent of Canada's total earnings from trade with the United States. But the government-controlled export price of Canadian gas was well above the average price of U.S. domestic gas. Gas consumers in states like Illinois, significantly dependent on imported gas, were faced with escalating prices as a result. The Canadian minister of energy, mines and resources announced an 11 percent reduction in the export price of gas April 11, 1983, but members of Congress and the administration wanted the price to be brought down further. A volume-related incentive-pricing scheme was presented by Canada July 6, 1983, that offered a 23 percent discount to U.S. importers purchasing gas above a base level. But the Canadians continued to find themselves defending their natural gas policies.

The Alaskan gas pipeline, a joint project between Canada and the United States to bring gas from Alaska through Canada to the U.S. Midwest, also had been the source of acrimony. Canadians feared they would complete their segment of the pipeline while the U.S. portion continued to be delayed due to insufficient financing.

Agriculture. Farm trade also has caused problems between the two countries. Both nations depend heavily upon it, and both governments have supported agriculture in a variety of intricate ways. The U.S.-subsidized sale of wheat to Egypt, for example, concerned the Canadians. The sale was intended as retaliation for West European agricultural subsidies, but it also affected Canada, which after the United States is the world's largest wheat exporter.

As noted above, potato and lumber imports from Canada also have been causing complaints in localized parts of the United States. But the Reagan administration had declined to take action in those cases as of late 1983, despite protectionist pressures.

Telecommunications. The telecommunications industry has opened vast uncharted lands. Some of the most difficult battles between the United States and Canada are likely to be fought in this arena because of the two nations' proximity and the expanding nature of the telecommunications field. The opening skirmish of this war was already in progress in the 1970s. In 1976 Canada enacted a law denying income tax deductions to Canadian companies advertising on U.S. border television stations. The Canadians argued that the tax discrimination against U.S. broadcasters was needed to boost the fledgling Canadian television industry. A stronger communications industry, the Canadian government determined, was necessary to strengthen the nation's cultural identity.

145

In Congress, Sen. Moynihan attempted to retaliate against Canada. In 1982 he proposed a measure to deny tax deductions to U.S. companies purchasing a video system manufactured by the Canadian company, Telidon. That proposal, however, ran into opposition from large U.S. firms wishing to use the Telidon system, and it was withdrawn. But U.S. border broadcasters, feeling the pinch, continued their pressure on Canada to modify its policy.

U.S. Trade Representative William E. Brock III proposed another retaliatory measure in 1983. In a message sent to Congress he recommended legislation duplicating the Canadian law and denying tax deductions to U.S. companies advertising on Canadian stations. Congress did not immediately respond to the proposal, but the Canadians expected the U.S. broadcasters to continue lobbying for an expansion of their markets.

The telecommunications trade had become a particularly sensitive subject by the 1980s. As the technology has become increasingly sophisticated, the significance of the telecommunications industry also has grown, both because it involves the transfer of critical information across borders, and because it is one of the key high-technology industries that both nations were hoping would generate employment growth in the future.

Outlook: Tough Times Ahead

U.S.-Canadian trade issues were likely to remain troublesome for the remainder of the decade due, in part, to a redistribution of industrial capabilities throughout the world. The global recession of the early 1980s underscored the structural problems of U.S. industry and prompted calls for a stronger protectionist policy. Although such calls were sometimes directed against Canada's trade and investment policies, the prospect that U.S. restrictions might provoke retaliation tempered those demands. The Canadian market clearly was one the United States could not afford to lose. Despite their numerous trade problems, the special interrelationship between the two countries remained firmly established. In most industries, new and old, Canada and the United States were closely tied and tended to share their fortunes on the world market.

"If Canada and the U.S., with the most extensive bilateral economic relationship in the world and a tradition of cooperation, cannot successfully manage their relations," said Ambassador Gotlieb, "then we might well ask, 'Who can?'"

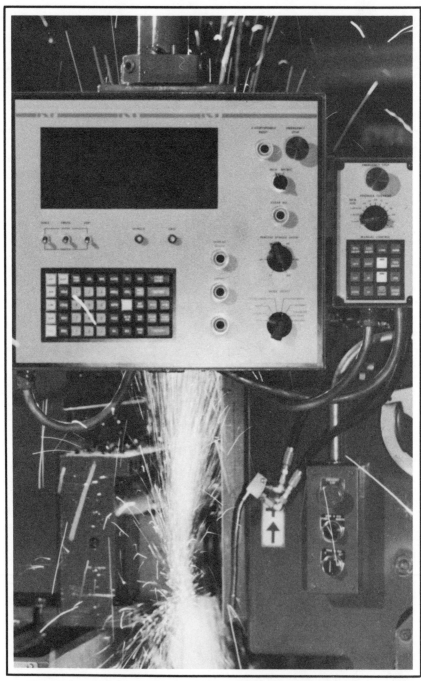

The marriage of machines and computers, like that shown here, has been hastened in Japan by aggressive government policies, while U.S. industry lags behind.

Chapter 6

TRADE ISSUES STRAIN U.S.-JAPAN TIES

U.S. Commodore Matthew Perry sailed into Tokyo Bay in 1853 and demanded that the Japanese begin trading with the United States. Japan at the time was wary of Western influence, but the United States persevered. The outcome of that contact was a trade relationship between the two nations that, during the decades after World War II — more than a century later — developed into one of the closest bilateral ties of any two countries in history. But by the early 1980s there was a glaring disparity in that relationship, straining economic ties as well as diplomatic bonds. In 1982 the United States had a trade deficit of nearly $17 billion with Japan. That deficit was likely to be even higher in 1983. Although the U.S. economy began to improve by mid-1983, the acrimonious debate over Japan's burgeoning trade imbalance with the United States remained a sensitive issue in relations between the world's two foremost economic powers.

Dissatisfaction with that state of affairs was dramatically apparent in the U.S. auto manufacturing capital of Detroit, where bumper stickers commanded drivers to "remember Pearl Harbor." Similar sentiments were expressed in West Virginia, where a charity raised money by selling sledgehammer hits on a Japanese-made Toyota car. As the U.S. economy faltered in the economic recession of the early 1980s, criticism of Japan's marketing impact could be heard throughout the United States. The reason: a growing conviction among Americans that the Japanese were taking advantage of relatively open U.S. markets and benefiting from the fact that they did not need to expend scarce economic resources on national defense, which was protected by U.S. security guarantees. Growing demands for revisions in trade practices and calls for Japan to shoulder more of the defense burden were the result.

The huge imbalance in trade between the two nations came at a time when American businesses, most notably the U.S. auto industry, were particularly hard hit by the recession. Japanese automakers, on the other hand, were enjoying unparalleled success, much of it in the United States. Almost 28 percent of the cars sold in the United States in 1982 were made in Japan. But observers pointed to another side of the economic coin: the fact that Japan had to export a high volume of manufactured goods to pay for the energy and food it needed. Moreover, a report by the Japan Economic Institute of America Inc. pointed out that the Japanese economy, also suffering from the effects of the global recession, was troubled by rising unemployment and a slowdown of its basic industries, including steel and autos. Japan's exports had fallen by more than 13 percent in the second half of 1982, that nation's biggest postwar decline to date.

Nonetheless, U.S. businesses continued to find themselves in stiff competition with the Japanese in developing and successfully promoting a number of products in the U.S. and world markets. Somewhat ironically, much of the raw material going into Japanese products that competed with American-made items came from the United States itself. Eleven of the top 15 U.S. exports to Japan in 1981 were raw materials. The relationship between Japan, the manufacturer, and America, the raw materials supplier, was an additional source of friction between the two nations. "Americans have some difficulty in seeing themselves mainly as a nation that supplies raw materials. . . . It defies America's industrial machismo," commented Daniel Yergin, a lecturer at Harvard's Kennedy School of Government.

Japanese Challenges to the U.S. Auto Industry

A prime example of exported raw materials returning home to threaten American manufacturers as a finished product was the Japanese automobile. In 1981 Japan sold $9.5 billion worth of automobiles to the United States and more than $2 billion worth of trucks. This influx of Japanese imports came in a year when American automakers were forced to close numerous plants, lay off tens of thousands of workers and cope with multimillion-dollar corporate losses. Even with the "voluntary" auto-import restrictions going into effect that year, 1.9 million Japanese cars and 443,500 Japanese trucks were sold in the United States, compared to 6.9 million American-made cars and 1.8 million trucks.

Much of Japan's success in the U.S. auto market has been attributed to better reliability and economy of the Japanese product.

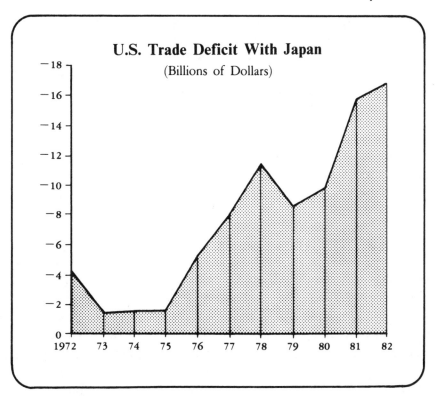

When asked in 1982 if the Japanese were to blame for Detroit's troubles, U.S. Trade Representative William E. Brock III responded, "I don't think you've ever heard anybody in this administration blame the Japanese for our domestic automobile problems. That is just not a valid point of criticism." Nonetheless, he did support the Reagan administration's efforts to limit Japanese auto imports.

Domestic Content Proposals. The dramatic inroads made by the Japanese auto industry produced a crescendo of demands for strict limitations on auto imports. Aided by the widespread sentiment that the United States somehow had been taken advantage of by Japan, numerous protectionist measures were introduced in the 97th and 98th Congresses.

One measure, passed by the House in November 1983 and similar to a 1982 House-approved proposal, would require that foreign auto manufacturers that sold more than 100,000 cars a year in the United States use substantial amounts of U.S. labor and parts in their products.

Depending upon the number of cars sold, the domestic content requirement would range from 3.3 percent to 30 percent during the first year the law was in effect. The content level would rise to a maximum of 90 percent for companies selling more than 900,000 autos in the United States in 1987 and beyond. By comparison, five Japanese car companies in 1982 had a domestic content level of 5 percent each for the cars they sold in the United States.

The major U.S. automakers also would have faced a domestic content requirement of 90 percent, limiting their ability to buy parts from abroad. Stiff quotas would have been applied to companies that failed to meet the bill's required ratios.

Although the Senate had not acted on the measure in 1983, supporters hoped to bring the legislation before that chamber in 1984, where they said election-year pressures could help secure passage. "Some people who find it easy to say no to this today just might find it harder to say that in an election year," said Owen F. Bieber, president of the United Auto Workers (UAW), after the House passed the legislation.

Voluntary Import Quotas. Because the U.S. market was critical to Japanese automakers, accounting for more than one-third of their total exports, it was not a market the Japanese wanted to offend. In response to growing American concern, Japan in 1981 imposed quotas or "voluntary restraint" measures on its auto exports to the United States. Under the arrangement the Japanese agreed to ship no more than 1,680,000 cars and trucks to the United States during the 12-month period beginning April 1, 1981. The agreement to maintain those import levels was extended for one year in 1982 and again in 1983.

The restrictions were to be lifted in March 1984. However, responding to the lobbying efforts of U.S. auto industry executives and Reagan administration officials to extend the limitation, the Japanese Nov. 1, 1983, agreed to renew the restrictions. That agreement, to take effect April 1, 1984, for a period of one year set the limits of Japanese auto exports to the United States at 1.85 million. While this figure was slightly higher than the 1.8 million level President Reagan requested, it was considerably lower than the 2 million vehicles Japan had hoped to export to the American market. The Japanese were amenable to the voluntary agreements in order to allow the U.S. auto industry the opportunity to recover and improve, and to forestall retaliatory legislation.

Under the voluntary restraint arrangements, the Japanese manufacturers still were able to increase the value of their exports to the U.S. market from $8.4 billion in 1980 to $10.3 billion in 1982 by concentrating on more expensive models. Although demand for automobiles in the United States contracted during the recession, the Japanese were able to increase their overall share of the market from 21.2 percent in 1980 to 22.6 percent in 1982. When the U.S. demand for autos began to revive in 1983, Japanese makers, who were facing depressed sales in their home market, wanted an opportunity to share in the revival. But the Japanese government and automobile manufacturers also were well aware that a flood of Japanese autos could increase the threat of congressional passage of domestic content legislation, resulting in far more drastic restrictions on their auto sales.

Japanese Dominance in VCR Industry

In addition to the large, established U.S. auto industry, Japan by the early 1980s had become a major competitor in the "high technology" field of consumer electronics equipment. The newest and brightest star in that field was the videocasette recorder (VCR). In 1981 Japan sold nearly $1.8 billion worth of audio and video recorders in the United States, a phenomenal 69.9 percent increase over 1980 sales. Japan dominated the booming U.S. market because no American electronics firms manufactured VCRs; all those sold by U.S. companies were built by the Japanese.

Ironically, the original idea and technology for videocasette recorders had been developed by American scientists and engineers. But the first two commercial U.S. ventures into the home VCR market by CBS and Ampex were costly failures. In the early 1970s, after American companies had given up on the idea, Sony and Victor Co. of Japan came out with successful home VCRs.

Worldwide, Japan shipped more than 7.4 million VCRs in 1981, more than doubling the 1980 total. For the first time, Japanese VCR exports surpassed those of its color television exports in 1981. Matsushita, Japan's leading electronics firm, had its best year ever, with nearly $13 billion in total sales, an 80 percent increase over 1980. Matsushita's exports of VCRs, marketed under the brand names of Quasar, Panasonic and National, rose 80 percent over 1980.

In addition to Japan's domination of the American VCR market, another aspect of the video battle had developed by 1983, when a royalty rights debate pitted the American motion picture industry against Japanese VCR manufacturers (and U.S. video retail outlets). According

Japanese Lobbyists Forge Coalitions . . .

Hideaki Otaka was quick to point out that he worked for an *American* company: Toyota Motor Sales, U.S.A. "We contribute lots of social benefits," he said in 1983. "We should not be special guests; we should be a part of American society. We should act as local companies." For Otaka, that included lobbying. In May 1982 he became one of the first representatives of a Japanese-owned firm to register as a Washington lobbyist.

It was a highly unusual move; Japanese executives tended to view congressional lobbying as a slightly sinister activity. But Toyota decided to take a different approach. "Lobbying should not be a bad word," said Otaka. "In America, especially in Washington, everyone has a right to speak." A career Toyota employee, Otaka, 42 in 1983, had been in the United States less than two years. He spoke English hesitantly, but seemed more comfortable with American ways than most of his Japanese colleagues. While his presence at the Capitol was unlikely to attract much congressional attention, it symbolized a new and more aggressive Japanese approach to lobbying.

Other Japanese companies, as well, seemed to be beefing up their lobbying efforts. Video-cassette recorder (VCR) makers, for instance, were playing a key role in a coalition of groups waging a high-powered campaign to stop legislation allowing film makers to collect royalty surcharges on VCRs and blank videotapes.

Aggressive lobbying was a distinct break with the past practices when Japanese business had relied for the most part on its government to handle international trade relations. But Japanese diplomats proved more effective when dealing with the executive branch and were less skilled in handling Congress. Increased congressional involvement in trade matters convinced some Japanese businessmen that they needed to do a better job of looking after their own interests on Capitol Hill.

Proposals that threatened to restrict drastically foreign auto imports by requiring a high percentage of U.S. labor parts in cars sold in America, forced the major Japanese automakers to quickly rethink their Washington strategies. They began to search for new sources of political influence, mobilizing their extensive networks of auto dealers and working with a large coalition of U.S. agricultural and business groups opposed to the bill.

They began with their networks of dealers. In September 1982 Toyota sent a telegram to each of its 1,100 U.S. dealers asking them to join the

. . . To Combat U.S. Protectionist Bills

fight against the domestic content bill. Nissan made a similar request. The dealers became the first major group to actively oppose domestic content legislation and provided the two auto giants with strong allies in every congressional district. Large groups of dealers began making regular trips to Washington to visit members of Congress.

The automakers also contacted other American groups that had reason to oppose the bill. They made special efforts to reach agricultural groups, which exported much of their product and were the most likely to suffer if Japan or any other country decided to retaliate against congressional protectionism. In 1982 U.S. farm exports to Japan totaled nearly $5 billion.

The Japanese automakers also worked with companies like IBM, Boeing, Xerox, and others that relied heavily on the free international flow of goods. And they found an unexpected ally in the International Longshoremen's Association, a union that refused to back the position of its umbrella organization, the AFL-CIO, in support of domestic content legislation. Longshoremen provided the manpower that unloaded millions of Toyotas, Datsuns and Hondas at U.S. ports. "We have got to protect our membership," said Ingo Esders, a Washington representative for the union.

Although the House passed a domestic content bill in 1982 and again in 1983 the Senate did not act on the measure. The administration opposed the bill, making it unlikely that President Ronald Reagan would sign domestic content legislation. Precisely how much credit the Japanese deserved for slowing the domestic content bill's progress was difficult to determine. The Department of Commerce and the U.S. Chamber of Commerce had both been active in organizing opposition to the bill. And some of the industry groups fighting the legislation undoubtedly would have been as fervent in their opposition regardless of the Japanese automakers' proddings.

Furthermore, Toyota, Nissan and Honda did not care to take much credit for their efforts. They feared their activity could cause resentment in Congress and among the American public. Instead, they let the dealer groups and other organizations take the spotlight, while they worked in the background. "I don't want to be so visible on Capitol Hill," said Otaka. "Toyota cannot really be the center of the campaign. But because we are a big organization, we can be the main source of statistics, help set up meetings, and so forth."

to The Motion Picture Association of America, the U.S. film industry produced an estimated $1 billion annual surplus trade balance by exporting its products to movie audiences abroad. That industry trade surplus was threatened, the association pointed out, by a growing video industry that balked at acknowledging royalty rights.

The controversy deepened after the 9th U.S. Circuit Court of Appeals in 1981 ruled that the Sony Corporation (maker of Betamax recording machines), its distributors and its advertising agency were liable for damages for contributing to copyright infringement by individuals who used the machines. The decision affected all VCR manufacturers, not just those made by Sony.

By the fall of 1983 VCR and tape cassette manufacturers, joined by video store owners throughout the country, were pressing for legislation to exempt from the ruling VCR owners who used their machines for personal use. At the same time the movie industry was lobbying for royalty surcharges to protect its dwindling trade surplus.

Japan's Hidden Trade Barriers

In addition to Japan's capture of the U.S. market in certain industries, another divisive trade issue concerned Japan's own trade barriers, or what critics charged was its closed market to foreign products. Those barriers included Japan's own stringent quotas on imports, rigorous inspection standards for foreign-made goods and agricultural products, a distribution system that was bewildering to outsiders and difficult for them to penetrate, as well as business traditions that were sometimes very different from Western practices.

Nontariff Restrictions

Those nontariff barriers were considered to be a more significant obstacle to U.S.-Japan trade than tariffs, which had been whittled away by both nations. Indeed Japanese officials pointed to tariff cuts on hundreds of items during multilateral negotiations in the 1970s. But U.S. officials responded that Japan had not gone far enough toward removing its trade barriers. Japan's tariffs, like those of most industrialized nations, had dropped to their lowest levels in history by the early 1980s as a result of several rounds of multilateral negotiations by the 88 members of the General Agreement on Tariffs and Trade (GATT). *(Background on GATT, p. 36; Tokyo round negotiations, p. 85)*

"Every member of Congress," wrote Sen. John W. Warner, R-Va., in response to a survey from the *Nihon Keizai Shimbun* (Japan Economic Journal), "has received letters of protest from farmers and businessmen explaining how their attempts to market their products [in Japan] have been thwarted, by rules and regulations which they believe to be discriminating."

"The perception, and indeed the reality," said U.S. Trade Representative Brock in 1983, "has been that the American marketplace has been much more open to Japanese goods than has the Japanese market to American ones." After World War II the Japanese government, encouraged by the United States, embarked on a closely coordinated effort to rebuild industry while protecting it from foreign competition. But by the early 1960s the Japanese realized they would have to liberalize their own import policy in order to be granted reciprocal access to foreign markets.

Dismantling Some Barriers. After the 1950s the Japanese government steadily, if at times reluctantly, dismantled the traditional barriers to trade. By 1982 it had abolished all but 27 of the 492 quotas that existed 20 years earlier. But in spite of those efforts, there was only a modest increase in the amount of manufactured goods imported into Japan. Merchandise imports actually declined as a percentage of gross national product (GNP) from 1.6 percent in 1960 to 1.5 percent in 1980.

Although tariffs were not a major issue in trade negotiations with the United States, Japan continued to maintain comparatively high quotas on some products that the United States was keenly interested in exporting, such as beef, citrus fruits, manufactured tobacco products and leather. However, bilateral discussions on loosening quotas on beef and citrus imports were in progress in September 1983, and an agreement on relaxing the quotas was likely to be reached by 1984. In addition, the Japanese agreed to put into effect in April 1982 tariff cuts on U.S. semiconductor parts that had been scheduled to go into effect in fiscal years 1983 and 1984.

Japan took other steps to remedy complaints about the difficulty of entering its market. On January 22, 1982, the Japanese government announced it would eliminate 67 nontariff barriers and set up an ombudsman's office to handle individual complaints on trade matters from abroad.

Japanese Tobacco Industry. U.S. trade officials pointed to Japan's cigarette industry as a particularly egregious example of how nontariff barriers shut out American products. Compared to about 20 percent of sales in some European countries, American-made cigarettes accounted for less than 2 percent of the Japanese market in 1981. One reason American cigarette manufacturers found it difficult to sell in Japan was the tight control of the industry by the Japan Tobacco and Salt Public Corp. (JTS), a government monopoly that regulated the cigarette market.

JTS was required to buy all the tobacco produced by Japan's 113,000 small tobacco growers, a commitment that supported the domestic industry at the expense of importers. JTS also limited the number of licensed retail outlets that could sell imported cigarettes, allowed only new brands of imported cigarettes to advertise on television and imposed a 57 percent excise tax and a 20 percent distribution and handling fee on imported brands. *Business Week* magazine characterized JTS in a March 22, 1982, issue as "an example of the closed nature of the Japanese market and a continuing irritant in our trade relations."

Standards and Testing. Quality regulations were another source of economic friction between the United States and Japan. American businesses complained that Japanese product standards were written by their Japanese competitors and that U.S. firms were not allowed to participate in the standards-setting process. Moreover, administration of standards was obscure and seemingly inconsistent, they charged.

U.S. companies also complained of large costs and delays resulting from Japan's refusal to accept much test data developed outside the country. One example was the refusal of the Japan Softball League to certify U.S. aluminum bats because they failed to meet certain design criteria that, U.S. makers claimed, were unrelated to the product's performance. Standards and testing problems were said to be blocking millions of dollars worth of trade in cosmetics, pharmaceuticals and medical and dental equipment, among other products.

Responding to those complaints, the Japanese government in January 1982 announced it would simplify testing procedures for certain types of automobiles, accept animal test data from abroad on medicines and cosmetics and relax certain safety standards for electrical appliances.

Tightly Knit Industrial Structure

A serious obstacle faced by U.S. exports to Japan was the nation's tightly knit industrial structure, much of which was dominated by business groups known as "keiretsu." Those groups are combinations of large banks, manufacturers and trading companies, joined together by cross-stockholding, financial links and informal ties. When purchasing goods or services, members of a group often gave preference to others in their group, in effect closing much of the market not only to foreign firms, but also to "non-group" Japanese firms. An example of the impact of "keiretsu" was provided in late 1982, when a successful Japanese elevator exporting firm without group ties announced plans to move its headquarters to the United States because it could make little headway in its home market.

The remarkably intricate and, in the opinion of some critics, inefficient, Japanese distribution and retailing system also made exporting to Japan more difficult. In recent years, the distribution and retail sector absorbed much of Japan's excess labor force, leaving the nation with almost as many wholesalers and even more retailers as the United States, which has twice the population. Furthermore, distributors often are governed by longstanding relations with their Japanese suppliers, making it difficult for new companies to break into the system. Some observers have pointed out that similar ties would violate antitrust laws if they occurred in the United States.

When U.S. officials complained about the nature of Japan's "industrial structure," the Japanese replied that it was part of their culture. Did the United States have the right to ask them to change their time-honored traditions for the sake of improved trade relations, they asked? "We are not telling them they have got to stop using chopsticks or listening to Japanese music, or do anything," said a U.S. Commerce Department official in 1982. "It's up to them to decide how to solve the problems or even whether they want to solve them."

Despite numerous obstacles, a number of American companies were successful in penetrating the Japanese market. The chemical giant E. I. Du Pont de Nemours Co. reported sales of $700 million in Japan in 1981, a 20 percent increase over the previous year. *Business Week* estimated that Texas Instruments (TI) Inc., a large manufacturer of semiconductors, sold $130 million worth of goods in Japan in 1981, a 9 percent rise over 1980. "TI recognized the market very early, and it started its operation with good people," said one industry observer in Tokyo. "They sent the first [string] team over here, not a second team."

In 1982 Matsumi Esaki, a special envoy to the United States on trade matters, listed several other U.S. firms that had been successful in the Japanese market. These included International Business Machine Corp, which had supplied 40 percent of the computer market in Japan; Caterpillar Tractor Co., with 32 percent of the Japanese tread-type tractor market; Warner-Lambert Co., with 70 percent of the razor blade market; Japan Procter & Gamble Co., with 85 percent of disposable diapers; Garrett Corp., with 64 percent of turbochargers; Borg Warner, with 54 percent of automatic transmissions; S. C. Johnson & Son, Inc., with 30 percent of floor waxes and between 20 and 30 percent of car waxes; Coca-Cola Co., with 33 percent of soft drinks; and Kimberly-Clark Corp. and Scott Paper Co. with 34 percent of the tissue paper market.

Criticism of Japan's Trade Practices

Concessions such as "voluntary" export agreements did not satisfy some congressional critics of Japan's trade practices, who introduced trade reciprocity measures that would strengthen the president's power to retaliate against what was seen as unfair foreign trade practices. One bill that received considerable attention in 1982 was sponsored by Sen. John C. Danforth, R-Mo. Danforth's bill would have required an annual report from the administration detailing any policy or practice of U.S. trading partners that denied the United States trade opportunities substantially equivalent to those offered by the United States to foreigners selling in the U.S. market. The measure also would have required the president to report to Congress on the impact the reported barriers had on U.S. commerce. At that point the president would have been required to propose actions necessary to correct any imbalance if initial efforts to obtain redress failed.

Even though the bill did not single out any country or make action mandatory, Japanese officials viewed the measure as an overt protectionist act directly aimed at retaliating against their nontariff barriers. The Japanese found an important ally in their opposition to the bill. Testifying before Congress in March 1982, Brock said the administration was committed to the concept of free trade and was firmly opposed to the proposed legislation. Although the president was pressing Japan to give American companies greater access to its domestic markets, Brock said the administration would not support any law "which will force U.S. trade policy to require bilateral, sectoral, or product-by-product reciprocity." He said such a law would give a "distorted view of reciprocity," and "could undermine an already vulnerable multilateral trading system, trigger retaliation abroad, further deprive the United States of export markets and erode, if not eliminate, our role as the world leader in liberalizing international trade."

Although the bill was not passed in 1982, another reciprocity bill

Overvalued Dollar vs. Undervalued Yen

While U.S.-Japan trade conflicts were many and varied, much of the blame for the large U.S. bilateral trade deficit was placed on the overvaluation of the dollar on foreign exchange markets.

According to Treasury Department statistics, the dollar appreciated 20.4 percent from the beginning of 1981 through January 1983 against the currencies of the 23 other countries belonging to the Organization for Economic Cooperation and Development (OECD). With each successive appreciation of the dollar's value, U.S. exports became more costly and less competitive with similar goods produced abroad. Dollar appreciation also made domestically produced goods less attractive than imports to American consumers.

During the last quarter of 1978, the Japanese yen traded at a rate of 190 to the dollar. As of November 2, 1983, that rate stood at 234 yen to the dollar. The implications of that huge swing were clear: Japanese products were far cheaper for the American buyer than they were five years earlier, and U.S. products exported to Japan were far more expensive.

Much of the discrepancy could be attributed to differing fiscal policies. The Reagan administration followed a loose policy, cutting taxes and permitting huge deficits, and fought inflation with a tight monetary policy. That resulted in extraordinarily high interest rates. High interest rates encouraged foreign investment in U.S. money markets, increasing the demand for dollars and pushing up exchange rates.

In Japan, the opposite policy was followed. Faced with huge budget deficits, the government launched a tight fiscal policy. A loose monetary policy, accompanied by low interest rates, was relied on to stimulate a sagging economy.

American business interests said the Japanese kept their interest rates at abnormally low levels to discourage foreign investment in Japan, preventing the yen from taking its place as a major reserve currency. This policy has protected the yen from fluctuations in the world market, avoiding deficit woes such as those experienced by the United States when the purchasing power of other nations was limited. A controlled currency that kept the value of the yen down was particularly important to Japan, because exporting was the mainstay of the economy.

was approved by the House Ways and Means Committee in September 1983. The measure gave the president the authority to restrict licenses to foreign services companies from nations that had barriers to U.S. services exports. No further action, however, was taken on the bill in 1983.

While numerous U.S. industries sought protection from import competition, each interest group pushed for its own particular relief measure and there was no agreement on what should or should not be sheltered from foreign imports. The failure of protectionist groups to join forces resulted in part from the nature of trade. Tariffs on steel or machine tools, for example, would be the equivalent of a tax on automakers, who must buy some of both. Quotas on textiles meant higher costs of cloth for airplane and automakers. And Japanese lobbyists were able to capitalize on U.S. industry's divisiveness. A strong Japanese auto lobby fighting domestic content legislation, for example, had garnered the support of not only U.S. foreign auto dealers, but also the International Longshoremen's Association. The union refused to back the protectionist position of its umbrella organization, the AFL-CIO. *(See Japanese lobby, p. 154)*

Most American business leaders, as well as some members of Congress, were not overly enthusiastic about the concept of reciprocity. An informal sampling of business leaders taken in April 1982 by *Fortune* magazine found "no one openly in favor of reciprocity legislation; most businessmen seemed fearful of retaliation." A House Ways and Means subcommittee report released in December 1981 concluded, "While we concede that Japan's trade barriers threaten the free world trading system, we believe that our prime focus should be on ways to make the U.S. economy more competitive."

The Japanese, on the other hand, took the position that American business executives had not been working hard enough to tailor their products to the Japanese market. "Forty years ago the American Army and Navy penetrated the Japanese islands physically," said Naohiro Araya, a trade advisor to the Japanese government, during a March 3, 1982, U.S.-televised interview. "We ... shuddered at the vitality and guts of the American soldier.... Now, they are complaining about the difficulty of getting into the Japanese market. I think we wish them to revitalize their vitality and guts.... What is important is to study the Japanese market and study what the consumers are wishing to have.... If they appeal to the consumers, there is no doubt that they can get penetration into the Japanese market."

Sharing the Defense Burden

Although the Reagan administration insisted that trade and defense were separate issues, in the halls of Congress they inevitably became intertwined. Democratic Sen. Carl Levin of Michigan, for example, pushed for a resolution in 1982 that would have asked Japan to increase its defense spending to more than 1 percent of its GNP. He also was a firm advocate of implementing trade restrictions to counter Japanese trade barriers in the 97th Congress.

Sen. Jesse Helms, R-N.C., made a more direct link between U.S. trade deficits and U.S. defense spending for Japan's security: "The real reason for the trade deficit between the U.S. and Japan is that the American people have shouldered the burden for years of providing security for Japanese trading activities. This has amounted to a subsidy worth billions annually from the U.S. taxpayer," Helms said.

At the end of World War II Congress clearly stated that it wished to see Japan completely disarmed and demilitarized. Under pressure from Gen. Douglas MacArthur's occupation staff and strong anti-war sentiment among their own people, Japanese officials included a clause in their constitution renouncing the "threat or use of force as a means of settling disputes."

The constitution did not prevent the Japanese from creating a large "self-defense" force, making them by some estimates the eighth largest military power in the world. But it restrained them from building that force to a size proportionate to their standing as the world's second largest economic power. While the Japanese allocated less than 1 percent of their GNP to defense in 1980, the United States allocated 5.6 percent, the United Kingdom, 5.1 percent, France, 4.1 percent and Germany, 3.3 percent.

As a result of Japan's limited defense effort, the United States shouldered the major burden for defending the Pacific. And while U.S. government officials were divided over how to deal with U.S.-Japan trade issues, almost all agreed that Japan should make substantial increases in its defense spending. Japanese officials, on the other hand, pointed to the fact that during the 1970s, the nation's defense spending increased in real terms by almost 80 percent. Among U.S. allies, that was the highest growth rate, with the exception of Turkey. In 1981, when growth of most other spending categories in Japan's budget was held at zero, defense spending rose by more than 7 percent.

One reason for U.S. pressure on Japan to increase its defense effort was a reported massive buildup of Soviet forces in Central Asia and the Far East, beginning in the 1970s. "The Soviet force in Asia is so complex that it may be possible for the U.S.S.R. to reach out with its nuclear might and destroy all the modernized sectors of China . . . within a matter of hours . . .," said Robert J. Pranger of the American Enterprise Institute in 1982 congressional testimony. "The sheer fall-out from such an attack, of course, could possibly bring havoc to Japan as well."

Although the Japanese appeared less concerned about a Soviet threat than did Washington, Zenko Suzuki, Japan's prime minister in 1981, increased defense spending by 7.75 percent, to about $11 billion overall. Japan also expanded its security commitments by agreeing to defend the sea-lanes (on which its economy is dependent) for a distance of 1,000 miles from the home island and to protect its own airspace. Most U.S. defense analysts argued that Japan could defend its sea-lanes only if its defense expenditures broke the self-imposed 1 percent ceiling. Yashuhio Nakasone, who succeeded Suzuki in November 1982, further emphasized the need to boost Japan's defense spending and shoulder more of the responsibility for its own defense.

Rearming Japan was strongly opposed by many Japanese voters and by some of Japan's Asian neighbors, including the Philippines and Indonesia, which suffered greatly at Japanese hands during World War II. And some U.S. observers believed that a Japanese military buildup would exacerbate the trade problem. Deputy Trade Representative David R. Macdonald, for instance, noted that military exchanges with Japan gave that country a great deal of technological know-how that might well be used to produce more exports.

Japan's Economic Prospects

Central to any discussion about Japanese trade policy is the nation's acute shortage of natural resources in the face of its constantly growing industrialization. Japan, with a population of approximately 117 million (about one-half that of the United States) has a land area of 143,000 square miles, roughly the size of Montana. But only about 20 percent of Japan's land is arable. The nation imports more oil, coal, iron ore, cotton, wood and lumber than any other country. Moreover, as already noted, Japan was feeling the effects of the global recession of the early 1980s. The nation's per capita GNP growth rate slipped from 4 percent in 1980 to only 2.3 percent in 1982, according U.S. Commerce Department figures.

In spite of the economy's sluggish growth rate, Japan did not experience the high unemployment or inflation besetting other nations. Its unemployment rate in 1982 was 2.2 percent, one of the lowest in the industrialized world. The primary reason for Japan's low unemployment was the widespread practice of "permanent employment," in which an employee went to work for a firm after leaving school and stayed through retirement, barring employee dishonesty or an economic catastrophe. Along with the near guarantee of lifetime employment went other benefits, which could include inexpensive company housing, low-cost company vacation resorts and company-sponsored sports teams and social events. Those dividends contributed to a permanent workforce that was loyal to the company or organization.

The strong worker-institution relationship also contributed to the high level of Japanese productivity. From 1950 to 1980 productivity in Japanese manufacturing rose an average of 9.1 percent each year. At the same time, American productivity rose only 2.4 percent annually. Productivity actually declined in the United States during 1978, 1979 and 1980. In contrast, Japanese productivity in 1980 grew 6.2 percent.

The High-Tech Challenge

Japan was counting on high technology to be the key to a successful exporting future. This strategy put the Japanese on a collision course with America because the United States had dominated the microelectronics industry since its inception. Indeed, American scientists invented the semiconductor, the core of microelectronics technology, and American businesses taught Japanese firms the mechanics of semiconductor manufacturing.

Japan as Industry Leader. Until recently, American companies — including Texas Instruments, National Semiconductor and Intel — built and sold about 70 percent of the world's semiconductors, with the Japanese manufacturers holding second place in production and sales. But by the early 1980s Japanese producers — especially Nipon Electronic, Hitachi and Fujitsu Fanuc Ltd. — with the help of hundreds of millions of dollars in government research and development funds, had cut deeply into the U.S.-dominated market. This came at a time when American semiconductor firms were experiencing rising research and equipment costs that, in combination with intense domestic competition in a depressed economy, had forced U.S. companies to sell their products at very low profit margins.

One reason for the success of many Japanese high-tech exports to the United States was that Japanese firms sold their products at prices below comparable American items. The Japanese made up the difference by selling at higher prices in their domestic market. Moreover, Japanese nontariff barriers prevented American microprocessor firms from selling significant amounts of chips to Japan. That led to charges that the Japanese were "dumping" semiconductors on the U.S. market, that is, selling them at less than cost.

The pricing issue was an important one because per-unit costs for high-technology products tend to drop rapidly as production volume rises, a relationship that business consultants refer to as the "learning curve." To enable high-volume production a company must have a high volume of sales, making competitive access in the international market vital.

One example of Japan's success in the microelectronics field involved the 64K RAM, a random access memory chip that could store 64,000 bits of digital computer data. It served as the main memory bank for many of the computers in use in the early 1980s. By the end of 1981 the Japanese controlled about 70 percent of the world market in 64K RAMS.

During the 1974-75 recession, U.S. semiconductor companies had been forced to cut their budgets and workforce. When the recession ended and demand returned, the domestic industry was not geared to meet it. Only two American companies, Motorola and Texas Instruments, were manufacturing the 64K RAM chips in 1981; three more firms joined the competition in 1982. According to the Commerce Department, the U.S. share of the world market grew to 40 percent during 1982 from 30 percent in 1981. While Americans were playing catch-up in this market, Hitachi forged ahead with work on a 256K RAM chip, with mass production set for 1983. Another Japanese firm, Toshiba Corp. of Tokyo, was planning to build an $86 million facility to manufacture the first 1 megabit unit, a chip capable of containing one million bits of data.

Robotics. Japan also dominated another sector of the high-technology arena in the early 1980s, robotics. Aided by government subsidies, Japanese industry made wide use of those labor-saving devices in factories; workers, with their guarantee of lifetime employment, welcomed their automated peers.

Again, it was the United States, not Japan, that pioneered the building of robots in the early 1960s. U.S. technology still was considered to be the most advanced in the early 1980s, particularly in the computer software that ran the so-called "smart robots." But Japan clearly led the United States in production, applications and worldwide sales. Robotics expert Paul Aron predicted that by 1985 Japan would have five times as many robots as the United States and that by then Japan would be producing about 32,000 robots a year.

A 1981 study by the U.S. House Ways and Means Committee, entitled "Report on Trade Mission to the Far East," underscored what the challenge meant to the U.S. industry: ". . .[I]n the high technology products that count — the products which will dominate the world trade and the economy for the rest of the century — the Japanese are second to none. . . . The trend lines indicate that they will surpass the United States and that the gap will widen dramatically, UNLESS the United States responds."

Japanese Industrial Policy. Much of the credit for Japan's successful high-technology industry was given to its industrial policy. The Japanese government consistently provided incentives to developing industries in the form of tax write-offs and subsidized loans. In the robotics industry, for example, the government pressured 24 manufacturers and 10 insurance companies to form Japan Robot Lease, which leased welding robots to small companies for $90 a month. Not only could a round-the-clock robot provide $1,200 worth of man hours for $90, but employers could exchange the robots for improved versions as they became available without tying up their money in an outright purchase.

The support given to Japanese semiconductor manufacturers by their ties with large corporations provided another illustration of the foresighted Japanese policy. While most leading U.S. manufacturers, at least initially, were relatively small, independent firms, most Japanese manufacturers were part of larger electronics companies, giving them a great financial advantage. "These [parent] companies are ready to provide the big sums needed for developing new microchips — and not just to earn profits from sales," a March 1982 issue of *The Economist* noted.

The success of Japanese industrial policy has been praised widely in the United States, and many economists have suggested adopting similar tactics. But Reagan administration trade officials complained that one result of Japan's highly touted policies had been to erect barriers to trade. "These [industrial] policy tools are not devised to restrict or exclude foreign participation from the Japanese market," said the U.S. trade representative's report presented to Congress in November 1982, "but that has often been the effect."

U.S. trade officials were particularly concerned about Japanese efforts to boost high-technology industries. It was these industries — such as computers, telecommunications, robotics and biotechnology — that increasingly would determine an industrialized nation's trade and economic strengths in the future. Although the United States continued to lead the world in most of those high-tech industries in 1983, it lagged behind in areas where Japan had taken the initiative. Japan's industrial policy, which encouraged the formation of research cartels and provided guidance, financing, tax incentives, and other benefits for high-technology companies, had given the Japanese a definite, and perhaps permanent, advantage in high-technology trade. *(See chaper on industrial policy, p. 217.)*

Future Trade Ties

It was clear that Japan would maintain its booming export economy throughout the decade. It also was clear that the United States would continue to press the Japanese to open their markets to foreign goods and to make additional contributions to the high cost of defense.

There were encouraging signs in the relationship between the two economic superpowers. In spite of numerous problems, U.S. trade officials said in private that they much preferred negotiating with the Japanese to negotiating with European governments. Japanese trade officials often expressed a similar sentiment about Washington.

"There are a broad range of communications between our countries that are open, and that will hopefully ward off callousness, protectionism and shortsightedness," said David Abshire, head of the Georgetown Center for Strategic and International Studies. "There is no relationship in the world today that is more important to the peace and prosperity of the world than the relationship between the U.S. and Japan."

Harvesting wheat in Washington state. Although farm products account for a large share of total U.S. exports, their value has been declining in recent years.

Chapter 7

U.S. FARM EXPORTS: SUBSIDIES AND BARRIERS

Agriculture long has relied for its economic well being significantly more on exports than have most other sectors of the U.S. economy. About 20 percent of industrial production depends on foreign markets for its existence, whereas one out of every three acres of farmland is planted for export. Each billion dollars in agricultural export sales creates at least 26,000 American jobs, according to Sen. Thad Cochran, R-Miss., a member of the Senate Agriculture Committee. It was little wonder that efforts to find foreign outlets for the food surplus had become a priority matter for members of Congress as well as Ronald Reagan's administration.

For nearly a decade, the U.S. government had counted on exports of farm commodities to siphon off excess production while boosting farm income. Between 1970 and 1981 farm exports grew sixfold, from $7.3 billion in 1970 to $43.3 billion eleven years later, comprising 18.9 percent of all U.S. exports and 19.5 percent of total world agricultural trade. By 1982, however, U.S. agricultural shipments abroad had fallen to $36.6 billion, or 17.7 percent of total exports. According to the U.S. Department of Agriculture (USDA), they were expected to slide to below $36 billion in calendar year 1983.

Dawson Ahalt, USDA deputy assistant secretary for economics, blamed the drop in trade on a "simultaneous recession around the world and a strong dollar. . . ." Both trends meant that foreign customers could not afford to buy as much from the United States. Moreover, other nations had become more efficient at growing their own food and more aggressive about exporting their surpluses.

From Optimism to Eroding Markets

The first of several massive grain sales to the Soviet Union, negotiated in 1972, injected strong expectations of prosperity into the farm community. That optimism was borne out during the early and mid-1970s, as net farm income and land values rose steadily. During that period grain production rose from 205 million metric tons annually to 303 million metric tons, nearly a 50 percent increase. (A metric ton is 2,200 pounds.) Of that growth, an average of about 18 million metric tons annually were consumed domestically, and 75 million metric tons were exported. But even as American farmers were beginning to rely more and more on foreign markets, those markets were eroding. The protective, highly subsidized common agricultural policy (CAP) of the 10-nation European Economic Community (EEC), adopted to stabilize markets and assure domestic food supplies, had become more effective during the 1970s. Western Europe reduced its need for other nations' food and became an aggressive exporter of its own surplus grain, livestock products and dairy goods. *(Background on EEC, p. 44)*

During this period, developing nations borrowed heavily to finance their own industrialization efforts, energy needs and food imports. The resulting debts meant that by the 1980s many could not finance additional U.S. food purchases.

Agricultural competitors of the United States, such as Canada, Australia and Brazil, stepped up their production, crowding America in world markets. And foreign customers found American food more expensive when the dollar rose in value compared to other currencies. "Even though the price of U.S. wheat was declining, the price to foreign buyers in their currencies increased by 160 percent over the last two years," Block told a group of U.S. exporters in late 1982.

Surpluses and Export Opportunities

In 1980 President Jimmy Carter's secretary of agriculture, Bob Bergland, announced that the federal government saw no need to pay farmers to take acreage out of production. What could not be sold at home could be shipped for sale abroad to satisfy a seemingly insatiable world market that already was absorbing one-third of the U.S. grain production.

By 1983 such optimism seemed unwarranted. As farmers prepared for spring planting, the message from Ronald Reagan's administration was dramatically different. Bumper crops in 1981 and 1982, falling demand, rising export competition and the dollar's strength abroad left farmers and the government stocked with price-depressing surpluses.

During 1981 and 1982 market prices for wheat, corn and other

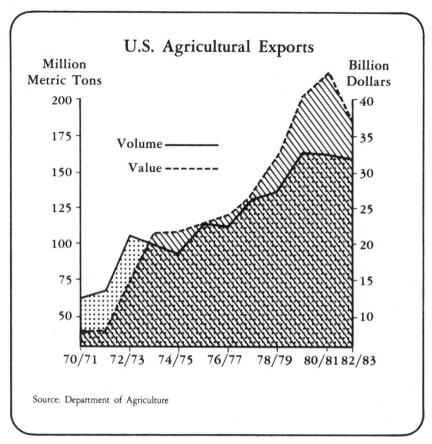

U.S. Agricultural Exports

Million
Metric Tons

Billion
Dollars

Volume ———
Value – – – – –

Source: Department of Agriculture

important grains dipped by one-third. Cotton prices dropped 25 percent. Net farm income nose-dived, too, from a historic high of $32.7 billion in 1979 to an estimated $19 billion in 1982. That was less than the interest payments on outstanding farm debt of $215 billion — a figure that had nearly doubled since 1977 and quadrupled since 1972, according to USDA. Adjusted for inflation, farmers' income in 1982 was the lowest since 1933.

As market prices sank in response to the surplus, the cost of government farm assistance programs soared to a record level of $11.9 billion in fiscal year 1982 — $7 billion in commodity loans, $2.6 billion for purchases primarily of dairy products, $1.5 billion largely for "deficiency" and disaster payments and $700 million mostly for grain storage. USDA projected that federal farm programs would cost $18.2

billion in 1983, when the impact of the 1982 bumper crop was felt. Costs were rising because the grain surplus depressed market prices and made selling less attractive to farmers than borrowing from federal price support programs. Farmers used their crops as collateral for price support loans, and USDA officials expected many to keep the money and let the government keep the grain.

The dilemma facing U.S. agriculture in the 1980s had not been experienced for two decades. The last time that American farmers and the government were left holding comparable quantities of grain was at the end of the 1950s. High demand and price supports had encouraged farmers to grow more grain than the United States could use. The supports discouraged export sales by pricing American grain above world markets. To rid itself of the surplus, the government resorted to export subsidies, paying farmers the difference between the world market price and what they would receive in the higher-priced U.S. market. Additionally, Congress in 1954 enacted Food for Peace (PL 480), a billion-dollar-a-year program authorizing gifts of U.S. commodities to help overcome world hunger and reduce domestic surpluses.

Farm bills after 1965 set relatively low crop price supports. The supports were sensitive to world markets, with supplementary income payments made directly to farmers in years of very low prices. The major assumption was that even when world prices were low, U.S. farmers would profit from the sheer volume of exports because they could produce more grain, more cheaply, than anyone else. Acreage controls limiting planting, a major feature of Depression-era farm programs, were to be used sparingly or not at all.

That thinking had changed by 1982. In November, Agriculture Secretary John R. Block unveiled a plan to pay farmers to reduce production. Under the "payment-in-kind" (PIK) program, some of the surplus grain was returned to farmers as a way of compensating them for reducing the amount they grew. Block estimated that PIK would take 23 million acres out of production in 1983, but the actual amount, announced March 22, 1983, far exceeded expectations. Farmers pledged to leave 82.2 million acres unplanted, about 36 percent of the farm land eligible for PIK and acreage diversion programs.

In addition to those programs, USDA officials also considered increasing food donations abroad. But no combination of government actions could make the surplus vanish quickly. "There's no magic solution," said Ahalt. The administration asserted that only drastic measures, such as PIK and increased exports, could reduce the American stockpile of surplus commodities. However, both domestic and foreign giveaway programs were expensive. The U.S. government spent $480 million on international food charity in 1982 and expected to spend $650 million in 1983 and 1984.

Impact of Embargoes on U.S. Farm Trade

There was general agreement by 1983 among farmers, members of Congress and administration officials that agricultural trade suffered not only from unfavorable economic conditions but from a decade of government trade restrictions, imposed both for domestic and foreign policy reasons. Those restrictions had jeopardized future export markets and created doubts in the minds of some potential foreign buyers as to the United States' reliability as a supplier.

1973 Soybean Export Restrictions. Trade experts said that 1973 restrictions on U.S. soybean exports, for example, sent an exceptionally damaging signal abroad: that even America's friends, such as Japan, could not count on contracted food deliveries. The soybean embargo was imposed on foreign markets in the belief that domestic supplies were too low to permit exports. Contracts were briefly suspended, then partially restored, as farmers were given permission to export only half the contracted-for quantity of soybeans. The cutback had a particularly significant impact on Japan; the price of tofu, the soybean curd common in Japanese meals, rose 50 percent. Before the embargo, Japan bought 98 percent of its soybeans from U.S. suppliers; afterwards, it began to buy large quantities from Brazil and invested in major expansions of soybean production there.

According to Bruce Hawley, assistant director of the American Farm Bureau Federation, the U.S. share of the world soybean market had dropped to 59 percent by 1981, compared with 95 percent in 1970. Hawley blamed the decrease on America's trade reputation, which he characterized as "somewhat beneath that of an unreliable used-car dealer." John Baize, who represented soybean growers in Washington, said the embargo even might have contributed to Japan's persistence in retaining its trade barriers on American farm goods and its reluctance to remain dependent on U.S. agricultural exports. One result of the 1973 soybean restrictions, Baize said, was that the Japanese "were shown how vulnerable they could be to their own lack of self-sufficiency in food."

(For a further discussion of trade barriers, see U.S.-Japan trade chapter.)

Soviet Grain Embargo. More damaging by far was the Carter administration's Jan. 4, 1980, decision to halt previously negotiated grain sales to the Soviet Union in retaliation for its invasion of Afghanistan. The embargo, imposed for foreign policy reasons, cost the U.S. economy an estimated $11.4 billion and triggered vociferous criticism from farmers. By the time it was lifted by President Reagan on April 24, 1981, the U.S. share of Soviet grain imports had dropped from 70 percent to 27 percent. *(Further discussion of embargo, p. 116)*

American grain found other foreign markets, however, and the U.S. share of the Soviet market by the end of fiscal year 1982 had climbed to 35 percent, representing 13.9 million metric tons, just shy of the record 15 million metric tons shipped in 1979. Nonetheless, American farm prices did not recover after the embargo was lifted. Members of Congress charged that U.S. sellers and communist buyers were reluctant to trade because of fears that a new embargo against the U.S.S.R. would be instituted by the administration in reaction to Moscow's role in the unsettled political situation in Poland. They insisted that only a new multiyear grain agreement could quell market jitters.

In fact, Reagan did break off negotiations for a new long-term, U.S.-U.S.S.R. grain agreement in December 1981 to protest the imposition of martial law in Poland. In the meantime, he extended the existing contract twice, each time for a year. In July 1983 U.S. and Soviet officials completed negotiations on a new five-year grain agreement.

The pact, which took effect Oct. 1, committed the United States to sell — and the Soviet Union to buy — at least 9 million metric tons and up to 12 million metric tons of wheat and corn each year. Agriculture Secretary Block said the pact generally followed the terms of the previous U.S.-Soviet agreement, guaranteeing delivery of the specified minimums and permitting either side to opt out under certain conditions, such as short supply in the United States. *(1983 grain agreement, p. 116)*

Phil St. Clair, vice president of Agri-Products Division of A. E. Staley Mfg. Co., had commented in 1982 that the Soviets needed the predictability of multi-year U.S. commitments to persuade them to rely again on the United States. After Carter's embargo, the Soviet Union sought other suppliers — as had Japan in 1973 — and negotiated major long-term grain trade agreements with Canada and Argentina, a barter agreement with India and informal grain agreements with Thailand and France.

U.S. Trade Policies Criticized

The cumulative effect of the grain embargo was to burden America with a tarnished reputation as a dependable trader, farm interests said. They noted that when the members of the EEC agreed to comply with Great Britain's trade sanctions against Argentina during the 1982 Falkland Islands crisis, the decision affected only new contracts, not existing agreements. Even Britain permitted delivery of goods to Argentina under agreements already negotiated.

Honoring existing contracts had been standard behavior for every nation except the United States, according to Joseph Halow, executive director of the North American Export Grain Association. "I find it unbelievable that a country built on free enterprise and business should be the first to cancel contracts. Nobody else does it," he said.

Other nations occasionally found excuses to back out of contracts if subsequent price changes made the agreement considerably less favorable to them, according to Jules Katz, who served in the Carter State Department as assistant secretary for economic and business affairs and later chaired a commodities brokerage subsidiary of Acli International Inc. But he stressed that the offending nations generally were the less developed countries. "If you ask what is the experience with Europe and the developed countries? No contest. We're the worst. We are certainly unique as a major developed trading country in using export policy as an instrument of other policies," Katz said.

Competing exporters, he added, "largely divorce their trade interests from political considerations, except in the most egregious circumstances." Katz suggested that other governments, faced with political pressures such as those following the Afghanistan invasion that prompted Carter's embargo, "would say, 'The Soviets have committed a dastardly act. They will be condemned for all time.' Period. Business continues."

'Contract Sanctity' Guarantee

Although the embargo tarnished America's reputation as a reliable supplier, there was little agreement on what should be done to remedy that lack of confidence. Some members of Congress and farm lobbyists wanted to enact legislation guaranteeing that export contracts would be honored despite any embargoes or other foreign policy actions. "The farm economy has a continuing problem [because] there is no guarantee that we will not have a similar embargo at any moment," Sen. Richard G.

Lugar, R-Ind., told a hearing of the Senate Banking, Housing, and Urban Affairs Committee early in 1982.

Donald E. Henderson, of the Indiana Farm Bureau, testified that "as long as there is the slightest indication in foreign countries that we will use food as a foreign policy weapon, we will continue to be the world's storage bins," with foreign customers buying from America only as a last resort.

On the last day before adjourning for the 1982 election recess, the Senate with little debate approved a "contract sanctity" proposal intended to improve the U.S. trade image abroad by guaranteeing that trade contracts would be honored. The proposal, offered by Sen. David Durenberger, R-Minn., required that except in time of war or national emergency, delivery be made on agricultural export contracts in effect at the time an embargo or other restraint on U.S. trade was imposed. "A strategy of market development can never succeed with the specter of the federal government hovering over the market every time it believes food can be used to achieve foreign policy objectives," Durenberger said.

The contract sanctity proposal was added to a bill reauthorizing the Commodity Futures Trading Commission. The House-passed version had no such provision, but the House accepted the proposal, and it was included in the final bill that cleared Congress in December. The bill's guarantee on delivery of agricultural exports, with an exception only for national emergency or war, drew objections from the State Department that it restricted the president's freedom to act. But because the trade guarantee had wide support within the financially troubled farm community, administration officials avoided objecting to it publicly.

Sen. Robert Dole, R-Kan., told House-Senate conferees on the measure Dec. 9 that he and other supporters of the provision had offered to soften the language in conference if the State Department would agree to negotiate a long-term grain sale agreement with the Soviet Union. But "to try to reason with the State Department is, as in any administration, impossible," Dole said. Although department officials did not respond to his offer, Dole added, "now, at the last minute, they're calling frantically and saying, 'you've got to change this.'"

Administration officials sought, without success, to convince farm lobbyists and their congressional allies that they did not need the statutory guarantee because Reagan repeatedly had pledged to avoid trade embargoes, except in extreme circumstances. (However, he did impose sanctions in 1981 and 1982 on U.S. exports for use in construction of a Soviet gas pipeline to Western Europe.) *(Pipeline issue, see pp. 117, 202.)*

The EEC, Congress and the Subsidy Issue

Most analysts contended that two years of worldwide recession and a strengthened dollar accounted for the decline in farm exports. Others pointed to an additional factor — export subsidies offered by the EEC (whose members are Belgium, Britain, Denmark, France, Greece, West Germany, Ireland, Italy, Luxembourg and the Netherlands), as well as a handful of other nations, that enabled their farmers to undercut American food prices in world markets. U.S. farmers decried Common Market food export subsidies (amounting to an estimated $6 billion in 1982) as unfair and pressed Congress to retaliate. A number of subsidy bills were introduced in the 98th Congress, raising the possibility that a trade war could break out unless the United States and the EEC arrived at a negotiated settlement.

The Common Market argued it was no more guilty of unfair farm export subsidies than was the United States. The main difference, said Ella Kruchoff, a spokeswoman for the European Community office in Washington, D.C., was "the U.S. government has a less transparent system of subsidies" than the Common Market. "Most congressmen are ignorant of the facts," she added. Kruchoff pointed out that the Common Market was the American farmers' biggest export market. It bought $9 billion in agricultural products in 1981, primarily soybeans and feed grains, while the United States bought only $2 billion in European farm products that year.

Common Market representatives defended their export subsidy practices at a November 1982 meeting in Geneva of the 90 nations subscribing to the General Agreement on Tariffs and Trade (GATT), an international trade forum for negotiating trade issues. Shortly before the meeting, a Nov. 8 EEC news release stated that the Common Market "does not see the need for any new negotiations on agriculture trade." The EEC contended its food export subsidies did not violate a GATT agreement that permitted such subsidies if they did not result in the takeover of traditional markets of other GATT nations. The United States claimed that Common Market wheat exporters violated that agreement. But a special GATT judicial panel announced in late February 1983 it could find no evidence to support the U.S. charge. *(GATT background, box p. 36)*

Reagan Administration Views on Subsidies

The administration shelved its aversion to export subsidies when it concluded that other nations would continue to refuse U.S. requests to alter their practices unless the United States fought back in kind. But Reagan officials clearly were reluctant to declare an all-out trade war. Testifying before the Senate Foreign Relations Committee on Feb. 15, 1983, Secretary of State George P. Shultz warned members that if subsidies were commonly used to market agricultural products, "the net result will not be good, and we will be in effect giving products away."

Yet the purpose of the subsidies, Agriculture Committee Chairman Jesse Helms, R-N.C., told the Senate, was to convince other nations "that the United States is serious when it said that their right to swing their export subsidy fist ends at Uncle Sam's nose."

Block and his colleagues likened the subsidies to warning shots to make foreign subsidizers reconsider their trade practices. But Glenn Tussey, assistant director of the American Farm Bureau Federation's (AFBF) national affairs division, wondered whether the administration would spend enough on export subsidy programs to be taken seriously. And if it did, farm lobbyists agreed, American agriculture would not easily return to life without subsidies.

The last time the United States began to directly subsidize farm exports, the procedure continued for more than 20 years. Between 1949 and 1972, the government paid commodity exporters the difference between high, federally supported domestic prices and lower world prices. The payments were suspended in September 1972, when the U.S.-Soviet grain sale agreement pushed world prices well above domestic prices, and they were never reinstituted. However, some foreign observers contended that such policies as the favorable credit provided to needy nations for PL 480 purchases of U.S. food and other programs constituted *de facto* subsidies.

In October 1982 the administration began to underwrite farm export sales with a $1.5 billion, three-year "blended credit" program. The program offered foreign importers of U.S. farm products loans with interest rates 2 percentage points below market rates. The lower rates were achieved by combining interest-free loans by the Agriculture Department's Commodity Credit Corporation with federally guaranteed commercial loans. In January 1983 Reagan announced the program would receive an additional $1.25 billion for loans. Block said USDA would be devoting a total of $5.1 billion to export financing in 1983. All but $350 million of that was in federal guarantees for private loans, which rarely cost the federal government substantial sums because of the low default rate.

The same month the administration negotiated the sale of one million tons of subsidized flour to Egypt, long considered one of France's principal markets for farm goods. The government gave U.S. millers enough surplus wheat to reduce the net per ton price to the Egyptians by $100, bringing it below the prevailing U.S. price of $255 a ton. The net cost to the government was expected to be about $130 million.

The sale was viewed by an unidentified Common Market official (quoted in the Jan. 21, 1983, *New York Times*) as "a brutal takeover of one of our major markets." In response, Block said the deal showed "We mean business when we talk about competing for export markets."

Export Subsidy Legislation Considered

Meanwhile, as disagreements over the subsidy issue persisted, the Senate Agriculture Committee in March 1983 approved a bill requiring the secretary of agriculture to sell at least 150,000 metric tons of federally owned surplus dairy products abroad annually for the next three years at prices substantially below U.S. market prices. (No comparable measure was considered in the House during the session.) The panel's bill also would authorize an export payment-in-kind program in which federally owned commodities would be given to buyers as bonuses, thereby lowering the overall purchase price. In addition, federal funds would be used to subsidize exports of eggs, raisins and canned fruit. Contrary to President Reagan's wishes, the bill contained a provision exempting export-PIK and commodities financed by the blended credit program from the federal cargo preference law. The law required roughly half of the goods exported under federal programs to be carried on U.S. flag ships. Farm interests disliked the requirement because U.S. shipping was more expensive, raising the cost of the exports to foreigners.

The committee members were almost unanimous in laying a large share of the blame for sagging U.S. farm exports on what they viewed as predatory trade practices by the EEC and others. Acknowledging that the legislation could invite international retaliation, Sen. Pete Wilson, R-Calif., said, "I don't think that's much of a risk because we're already suffering." The trade bill, he said, "will send a message that we're willing, however reluctantly, to escalate the arms race" in agricultural trade.

Only Lugar opposed the thrust of the legislation. He warned that such actions as actively promoting foreign sales of heavily subsidized

U.S. butter, cheese and dry milk were "likely to be disruptive of our agriculture policy and our foreign policy."

Farm Response to Subsidy Proposals

Farm leaders generally agreed that export subsidies were unwise in the long term. But many of them added that subsidies were increasingly necessary if the United States was to compete effectively in the commodity markets of the 1980s.

The American Farm Bureau Federation welcomed the subsidy proposals, albeit reluctantly. "The one group that might have philosophically come out against it is us," said Tussey. He said the organization disliked the economic distortions caused by subsidies but decided that the United States had to fight for foreign markets. The $6 billion a year that it would take to match EEC subsidies, or "rebates" as European officials termed them, seemed cheap, compared to budget estimates of $18 billion in outlays for fiscal 1983 for domestic price support loans and payments to farmers who could not sell their crops. But it was double what the price supports had averaged between 1972 and 1982. "The Europeans are saying that Reagan won't spend that much money," said the AFBF's Tussey. "They're probably right."

The National Farmers Union was even more skeptical about the impact of the export aid programs, holding that the subsidies would not put cash in farmers' pockets in the near future. The NFU feared that subsidies would drive world prices dangerously low and keep them there, according to NFU's Mullins. "We're still exporting for less than it costs to produce. This destabilization could come back to haunt us," he said.

"I'm concerned about this move to trade barriers. I don't think it's the best way to go," said Baize of the American Soybean Association. He warned that indiscriminate use of export subsidies would stimulate retaliatory trade barriers. Yet the soybean group had asked the Reagan administration to put together a subsidized export sales program for soybean oil. Baize contended that Brazilian export subsidies had severely damaged American sales of soybean oil to India. In 1977-79 India bought $155 million worth of American oil a year; at the end of 1980 those purchases had dropped to $22.1 million. The time had come, Baize said, for the United States aggressively to assert itself in subsidized markets.

Poultry, egg and rice producers also were seeking export-PIK sales, and Rep. Charlie Rose, D-N.C., told Block that his tobacco and peanut growers wanted help for their products as well. The National Cotton

Council sought legislation to permit U.S. textile manufacturers to use free surplus cotton to lower their export prices for finished cotton clothing. That way, according to the council's Macon Edwards, "we could ship our cotton out in blue jeans" and combat subsidized foreign clothing manufacturers.

Costs of Subsidies, Potential Dependency

Some administration officials warned the U.S. farm subsidies could prove costly, ineffective and difficult to turn off. They suggested that competing nations were unlikely to retrench on subsidies unless they felt the United States would spend as much or more than they did, for many years. That level of spending, they added, could draw American farmers and related industries into an unhealthy dependence on subsidies. And even without approaching European expenditures, the United States could create "chaos" in world markets, according to Deputy Agriculture Secretary Richard E. Lyng. Asked whether he worried about weaning U.S. agriculture and related industries from subsidies, Lyng said in a 1983 interview, "Yes. We all worry about that potential. And over time, government involvement [in trade] gets greater and greater, and a lot of us don't like that."

Gary Hufbauer, a specialist in trade subsidies at the Institute for International Economics (a Washington, D.C., research organization), suggested that American beneficiaries could become so dependent on subsidies that they would lobby against international negotiations to end them. "Once the government starts giving subsidies, you see a buildup of powerful internal groups that oppose international agreements. They will hire very good lawyers. They will hire very good lobbyists," he warned.

The GATT talks in Geneva in November 1982 illustrated Hufbauer's warning about dependency on subsidies, according to one high-ranking trade expert. The agriculture ministers of the Common Market nations took the unusual step of accompanying their spokesmen to Geneva. Like lobbyists in a congressional committee session, the official said, the ministers watched closely as the negotiators flatly told the American team they would not discuss the U.S. proposals. The United States had gone to the talks hoping to persuade other members to freeze and then reduce their agricultural export subsidies.

Lyng, who also took part in the November talks, said that it was the European resistance there that finally persuaded the Reagan administration to increase the limited U.S. export subsidy programs. Lyng told reporters shortly after the talks that the subsidies would be applied to commodities that were the subject of unresolved complaints to GATT — wheat, flour, poultry, pasta and raisins, among others. *(GATT meeting, p. 15)*

In spite of those actions, it was far from certain that an expansion of U.S. subsidies would influence the larger political and economic concerns underlying foreign trade practices. For instance, Brazil, which was selling in markets once considered to be American, was under stiff pressure in 1983 from international and U.S. banks to increase its export earnings to pay off its massive debts and was likely to continue marketing subsidized exports despite opposition from Washington.

Additionally, the EEC-initiated agricultural rebates were part of a protective internal farm policy grounded in memories of hunger and food shortages, according to Ulrich Knueppel, first secretary for agriculture with the EEC's Washington, D.C., delegation. Knueppel added that the European community was taking steps toward making its farmers pay some of the costs of their surplus production. The long-term goal, Knueppel said, was to reduce the need for subsidies by bringing European prices closer to world levels.

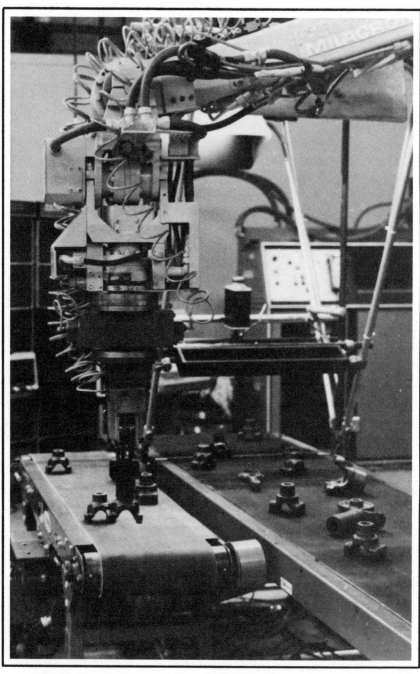

U.S. export control policy must balance national security considerations against the economic advantages of exporting high-technology products. Shown here is a large industrial robot equipped with vision capability being tested at General Motors.

Chapter 8

AIDING EXPORTERS: THE EX-IM BANK'S ROLE

In 1981 Rep. David R. Obey, D-Wis., helped lead a congressional attack on the Export-Import Bank, a little known government institution that provides low-interest loans for the purchase of U.S. goods by foreign nations and companies. To Obey, the bank was initially viewed as a symbol of government largess toward big business. He felt the vast majority of its subsidized loans benefited only a handful of huge U.S. corporations. In 1981 he proposed cutting nearly half a billion dollars from its loan authority. By 1983, however, Obey was on the other side of the fence, advocating greater loan authority for the bank.

The increasing use of export credit subsidies by France, Britain, Japan and other nations had caused Obey — and many other members of Congress — to take a second look at the Export-Import ("Ex-Im") Bank. Even such a free enterprise proponent as President Ronald Reagan, who attempted to cut the bank's operations in his first two annual budgets, by 1983 was supporting a modest expansion of its lending authority.

Much of the change in attitude was caused by high U.S. unemployment. In that situation, subsidized export credits were viewed less as solely a bounty for big business. They were seen more and more as a way to sustain employment and create jobs. "As much as I detest the idea of export subsidies, I guess we have no choice but to participate in the stupidity," Obey said. "Given the general economic collapse, we have to grab at whatever life preservers are around when the ship is going down."

Importance of Exports to the U.S. Economy

Compared to the importance of trade in other major industrialized nations, exports' share of America's gross national product (GNP) is small. Merchandise exports in 1982 accounted for 6.7 percent of GNP in the United States. (In comparison, West German exports were 26.7

percent of its GNP. Merchandise exports include such items as capital and consumer goods, automotive vehicles, food and energy supplies and exclude military grants in aid). Although the ratio of U.S. exports to GNP is relatively small, exports have come to play a crucial role in the nation's economic health. Eighty percent of the jobs created in the United States between 1977 and 1980 were due directly and indirectly to exports, according to government statistics. And more than a million of the jobs lost in the early 1980s could be traced to the deterioration of trade.

Given that situation, some members of Congress reached the conclusion that a number of U.S. trading partners had held for years: Subsidizing exports was a good way to create jobs. On the other side of the coin, there was a growing feeling in Congress that subsidies by other countries had eroded U.S. employment by making those nations' products cheaper than U.S.-made goods. "The United States has been a patsy for what our trading partners have been doing for too long," said Sen. Mack Mattingly, R-Ga. His sentiments typifed those of many on Capitol Hill.

Many U.S. businessmen contended that European, Canadian and Japanese firms had snatched multimillion-dollar export contracts from U.S. companies simply by offering government-sponsored, low-interest loans to foreign buyers. If the United States could provide similar government credit, they argued, its exporters could bring in more business and create thousands of jobs at a cost to the government far lower than any of the highly touted "jobs programs" considered by Congress and the administration in 1983.

To reverse the grim U.S. employment picture, Congress began to consider various plans that would, in effect, fight fire with fire. Among them were proposals to authorize subsidies for agricultural exports, to expand low-interest loans to foreigners buying U.S. products and to provide tax breaks for U.S. manufacturing exporters — all designed to improve the ability of U.S. companies to outbid their competitors overseas. *(Agricultural exports, p. 181)*

The Ex-Im Bank figured prominently in those efforts. Bills were introduced in 1983 that not only reauthorized the bank through Sept. 30, 1989 but also strengthened its mandate to provide financing for the purchase of U.S. exports in amounts and terms that were competitive with the financing foreign exporters received from their governments. "The Export-Import Bank is a powerful instrument of job creation," said

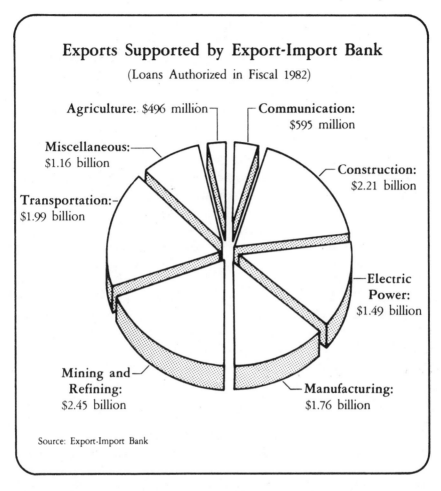

Exports Supported by Export-Import Bank
(Loans Authorized in Fiscal 1982)

Agriculture: $496 million

Communication: $595 million

Miscellaneous: $1.16 billion

Construction: $2.21 billion

Transportation: $1.99 billion

Electric Power: $1.49 billion

Mining and Refining: $2.45 billion

Manufacturing: $1.76 billion

Source: Export-Import Bank

John Heinz, R-Pa., principal sponsor of the bill. "By annually supporting over $18 billion in U.S. exports, it is providing jobs we would otherwise lose to 550,000 Americans."

Subsidies and Job Creation

Since the Depression, the United States has led the steady progress toward a freer world trading system. But it sometimes has deviated from the free-trade path. Agricultural subsidies, textile trade restrictions, "Buy American" provisions and other U.S. practices have done their share to distort world trade.

Nonetheless, as the world's largest economic power, the United

States frequently has been willing to give up more than its trading partners in order to ensure movement toward more liberal trade policies. The United States also has played a key role in establishing international agreements, primary among them the General Agreement on Tariffs and Trade (GATT), that set limits on the use of tariffs, subsidies and other measures that hindered free international exchange of goods and services. *(GATT background, p. 36)*

Given the state of the economy in the early 1980s, however, Congress appeared to be losing its willingness to maintain that role. Its commitment to international agreements seemed to be weakening. Members were demanding a "level playing field" in world trade, and if that meant they had to adopt the same practices they had so fervently criticized in the past, many appeared ready to do so.

The move to broaden the Ex-Im Bank's activities resulted largely from the international credit subsidy wars that took place in 1981 and 1982, when market interest rates soared and companies able to get low-rate government financing had a significant advantage in world markets.

According to Senate Banking Committee Chairman Jake Garn, R-Utah, the United States lost more than $1 billion in export sales in 1982 because of the Ex-Im Bank's failure to provide competitive credit. By most estimates, that translated into 25,000 lost jobs.

But some economists — including the three members of President Reagan's Council of Economic Advisers — argued that export subsidies would not create new jobs. The increased demand for a nation's subsidized products also increased demand for that nation's currency to pay for those products, these economists argued. That forced up the exchange rate and made the nation's non-subsidized goods more expensive overseas. The result was that the general level of exports, and overall employment, would not increase.

Exchange rates, however, did not work nearly as well in fact as they did in theory. Trade flows sometimes seemed to have little effect on their movement. And, in any case, economists' theoretical arguments did not seem to carry much weight on Capitol Hill. The majority sentiment among legislators was that foreign export subsidies had cost the United States jobs, and similar U.S. subsidies might win back those jobs.

Sponsors of proposals to strengthen the bank claimed the measures were defensive. "This is not what we want," said Rep. Stephen L. Neal, D-N.C., chairman of the Subcommittee on International Trade, Investment and Monetary Policy of the House Banking, Finance and Urban

Affairs Committee. "This is not the ideal way to create employment. But we are going to stop being patsies to the rest of the world."

Export Financing Competition

An example of the problem faced by potential U.S. exporters was provided by Petrotech, a small Louisiana company that manufactured equipment used by oil and gas pipelines. In 1982 it entered a $15 million bid for a pipeline project in Egypt. Competing for the job were British, French and Italian firms.

"From an engineering and technical standpoint, Petrotech was the winning company," said Frederick Amling and Fariborz Ghadar, two George Washington University professors and experts in export financing. But, according to Amling, an Italian firm — Nuovo Pignone — won the contract because the Italian government reportedly agreed to provide loans at 6.5 percent — several percentage points below the market level — to finance the purchase. The cost to the United States: 300 man-years of employment lost.

The Cross Company, a Michigan manufacturer of equipment for the automobile industry, offered a similar example. In 1981 a Ford subsidiary in Mexico asked it to bid on a $20 million project. The Ex-Im Bank offered to finance the project at 12 percent interest. But Cross routed the bid to its United Kingdom subsidiary because the British government was willing to provide 7.75 percent financing, in dollars, according to Amling and Ghadar.

In another case, export credit subsidies were used by a foreign company to win a contract in the United States. New York's Metropolitan Transit Authority (MTA) awarded a $622 million contract for new subway cars to Bombardier Inc. of Canada, passing over a Michigan firm that also had bid for the contract. According to the Commerce Department, the Canadian government offered MTA 9.7 percent fixed-rate financing, which over the term of the contract amounted to a subsidy of $91.2 million.

Examples such as these convinced many members of Congress that the United States needed to strengthen its Ex-Im Bank.

Compared to government credit agencies in other nations, the U.S. bank's efforts were small. In 1980, for instance, U.S. government export credits covered only 12.8 percent of all manufactured exports. Meanwhile, the French government financed 25.2 percent of its exports; the British, 50.8 percent; and the Japanese, 42.4 percent, according to a study

DISCs: A Boon to Exports . . .

Since 1971 the United States has offered large tax breaks to U.S. exporters through a device known as the Domestic International Sales Corporation (DISC).

DISCs, in most cases, are paper companies, with no employees and no real operations of their own. They "exist" in order to allow a company to attribute a certain portion of its export earnings to the DISC; those revenues are thereby exempt from U.S. income taxes.

The tax break, according to the Treasury Department, has been successful in promoting exports. Though DISCs cost the federal government about $2 billion a year in lost revenue, the department estimated that in 1980 they created between $6 billion and $9 billion in additional exports for U.S. businesses.

Business organizations have enthusiastically supported the DISC program. "The DISC has contributed strongly to our export competitiveness and should not be abandoned," said Michael A. Samuels, vice president of the U.S. Chamber of Commerce.

The DISC, however, has been an albatross around the necks of U.S. officials participating in international trade negotiations. A council of the General Agreement on Tariffs and Trade (GATT) ruled that the DISC was an export subsidy that violated GATT agreements. European members of GATT took the United States to task at every opportunity for refusing to acknowledge that ruling.

In October 1982 U.S. officials told other GATT members they would eliminate the DISC. However, they planned to replace it with another tax

by Gary Clyde Hufbauer, a senior fellow with the Institute for International Economics, and Joanna Shelton Erb, an economist at the Treasury Department.

Ex-Im Operations and Policies

The Ex-Im Bank provides both direct loans and loan guarantees for five years or more to finance the export of major capital equipment. Traditionally, the vast majority of the bank's loans covered major capital exports, such as nuclear power plants, airplanes and manufacturing plants,

. . . Or an Unfair Trade Practice?

break that would not violate GATT, while providing the same benefit to exporters.

A number of nations — including France and the Netherlands — had territorial tax systems that allowed exporters to escape taxes on income attributed to overseas branches. These systems had been supported by the GATT council. The problem with DISCs, according to the GATT ruling, was that they were domestic companies.

The Reagan administration in 1983 was working with Congress on a plan that would allow companies to channel exports through tax-exempt sales corporations outside the 50 states, instead of domestic sales corporations. The new entities, called Foreign Sales Corporations (FSCs), would be set up by exporters seeking tax relief and would operate similarly to DISCs, except they would have to maintain an office outside of the U.S. customs jurisdiction. The program was expected to cost the Treasury the same amount, and have the same impact on exports, as DISCs.

A study by the National Planning Association in 1977 found that DISCs, in conjunction with other tax provisions, made the effective rate of tax on corporate export income 27.4 percent, compared to a rate of 36.7 percent on domestic income.

In France, the study found, export income was taxed at an effective rate of 8.7 percent compared to 34.3 percent for corporate domestic income. In Japan, the export rate was 17.9 percent compared to 29.2 percent for domestic income. Germany's effective tax rate was the same for export and import income: 39.7 percent.

made by a handful of very large firms, such as Boeing, Westinghouse and General Electric. The bank did far less for smaller capital goods exports that could get adequate financing, although at higher rates, from commercial banks.

Furthermore, the bank has been handicapped by its commitment to self-sufficiency. The bank, a federally chartered independent corporation, does not receive government funds from Congress. Rather, it borrows money from the Federal Financing Bank (FFB), which in turn borrows from the Treasury; the Treasury raises its funds by the sale of government securities. Because the interest the Treasury has to pay on the securities it sold was generally lower than commercial loan rates, Ex-Im can make loans somewhat below market rates.

Historically, the bank has followed conservative lending policies, attempting to keep its interest rates high enough to cover the cost of borrowing from the FFB. In the last few years, however, increased export credit subsidies by foreign governments has required Ex-Im to keep its rates low to be competitive — while high interest rates in the United States required it to keep its rates high enough to cover costs.

"The bank's charter requires Ex-Im to walk a fine line," said Neal. "It must make a profit and at the same time encourage exports."

Under the leadership of William H. Draper III, a Reagan appointee who became chairman of the bank in July 1981, Ex-Im became more fiscally conservative. When Draper took over, the bank was losing money rapidly as it attempted to stay competitive with European countries. Draper unilaterally raised the bank's interest rates twice to prevent losses from its loans — and to avoid having to ask Congress for a direct appropriation.

Some members of Congress, however, have indicated they would be glad to give the bank an appropriation in order to keep its rates competitive. "During the first two years of Bill Draper's stewardship, the bank, in my view, has been shortsightedly conservative in supporting American exports," said Sen. Heinz, chairman of the Senate Banking Committee's International Finance and Monetary Policy Subcommittee. "The result was that many opportunities to export were missed, because Ex-Im offered terms that were not competitive with other nations."

"It has been a very non-activist bank under the current [1983] policy," Neal agreed.

Chairman Draper made no apologies for his performance. "This administration does not believe in subsidies," he said. "This country has never believed in as much government involvement in business as other countries do." While he admitted that Ex-Im interest rates had remained above European rates, Draper said the bank had competed successfully with foreign countries by offering longer loan terms than other nations were willing to give. That gave the bank some bargaining leverage in international negotiations to reduce foreign loan subsidies. As a result, Draper said, "we have through negotiation reduced the amount of subsidy and become more competitive than we ever have been in interest rates."

1982 OECD Interest Rate Agreement

In July 1982 the Organization for Economic Cooperation and Development (OECD), which includes the major industrialized nations of the free world, agreed to keep most interest rates on export credits above 11 percent and to limit other concessionary lending terms. However, 11 percent still was well below market interest rates in the United States.

Subsequently, however, interest rates in the United States fell, due to the recession. Market rates in early 1983 were close to the official OECD rate, which left OECD member nations little room to subsidize their export loans. "Winning orders by credit deviation alone is occurring far less now in the world market," said Draper. Heinz generally agreed. "We are no longer at the kind of competitive disadvantage we were previously."

Nevertheless, Heinz and others feel there remains a pressing need to strengthen the Ex-Im Bank. For one thing, given existing worries about potential economic and political instability in the debt-ridden developing countries, commercial banks could lose their desire to make export loans. The Ex-Im Bank must be prepared to provide credit or guarantees in those cases, Ex-Im promoters contend. Furthermore, the OECD interest rate agreement — like most international agreements — lacked teeth. "Questions are always raised with the effectiveness of the arrangement, especially with regard to the French," said Heinz.

By early 1983 businessmen were claiming the agreement was being violated. Said Howard Lewis of the National Association of Manufacturers: "I don't think you need to be overly cynical to expect that you would find violations."

And even within the confines of the agreement, there were significant loopholes. For instance, low-interest financing deals that were in the works before the agreement took effect were allowed under a "grandfather" provision, and agricultural exports were excluded from the interest rate floor.

In addition, the OECD agreement did not cover all "mixed credits" — combinations of export loans and government development assistance. By mixing development assistance in with loans to developing countries, foreign governments could achieve the same effect as low export interest rates.

According to Theodore A. Chapman, head of the business and international review office at Ex-Im, 99 cases of mixed credit financing were reported during 1982. "More countries are doing this," Chapman said. "It is mostly the French, but recently other countries have been doing it as well." Chapman said the total value of exports covered by mixed credit plans probably was several billion dollars.

Expanding the Bank's Authority

In October 1982 the Ex-Im Bank instituted a new program for "medium-term" exports — exports that required only one to five years of financing. Chairman Draper hoped the new program would allow more medium-sized companies to use the bank's services. "We recognize that our relatively new medium-term credit facility does not match what our competition is offering," said Ex-Im Vice Chairman Charles E. Lord. "Since the U.S. government does not believe that export financing should be run as an entitlement program, it behooves us to move cautiously as we enter any new field."

For fiscal 1983 Congress set a limit of $4.4 billion on the bank's direct lending and a ceiling of $9 billion on its guarantees of commercial loans. In its fiscal 1984 budget request, the Reagan administration asked for only $3.8 billion in direct lending authority, but said it would offer a supplemental request for $2.7 billion if a need for the funds arose. The budget also requested a raise in the loan guarantee ceiling to $10 billion.

Members of Congress saw the president's new initiatives as a step in the right direction, if a small one. "I'm delighted," said Heinz. "It's a welcome and overdue commitment." But Neal was less impressed. "They [the administration] say a lot of things and then don't do them," he said.

Heinz and Neal believed that increasing lending authority alone was not enough. Under existing economic conditions and bank policies, Ex-Im was not using all of the lending authority available to it. As the economy recovered, lending was expected to increase. But the two legislators argued that bank policies also had to change if the United States was to become competitive.

Heinz proposed rewriting the bank's charter to make it clear that its primary responsibility was to provide government financing that was competitive with what was offered overseas. Under Heinz' plan, self-sufficiency would become a secondary goal. "The bank fails to fulfill its very reason for existence when it provides loans at uncompetitive rates because of fears of temporary losses in its own financial condition," said Heinz. "It seeks to become self-sustaining, but self-sustaining for what?"

Neal supported a more ambitious proposal. He wanted to create a

$1 billion "war chest" that could be used to subsidize interest rates on billions of dollars' worth of exports. Neal also hoped to create a mixed credit program to compete with such programs used overseas. A similar proposal was backed by the U.S. Chamber of Commerce. "On the whole, the Chamber does not support subsidies," said Ava Feiner, director of international trade policy for the Chamber. "With the Ex-Im Bank, however, we make a small exception." Feiner further explained, "This is not an offensive program we are proposing, it is only a defensive program."

Various other proposals for strengthening the bank were discussed in Congress during 1983. For instance, Rep. Stan Lundine, D-N.Y., introduced a bill Feb. 8 that would force Ex-Im to provide low-interest financing in cases where credit subsidies had been used by foreign nations. And a number of members would like to see the bank expand its operations to cover more medium-term export efforts.

The administration seemed likely to resist most of these proposals. "Quite frankly, we are concerned about the well-meaning efforts of our friends and supporters to try to fix something that ain't broke," Lord said. "A little change here and a little change there soon adds up to a big mess. Accordingly, we are recommending that our charter be renewed without modification for another five years."

Given the rising support in Congress for a stronger Ex-Im Bank, however, Lord might well have ended up with more than he asked for. The final version of the bill, extending the bank for three years (through Sept. 30, 1986) mandated that, while the bank should consider the cost of money in setting interest rates on loans, all Ex-Im programs should be competitive with the export promotion programs undertaken by other governments.

The bill also established a "tied aid" credit program for U.S. exports that would permit foreign nations to receive a combination of Ex-Im Bank credits and foreign aid, resulting in very generous credit terms. The legislation specified that the bank could provide financing for the export of services, such as insurance, as it did for exports of manufactured products, equipment and other capital goods.

The bill required the Ex-Im board of directors to include at least one small-business representative. The bill changed the terms for board members by providing for staggered terms of four years except for two directors first appointed on or after Jan. 21, 1985, who would serve for two years.

The Export-Import Bank historically has subsidized "big-ticket" U.S. exports — such as airplanes, power plants and satellite communications systems — with its below-market-rate loans and loan guarantees.

Chapter 9

HIGH-TECH TRADE AND NATIONAL SECURITY

Electronics advances in the latter half of the 20th century spawned a new generation of sophisticated computers possessing the potential for radically changing every aspect of society, including international trade. President Ronald Reagan addressed the opportunities opened by "the frontier of high technology" in his 1983 State of the Union address.

A decade earlier, the U.S. defense establishment led the world in the development of new technology. By the 1980s, however, products on the shelf at Radio Shack often were as sophisticated as those under development in Pentagon research laboratories. "It is the commercial sector, the private sector, that is now the cutting edge of technological development," said Commerce Under Secretary Lionel H. Olmer in 1983.

That fact of "high-tech" life posed a difficult problem for members of Congress and President Reagan. In the name of national security, they felt compelled to constrain the flow of technology to the Soviet Union. But for the sake of the nation's economic health, they felt the export competitiveness of America's high-tech products should be promoted.

"This is a genuine dilemma for both the legislative branch and the executive branch," said Rep. Don Bonker, D-Wash., chairman of the Foreign Affairs Subcommittee on International Economic Policy and Trade. "We have to be more competitive. We must increase export opportunities if we are going to have economic recovery. But we have certain national security and foreign policy objectives which are responsibilities of the United States as a world power."

The United States has restricted exports for national security or foreign policy reasons since the 1940s. The original Export Control Act was passed in 1940 and rewritten during the Cold War in 1949. After periodic extensions through the 1950s and 1960s, the law was revised in 1969 and renamed the Export Administration Act. The act was extended several times in the 1970s, with few major changes. It was due to expire

Sept. 30, 1983, but Congress extended the act to Oct. 14, and Reagan subsequently invoked emergency powers to prevent the controls from lapsing while Congress debated revisions. *(Background on export control legislation, see chapter on Trade With Communist Nations.)*

Policy Reasons for Controls

Export controls based on national security considerations traditionally have been invoked to prevent high-technology items that could have military applications ("dual-use" items) from falling into the hands of U.S. adversaries. Products placed on the act's Commodity Control List could not be exported without a license issued by the Commerce Department.

Many presidents have imposed foreign policy controls, such as Reagan's ban on gas pipeline equipment sales to the Soviet Union, to punish a nation or to attempt to influence its behavior. Such controls for foreign policy reasons usually are temporary measures.

Under the Export Administration Act, the government also limited some trade with nations that violated human rights or supported "international terrorism" (such as Libya) and required special licenses for equipment and technology that could be used to create nuclear bombs. Several foreign aid laws also imposed companion restrictions on commercial arms sales overseas.

Complicating Congress' consideration of the use of export controls was the fact that since World War II, the United States had imposed economic sanctions on a number of countries for a wide variety of reasons, and each set had been supported or opposed by a relatively narrow constituency. In addition to controlling trade with communist countries in general, restrictions have been placed on exports to some right-wing authoritarian regimes in South America and elsewhere as well as on African nations following a policy of apartheid. Conservatives resisted lifting controls on the communist nations, and liberals took the same position on trade bans imposed on the latter groups.

The Reagan administration in February 1982 relaxed some controls on exports to South Africa, Syria, South Yemen and other countries. That action produced loud outcries in Congress, and the House Foreign Affairs Committee unsuccessfully sought to reinstate some of the prohibitions. Members of that panel and the Senate Foreign Relations Committee complained especially that the administration was changing export policies without consulting Congress.

Promoting Trade vs. Protecting National Security

Export controls long have been controversial. But the increasing commercialization of high-tech products made the battle over controls in 1983 more difficult than ever before. Within the administration, the Defense Department generally advocated tougher controls, while the Commerce Department was anxious to ease the red-tape burden on exporters.

According to Richard N. Perle, assistant secretary of defense for international security policy, the late 1970s and early 1980s had seen "a virtual hemorrhage of strategic technology to the Soviet bloc countries." Perle was one of the leading advocates in the Reagan administration in favor of tightening export controls. He believed that during "the euphoria that surrounded the détente policies" of the late 1960s and early 1970s, the administration of export controls had been allowed to deteriorate. The resulting leakage of Western technology, he argued, boosted the Soviet Union's military buildup and saved the Soviets hundreds of millions of dollars in research and development costs. "In certain applications, the Soviet bloc has narrowed its technology gap with the West from 10 years to within two years," Perle said during testimony before a House Foreign Affairs subcommittee in March 1983.

Jack Vorona of the Defense Intelligence Agency told a Senate Governmental Affairs subcommittee in 1982 that the Soviet Union tapped into U.S. research and development so often "that one must wonder if they regard U.S. research and development as their own national asset." To Perle, Vorona and others in the defense establishment, regaining control over the "hemorrhaging" of U.S. technology was a top priority.

Commerce Under Secretary Olmer, on the other hand, was concerned about the adverse impact of export controls on the U.S. trade position. Over the last decade, total exports of goods and services had grown to 12 percent from 6 percent of U.S. gross national product (GNP). Estimates suggested that as many as 80 percent of the new manufacturing jobs created between 1979 and 1981 came from the expansion of export industries. Most economists agreed that the United States had to depend on export expansion to spur economic growth.

Businessmen complained that the existing export control system hampered overseas sales. The number of export license requests turned down by the government was relatively small — in 1982, for instance, only 885 of 80,369 export license applications were denied. But companies faced delays of up to 180 days while waiting for licenses to be granted. And those companies that had not mastered the art of applying for licenses often had their applications returned without action. For exporters facing tough competition overseas, the delays were more than just a nuisance; they sometimes meant lost business.

"During the 1970s the U.S. lead in many aspects of high-technology dwindled or disappeared," said Paul Freedenberg, an economist on the Senate Banking Committee. "For the first time in the postwar era, U.S. high-technology firms saw their foreign markets taken away by aggressive new competitors, and even their domestic market share was challenged. This meant that export controls and other constraints, which served as a nuisance in earlier times . . . , could possibly make the difference between holding on to an important market or losing it."

Many of the export controls, advocates of free trade argued, not only damaged the U.S. economy but also failed to achieve their purpose because many of the U.S.-controlled products were readily available from other nations. Those who supported strict trade prohibitions operated "under the myth that the United States has a monopoly on everything on the control list," complained one House committee aide.

The value of goods exported to the Soviet Union under export licenses was relatively small ($32 million in 1982), representing about 2 percent of total U.S. exports to the Soviet Union. Most of those goods involved high-technology products and sophisticated capital equipment.

Issues Raised by Pipeline Sanctions

One of the most controversial applications of export controls in recent years were the sanctions imposed by Reagan prohibiting U.S. companies, their foreign subsidiaries and foreign companies using U.S. licenses from selling to the Soviet Union equipment or technology for transmission or refining of oil and gas. The sanctions cost American companies and their subsidiaries hundreds of millions of dollars worth of business and became an issue in several 1982 congressional election campaigns. Opposition to the sanctions was so strong that a measure to overturn them was considered by the House Sept. 29, 1982, and rejected by only three votes. *(Background, p. 117)*

Reagan initially ordered the sanctions in December 1981 as a protest against Soviet pressure on the regime in Poland, which had declared martial law and imprisoned leaders of the independent Solidarity labor union. But it quickly became clear that the sanctions were having

Caterpillar Tractor and the Soviet Pipeline

In September 1980 the Caterpillar Tractor Co. applied for a license to export 200 pipelaying tractors to the Soviet Union for use on construction of a natural gas pipeline from Siberia to Western Europe. After several months, the license was granted. But negotiations on the sale were suspended while Moscow sought to arrange financing. In the interim the company also was granted permission to sell $40 million worth of pipelayers for use in other projects in the Soviet Union. The Pentagon opposed the sale, arguing that the equipment could be used on projects that would bolster Soviet defense production. The State Department generally favored the sale, arguing that the equipment was not technically sensitive and that the Russians could easily buy similar machines elsewhere.

The issue became moot, however, when Reagan Dec. 30, 1981, prohibited the export of all equipment involved in the transmission or refining of oil and gas to the Soviet Union. "We lost $90 million in machine sales," said Timothy L. Elder, the company's Washington, D.C., manager for governmental affairs.

The Caterpillar Tractor ban had little effect on the Soviet Union because it could buy tractors from Caterpillar's Japanese rival, Komatsu. And the damage to Caterpillar, said Elder, was far greater than just the lost sale of 200 machines. It effectively closed the large Soviet market to the company, and injured Caterpillar's reputation for reliability in other countries. "If you couple the lack of reliability with the long delays, . . . how many times is a country going to be burned by a U.S. company before they finally smarten up and buy from someone else?" Elder asked.

When the Soviets decided to buy 500 new pipelayers in 1983, Caterpillar was not even asked to bid on the project, although the Reagan administration sanctions had been lifted. The $200 million contract went to Komatsu, creating thousands of Japanese jobs. Before 1978 Caterpillar had 85 percent of the Soviet market for track-type tractors and pipelayers; by 1983 Komatsu had captured 85 percent of that market.

To salvage their reputation for reliability, Caterpillar and other U.S. exporters supported a contract sanctity measure that would prohibit imposition of sanctions that broke existing contracts.

no effect on Soviet behavior, and Reagan shifted their focus by applying them in a way that would disrupt construction of a 2,600-mile natural gas pipeline from Siberia to Western Europe. Reagan imposed additional sanctions June 22, 1982. However, he lifted the restrictions Nov. 13, 1982, saying it was possible to do so because the United States and its European allies had agreed to study ways to limit trade with the Soviet Union in the future. However, European leaders said they had not agreed to any specific steps that would create an effective substitute for the sanctions.

Even after Reagan lifted the ban on pipeline-related exports, congressional leaders continued to debate the wisdom of using trade as a foreign policy tool. At a U.S.-Soviet trade conference in Moscow Nov. 16, Finance Committee Chairman Robert Dole, R-Kan., said flatly that he opposed using trade sanctions for foreign policy purposes "unless bilateral relations are curtailed across-the-board."

Virtually all the issues that were debated in 1983 in connection with the export law were raised by the Soviet sanctions. Among the major issues were:

● Contract Sanctity. Should the government have the right to interrupt overseas sales for which contracts already had been signed and export licenses approved? The pipeline sanctions voided several sales that already were in process, prompting bitter complaints from the companies that lost business. *(Box on Catepillar Tractor sales, p. 203)*

Numerous members of Congress introduced bills to prevent future trade sanctions from interrupting existing contracts. In the last days of the 1982 session, largely in reaction to the embargo imposed by President Jimmy Carter on grain sales to the Soviet Union, Congress passed a contract sanctity measure for agriculture exports. *(See chapter on U.S. Farm Exports, p. 177.)*

● Extraterritoriality. As widened on June 22, Reagan's pipeline sanctions imposed U.S. law on foreign subsidiaries of U.S. companies and on foreign firms holding U.S. licenses to manufacture products developed in the United States. British Prime Minister Margaret Thatcher and other allied leaders rejected the sanctions, arguing that Reagan had no right to impose U.S. laws outside U.S. territory. Many American business groups agreed. "It can make having a foreign subsidiary worthless," said Howard Lewis III, assistant vice president for international economic affairs for the National Association of Manufacturers.

● Effectiveness. A basic issue in the Soviet sanctions controversy was whether they accomplished their stated purposes: to demonstrate U.S. unhappiness with Soviet pressure on Poland and hamper construction of the natural gas pipeline. Soviet leaders almost certainly got the message on Poland, but even administration officials admitted there was no evidence the sanctions altered Soviet behavior toward Warsaw. Although the administration said the sanctions might delay construction of the pipeline by up to two years, U.S. industry spokesmen disputed that claim, maintaining the pipeline could be completed nearly on time with parts from other countries.

● Congressional Role. Congress had no formal role in the decision to impose the sanctions, but congressional unhappiness over the damage done to American business helped persuade the administration to seek a face-saving way to lift the Soviet pipeline embargo. The 1979 Export Administration Act required the president to explain why he was imposing sanctions and certify to Congress that they would work. But a House Foreign Affairs Committee aide said reports submitted previously under that law had been "pro forma." The Reagan administration itself provided fuel for criticism in Congress by failing to submit a required report on the June 22 sanctions.

Commodity Control List and the Coordinating Committee

Under the Export Administration Act, exports are controlled for three purposes: to protect national security, to achieve foreign policy goals, or to prevent the depletion of goods in short supply. The act is administered by the Office of Export Administration in the Department of Commerce. That office maintains the Commodity Control List of items that may not be exported without a license. The list has grown steadily, particularly since 1979, and in 1983 it included more than 100,000 items.

Most of the goods on the control list are there for national security reasons and require a validated export license regardless of their destination. If the goods are to be exported to a communist country, the secretary of defense may ask to review the license application. The Department of State, the CIA, the National Aeronautics and Space Administration (NASA), the Treasury Department and even the National Bureau of Standards also have roles in reviewing licenses.

The United States coordinates export controls with its allies through a Coordinating Committee (COCOM) that includes the North

Atlantic Treaty Organization (NATO) nations (minus Iceland and Spain) and Japan. But the U.S. government is a more ardent controller of exports than its allies, and it restricts many products not on the COCOM list. "They [other COCOM countries] neither license as carefully or enforce as rigorously as we do," said Freedenberg.

The Coordinating Committee operates informally, without a treaty and without means of enforcing its decisions or imposing penalties for violations. "COCOM occupies a couple of borrowed offices in an annex of the American Embassy in Paris," said Perle during his appearance before a House Foreign Affairs subcommittee in March 1983. "It has a budget that I would guess is smaller than the budget certainly of the full committee and maybe even this subcommittee.... COCOM has been allowed to decline in my judgment to an appalling degree."

The administration in 1983 was negotiating with the COCOM countries in an attempt to add to its list many of the items that were controlled unilaterally by the United States. It was unlikely, however, that the effort would be successful.

The major concern for most U.S. exporters, however, was their competitiveness in other Western markets, not in the communist bloc. "The United States has only 1 percent of the Eastern European market for manufactured goods," said Freedenberg, "and an even smaller percentage in the high-technology field." As a result, exporters were lobbying for a proposed 1983 amendment to the Export Administration Act that would eliminate the need for licenses to export "dual use" items (that is, goods that could be used either for military or civilian purposes) to other nations that participated in COCOM. That would greatly reduce the problems caused by licensing delays, proponents argued. But as long as the U.S. government felt that COCOM nations were violating the control agreement, defense hard-liners in Congress were expected to oppose such a relaxation.

Effectiveness of Curbs Questioned

Writing in the May 30, 1983, issue of *Fortune* magazine, Walter Guzzardi Jr., on the magazine's board of editors, noted that "in a kind of vote of no confidence" in the organization, the United States required many of its exports to COCOM members to have licenses. Because licenses for similar exports were not always needed among other members, "security can thus be reduced to the level provided by COCOM's leakiest member."

Guzzardi was one of many observers challenging the effectiveness of COCOM. One example of the lack of real coordination among the members was provided by the machine tool industry. Machine tool products they made are controlled by the United States as well as its COCOM allies. But according to James A. Gray, president of the National Machine Tool Builders' Association, some of the COCOM nations were less than thorough in enforcing export controls. "The Japanese and others continue to ship machine tools to communist countries despite the COCOM proscriptions," said Gray.

Because the communist nations consumed large quantities of machine tools, Gray contended that selling to the Soviet bloc and China enabled Japanese companies to expand their production and achieve greater economies of scale. As a result, U.S. producers lost business not only in the communist countries, but also in Western nations and even in the U.S. market. For the U.S. machine tool industry, lost business became a serious problem. Imports had captured a third of the domestic market. Export controls certainly did not deserve all, or even most, of the blame for that decline. But they were not helpful. A proposal by the machine tool builders to force COCOM nations to abide by controls found support in Congress and the administration. Under the proposal, if a foreign company violated COCOM restrictions, its exports to the U.S. market would be restricted.

The experience of the Scientific Apparatus Makers Association (SAMA) brought forth similar complaints. SAMA included nearly 200 companies that made a variety of scientific instruments and measurement and testing equipment. Many SAMA instruments used microprocessors, and because they did, they had to be licensed for export. SAMA members complained, however, that the controls were ineffective because they covered only U.S. makers and not their overseas competition. The instruments were not covered by the COCOM agreements.

According to Eben Tisdale, director of public affairs for SAMA, the members of the organization faced severe competition from foreign companies. Applying for an export license caused delays — four to eight weeks when exporting to another Western nation; four months or more when exporting to the communist bloc nations. And any delay created a competitive disadvantage, he said. Tisdale also argued that the controls did little for national security, since most SAMA products were readily available from other countries.

To illustrate what he called the absurdity of the control system,

Tisdale said that Du Pont was required to get an export license for a liquid chromatograph even though the microprocessor used in the instrument had been made in the Soviet Union.

The issue of foreign availability, however, raised questions of definition. If a U.S. product clearly was superior, control advocates argued, there still could be justification for preventing its export to the Soviet bloc.

Enforcement Efforts Criticized

Senate Banking Committee Chairman Jake Garn, R-Utah, who opposed relaxing the controls, argued that the Commerce Department could not administer the act effectively because of its traditional commitment to export promotion. He proposed placing the administration of export controls in a separate agency. "We cannot afford to give the Commerce Department more time to improve an operation for which it has had responsibility for over three decades and for which it is institutionally unfit," said Garn. But Rep. Bonker took the opposite view. Commerce was the appropriate department for the job, he said.

In May 1982, at the insistence of Sen. Sam Nunn, D-Ga., the Senate Governmental Affairs Subcommittee on Investigations held a series of hearings on the transfer of U.S. technology to the Soviet Union. In preparation for those hearings, the subcommittee's staff documented several cases of technological espionage by which U.S. high-technology products and information found their way to the Soviet Union. The investigation also brought to light inadequacies of the enforcement branch of the Commerce Department's Office of Export Administration.

"The staff concluded that the compliance division [of the Office of Export Administration] was an understaffed and poorly equipped and, in certain instances, undertrained and unqualified investigative and intelligence unit," the subcommittee's report said. "One compliance division agent ... said the Kremlin's spy organization, the KGB, could not have organized the compliance division in a way more beneficial to Soviet interests."

To buttress the export control enforcement efforts of the Commerce Department, the Department of Defense provided $25 million to the U.S. Customs Service, a Treasury Department agency, for its "Operation Exodus," designed to stop unlicensed exports at U.S. ports. According to Perle, by March 1983 the project had interdicted 1,100 shipments valued at more than $71 million. "Some involve extremely sensitive equipment that would have gone to the Warsaw Pact [Soviet bloc countries]," he said.

Nunn introduced legislation that would transfer all enforcement of export controls to Customs. The proposal had strong support in the Senate, and even Sen. John Heinz, R-Pa., chairman of the Banking Subcommittee on International Finance and Monetary Policy, who was generally supportive of exporters' calls for relaxing restrictions, endorsed the plan. In the House, however, Operation Exodus came under heavy criticism. Rep. Bill Frenzel, R-Minn., labeled it a "paramilitary operation" aimed at U.S. exporters. Critics told stories of shipments being detained on the docks for days or weeks while inexperienced Customs officers attempted to determine whether the products had or needed a validated export license.

Bonker said he recognized the shortcomings of the Commerce Department's enforcement efforts but still believed Commerce was best suited to do the job. "If there is a hemorrhage," he said, "the answer is to beef up Commerce's authority."

Administration Proposal: Tighter Controls

President Reagan April 4, 1983, sent Congress legislation renewing the Export Administration Act. Reagan recommended giving the executive branch more power to enforce restrictions on exports of strategically sensitive goods and technology. One provision gave the president new authority to control imports from foreign countries thought to have violated U.S. national security controls. Another would establish new statutory crimes for conspiring and attempting to violate the Export Administration Act. A third restricted the sale of controlled goods to officials of foreign embassies inside the United States. In a concession to business, the bill contained a contract sanctity provision in which the administration agreed that when an embargo was imposed for political reasons, the restrictions would not affect existing contracts if they called for delivering the goods within 270 days of the imposition of controls.

The proposal also called for "bilateral and multilateral negotiations to eliminate, wherever possible, the foreign availability of comparable goods and technology."

Apparently bowing to Reagan's more hard-line position, Commerce Under Secretary Olmer said in presenting the bill to Congress, "The U.S. and its allies simply must curtail the flow of strategic technology to the

Soviet Union. This administration views this as a very high priority. Clearly, export controls may impose economic costs to business firms. But these are sometimes necessary costs." At the same time, however, Olmer pledged that the administration would pursue measures to ease controls on trade with non-communist nations.

Action on Export Act Revisions

In Congress opinion about revising the export control statute also was divided. Sen. Garn, chairman of the Senate Banking Committee, which has jurisdiction over the Export Administration Act, maintained that billions of dollars in defense costs could have been saved in recent years if U.S. export controls had been tighter. "We cannot preserve our national interests and keep defense costs down while supplying our adversaries with the means to threaten those interests," Garn said.

Heading in an opposite direction was Sen. Heinz, who was concerned about the damage that controls had done to exports and the U.S. economy. His Subcommittee on International Finance and Monetary Policy had held hearings on revising the restrictions. Both Heinz and Garn introduced sharply different proposals to amend the act. However, the two worked out a compromise whereby Garn gave Heinz — and exporters — many restrictions they wanted on presidential power to impose foreign policy controls, and got in return many provisions he wanted to tighten national security controls.

In the House, exporters found their surest advocate in Rep. Bonker. As chairman of the Foreign Affairs Subcommittee on International Economic Policy and Trade, Bonker easily shepherded through the committee a bill that addressed many of the exporters' concerns. The bill provided a two-year reauthorization of the act. It eliminated the need for licenses to export high-tech goods to U.S. allies participating in COCOM; removed restrictions on goods controlled by the United States but not by COCOM; included broad contract sanctity provisions; and eliminated the president's authority to impose controls on companies outside U.S. territory without the specific authorization of Congress. The major elements of the subcommittee's bill were approved by the House Foreign Affairs Committee May 26, 1983.

"When the bill reaches the House floor, it [will take] on a new dimension," Bonker predicted. "That is when the national security advocates come up with highly emotional and appealing arguments to support certain amendments. Congress can do all kinds of harm or damage to the legislation."

However, an intense lobbying effort by representatives of the business community, including the U.S. Chamber of Commerce and Business Roundtable (a group of the chief executives of major U.S. firms) led the House to reverse itself Oct. 27, 1983. Overturning a previous decision, representatives voted to reinsert a provision that restricted the president's power to control high-tech exports. The House Oct. 18 had voted to delete the provision.

Other provisions of the House-passed bill eliminated licensing requirements for exports to COCOM countries (a provision strongly opposed by the administration); required the president to drop national security controls on a product that was readily available from other countries if, after 18 months, he had failed to persuade other nations to control the product; prohibited the application of foreign policy controls to companies outside the United States, including overseas subsidiaries of U.S. firms; barred the export of nuclear technology and nuclear components to nations that failed to comply with the safeguards established by the International Atomic Energy Agency; urged the president to seek the counsel of other foreign countries and Congress before imposing foreign policy controls and required the president to report to Congress before he implemented foreign policy controls; barred the president from enacting foreign policy controls that broke existing contracts unless the controls were in retaliation for actual or imminent acts of aggression, terrorism, human rights violations or nuclear weapons tests, or unless Congress approved; and required the president to lift foreign policy controls after six months if the products were readily available from other nations and attempts to eliminate the foreign availability proved unsuccessful.

Meanwhile, the Senate Banking Committee May 25 approved its version of the legislation. Unlike the House bill, the Senate measure generally followed the recommendations of President Reagan and defense hard-liners in Congress. The Senate panel's version maintained and in some cases tightened national security controls. The bill gave new authority to the Defense Department to review exports to U.S. allies, in addition to its existing authority to review exports to Soviet bloc nations. The measure transferred enforcement of the act to the U.S. Customs Service. The Senate measure, however, did contain a contract sanctity provision that pleased pro-export forces.

As of the end of 1983 the outlook for passage of the House version was highly uncertain. The administration Nov. 11 came out in support of the more restrictive Senate committee bill. In the interim, Congress extended the export controls through February 1984.

Assessments of the Act

A 1981 study by the Rand Corp. concluded that to be feasible export controls should be applied narrowly to protect military technology. Controls aimed broadly at impeding Soviet economic development were likely to be self-defeating, it said.

Two years later, a report by the congressional Office of Technology Assessment reached somewhat the same conclusion. The study, released in May 1983, found there were severe constraints on the capacity of the U.S. export licensing procedures to deny the Soviets access to Western technologies. "It is foolhardy to expect that even drastic changes in U.S. export control policy could materially alter the fact that the U.S.S.R. benefits militarily from Western technology. But it is extremely rare to find examples of military technologies obtained from the West which the U.S.S.R. could not have produced itself, albeit later and at additional expense," the study said.

The report cited the following factors that cut down on the effectiveness of U.S. export curbs:

● The extent of illegal Soviet methods of procuring the technology.

● Failure of the United States and its allies to formulate a mutual and enforceable export control policy.

● The difficulties inherent in identifying in advance which technologies have important military payoffs.

● The increasing worldwide diffusion of technology.

A realistic export control program could not be expected permanently to deny Soviet access to specific technologies, the report said. "It is successful to the extent that it increases the cost to the U.S.S.R. — in time, money, effort and efficiency — of obtaining the technologies it desires; and to the extent that the roadblocks it creates limit the rate and volume of Soviet technological acquisitions. In the long run, technological leads can only be maintained through effective research and development efforts."

In his May 1983 *Fortune* article, Guzzardi concluded that to meet the threat of Soviet inroads into U.S.-developed high-technology products, the United States "must accept a paradox: by attempting to cut off the Russians from too much, the U.S. will only continue to lose more; by recognizing that U.S. power is sharply limited, this country can do a good deal to keep high technology out of the Russian reach." Guzzardi went on to suggest that:

> By paring to the core what we seek to deny the Soviets, limiting it to what has immediate military use, the U.S. will get more allied support, and as a result the Russians will get less technology. By refraining from general sanctions that amount to declaring economic war on the Russians . . . the U.S. could avoid inflicting damage on itself and straining relations with its friends. And by heeding the business community's legitimate complaints, the U.S. would strengthen its own technological capacity, because it would be putting more of its products into international competition and would be more innovative as a result. The best security of all lies there.

An interesting viewpoint was offered by John W. Kiser III, a consultant specializing in various aspects of East-West relations, in an article in the March-April 1982 *Harvard Business Review*. Kiser commented that as the international economy becomes increasingly competitive, the United States might well be missing out by ignoring new technological developments in Eastern Europe and the Soviet Union. Kiser noted that the Japanese steel industry had exploited and improved on many Soviet inventions; and in the textile machinery industry, Enshu, a Japanese licensee of Czechoslovakia, made almost 75 percent of the high-productivity water jet looms sold in the United States.

As Congress and the administration wrestled over revising the Export Administration Act, many academicians and business groups agreed that excessive regulation undermined the advancement of science and technology and damaged the U.S. economy. Some industry leaders viewed the Reagan administration's move to tighten export controls as ironic, in light of its pledge to reduce government's role in business by eliminating excessive regulation. For companies with foreign subsidiaries, information could not flow freely between different parts of the same company. Tight controls would constrict the flow of information between academia and industry as well. Peter J. Denning, head of Purdue University's computer science department, said at an American Association for the Advancement of Science symposium in January 1982: "It is no accident that the computing field has been free of government regulation and has an impressive record of accomplishment. . . . If you

213

want to win the Indy 500 race you build the fastest car. You don't throw nails on the track."

There also were questions about how well the Soviet Union could apply whatever expertise it gained through technology transfer. According to Thane Gustafson, a political science researcher for the Rand Corp., the Russians' ability to learn from foreign technology was high only in areas where their skills were high. For that reason, Gustafson supported a control system of case-by-case evaluation, much like the one in existence. In an article on U.S. export controls and Soviet technology adapted from his book, *Selling the Russians the Rope* (1981), Gustafson wrote, "History teaches that the control of technology transfer is at best a rear-guard action, achievable (and then only briefly) at the cost of regulations and secrecy that carry harmful side-effects. . . . Regulation, however well-intentioned, introduces screens and filters between the perception of an opportunity for innovation and the inspiration and incentive to take advantage of it. Consequently, if the national purpose is to maintain the U.S. technological lead, our first concern should be to be good innovators ourselves."

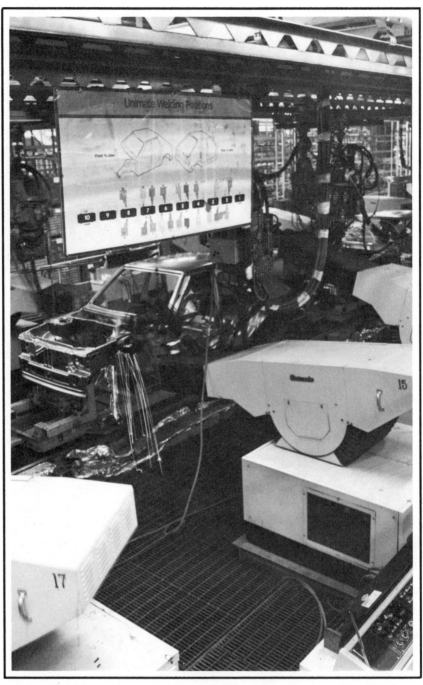

Chrysler assembly plant. Advocates of an industrial policy cite Chrysler's success after it received a $3.5 billion aid package, the largest-ever government bailout of a private company.

Chapter 10

DEVELOPING AN INDUSTRIAL POLICY

Machine toolmakers in the United States were understandably worried. The high-technology segment of their market — computer-controlled machine tools — was rapidly being devoured by foreign manufacturers. By 1981 Japanese computerized machining centers had captured roughly half of all U.S. sales.

The reason, said U.S. toolmakers, was that Japanese companies had benefited from their nation's industrial policy. Japan's government supported mergers, created research and development (R & D) cartels, provided tax benefits and subsidies for the machine tool industry and encouraged other industries to use computerized tools. This coherent industrial policy had converted Japan into the world's leading producer, consumer and exporter of those products by the early 1980s.

The effects of Japan's policies could be seen throughout high-technology industries, considered by many U.S. economists and business leaders to be the key to a viable U.S. trading economy of the future. By 1980 Japan dominated the world consumer electronics market; 20 years earlier the country barely had a domestic electronics industry. And on the agenda for the remainder of the decade was a government-supported initiative for development of a strong semiconductor industry through subsidies, tax exemptions, a generous research budget and trade policies to protect the young industry on the home market.

Japan has created a burgeoning robotics industry in much the same way. Through tax write-offs, subsidized loans and lucrative offers to stimulate the use of robots, the Japanese government has actively participated in developing a vigorous industry. Yet, as some American economists were quick to point out, most of the initial research and development that underlay the Japanese robotics industry was carried out in the United States. And although the U.S. robotics industry was keeping apace of the Japanese in the development and commercialization of the products, it was doing so largely without benefit of government subsidies.

One of the principal Japanese programs to support robotics was a Ministry of International Trade and Industry (MITI) plan to promote the development of machines that could "think" for themselves. By 1991 the government wanted to have a working robot that could automatically translate languages, convert speech into print, as well as make decisions.

Japan was not alone in the development and practice of successful industrial policies that were able to respond to the shifting economic bases of the 1980s. West Germany and France also had adopted policies of aiding industries that promised to capture a large share of international markets while easing the shift away from declining industries. Again, through the use of a comprehensive policy of tax incentives, loans and subsidies, those governments financially encouraged the development of growth industries.

Confronted by the fact that many of the older, basic manufacturing industries of the United States were in rapid decline, while at the same time many new industries could not obtain the financial backing to compete successfully both in the United States and in international markets against heavily-subsidized overseas competitors, numerous members of Congress began to call for an industrial policy. Congressional Democrats, taking the lead, proposed legislation that would establish a national council on industrial policy. But it was the fear of stiff foreign competition in industries both new and old that made industrial policy a growing political issue in time to heat up the 1984 election campaigns.

Industrial Policy and U.S. Attitudes

Industrial policy is a term broad enough to accommodate a variety of definitions. In general, the term has come to signify coordinated policy making by government and industries in short- and long-term economic planning. Contrary to prevailing U.S. practices, an active industrial policy would move government beyond the realm of macroeconomic policies — designed to influence overall levels of spending or investment — and into the forest of microeconomic policies that would require specific policies targeted to affect specific industries.

Policy Goals. Ideally, an industrial policy would include long-range analyses of global markets to foresee structural changes in economies, thereby putting the United States in a better position to make the necessary changes within industries to meet new challenges. Under a model industrial policy, government officials and representatives from the private sector would agree to allow some industries or firms within a particular industry to shut down in order to reallocate resources to other, more competitive enterprises. An active industrial policy thus suggests a strong working relationship between government and industry — with a certain amount of power on the part of that coalition to override regional and political demands.

Industrial policy advocates cited an earlier policy experience begun in the Depression when the government went to the aid of business and industries in need. The Reconstruction Finance Corp., founded in 1932 during the administration of Herbert Hoover, was a federally funded agency that loaned money to corporations, small businesses and farmers who met the qualifications. Recounting the success of the operation from experience, Rep. Claude Pepper, D-Fla., said, "Not every Dick, Tom or Harry who came along was able to get an RFC loan, just a Jones who was shrewd, who showed he had a good prospect. Those were the people the RFC was designed to help and did help." The RFC operated until 1957. *(See Reconstruction Finance Corporation box, p. 220.)*

Free-Market Approach. The philosophy underlying an industrial policy, however, was contrary to the Reagan administration's adherence to a "supply-side" economic theory. Ronald Reagan's free-market approach was based on the classical laissez-faire doctrine of Adam Smith that held economic "boom-and-bust" cycles as an inevitable consequence of a free-market economy. According to Smith, an 18th century economist who laid the groundwork for many subsequent economic theories, any attempt by government to intervene in the natural law of the market place would be at best ineffective and, more likely, deleterious to the economy.

The United States largely has followed this doctrine, not always out of conviction, but because of an American tradition that distrusts central planning and a political system strongly influenced by diverse interest groups and partisan politics that did not permit a consensus to be formed on the government's role in microeconomic policy making.

Countering the recent demands for a more active federal role, many people pointed out that the government already had a vast array of tax incentives, trade protection and promotion policies, subsidies and loan programs targeted to specific industries. But most were ad hoc, developed in response to a particular emergency, political pressures, or the requirements of the Defense Department, and did not form an

Reconstruction Finance Corp. . . .

For Rep. Claude Pepper, the octogenarian Democrat from Florida, recent interest in developing an industrial policy brought back memories of an earlier experience. Like many other congressional advocates of a comprehensive government/industry program to formulate economic goals and policies, he supported creation of a national industrial development bank to foster that effort. As Pepper saw it, that bank would be a re-creation of the Reconstruction Finance Corp. (RFC), an institution that had its origins in the Depression.

Established in 1932, the RFC distributed during its 25-year existence more than $11 billion in loans to banks, railroads, corporations and farmers teetering on the brink of financial disaster. "That was a wonderful institution," said Pepper. "It was founded in the [Herbert] Hoover administration, but it didn't amount to anything much until the [Franklin D.] Roosevelt administration. Then it became important." As a U.S. senator (1936-51), Pepper had firsthand experience helping a number of Floridians secure loans from the RFC.

The RFC became embroiled in controversy during the administration of Harry S Truman, following a spate of charges that its lending policies were unduly influenced by high Democratic officials. A Senate Banking subcommittee uncovered questionable transactions, such as a $1.5 million loan to a Florida hotel in which a presidential assistant, Donald S. Dawson, vacationed free of charge. The subcommittee concluded in 1951 that the RFC had been plagued with "improper use of the corporation's vast [lending] authority," and named three other prominent Democrats, in addition to Dawson, who had been guilty of influencing bank loans. The bank was reorganized, and then finally abolished in 1957.

Pepper, however, attributed the bank's fall to "growing reactionary political sentiment." He believed it never should have been allowed to die and could have proven particularly useful today. "I have been unable to understand why [the Reagan] administration has utterly ignored the things

overall economic strategy. Lester Thurow, professor of economics and management at Massachusetts Institute of Technology, described those random practices as amounting to a "back-door industrial policy," one that the United States could pretend did not exist. In the view of Thurow

. . . Policy Model for the Future?

that Roosevelt used to get this country off of its knees and onto its feet," he said.

Pepper's fond memories of the RFC were shared by a number of the House's senior Democrats. Rep. Jamie L. Whitten, D-Miss., 10 years Pepper's junior, also proposed reviving the institution. "It is always good, in my opinion, to start with something that is tried and true," said Whitten.

In the Senate as well, bank supporters looked to the New Deal for their model. Sens. Daniel Patrick Moynihan, D-N.Y., and Robert C. Byrd, D-W.Va., proposed reviving the RFC. Moynihan noted that during the 1970s, Congress felt compelled to make controversial loan guarantees for the Penn Central Railroad, Lockheed Aircraft Corp., New York City and the Chrysler Corp. A bank, he argued, could at least bring some order and discipline to this process.

But the economy of the early 1980s was a far cry from that of 50 years earlier. Many members from both parties questioned whether a federal bank had a role to play in the modern U.S. financial system. It would drain money from the nation's credit markets, which already were feeling the strain of a nearly $200 billion federal deficit, they argued. Furthermore, remnants of the RFC were still scattered throughout Washington at institutions such as the Export-Import Bank and the Small Business Administration.

A development bank, said Pepper, "will always have a place in our economy. Private banks that make relatively short-term loans can never perform the same service that an institution like the RFC performs."

Development bank supporters got a boost in June 1983, when House-Senate budget conferees agreed to put $50 million for an RFC-like development bank in a fiscal 1984 "reserve" fund for projects not yet authorized. Passage of any development bank legislation in the 98th Congress, however, was unlikely, since the administration and most Republicans opposed the idea.

and others, the real question facing the United States was not whether to have an industrial policy. Rather, it was whether to face up to the fact that an industrial policy already existed and by that admission make possible a more rational coordination of those efforts.

Japanese Experience With Industrial Policy

The Japanese, in particular, never shared the U.S. enthusiasm for laissez-faire economics. Emerging from the devastation of World War II, they spurned the notion that uninhibited markets offered the fastest route to economic recovery. With so much of their industrial base destroyed, they feared free-market forces would relegate their economy to low-wage, labor-intensive enterprises.

Consequently, the Japanese government adopted policies designed to speed development by actively promoting those industries with the most promise for future growth. Selective credit allocation, import protection, tax incentives, an antitrust policy favorable to mergers and the bureaucracy's considerable powers of persuasion were used to nurture selected industries and push the economy in a highly industrialized, high-technology direction.

The development of machine tool manufacturing was an example of the success of that policy. Beginning in the 1950s Japan's MITI took steps to encourage its machine tool manufacturers to develop computerized, numerically controlled machine tools. Those automated tools, wired to perform a single function, promised a high productivity return per worker.

To help accomplish its goals, the government shielded the industry from international competition in its early stages of development. At the same time it provided tax benefits, concessionary loans and research and development grants. Manufacturers with small shares of the fragmented market were forced to drop out, and those remaining were encouraged to cooperate in product R & D. The government also funded a program to promote the use of computerized machine tools by other industries. For example, the government subsidized an institute in Tokyo that developed software for a watch company to use in making watches, thereby convincing the watchmaker to buy a numerically controlled machine tool. As a result of those policies, Japanese industry as a whole made the transition from traditional to computerized machine tools far faster than the industry of any other nation. By 1980, according to a study by a French consulting firm, Japan was utilizing as many numerically controlled tools as the United States, even though Japan's economy was less than half the size of the U.S. economy.

U.S. machine tool manufacturers, once considered the best in the world, were lagging behind by the early 1980s. A U.S. Commerce Department analysis noted, "U.S. manufacturers find themselves in a disadvantaged position relative to their government-supported competitors. . . . Few of them have the resources to pursue an aggressive catch-up program in the current economic environment."

Faced with this unfavorable situation, the U.S. manufacturers were crying foul play. Their concerns were acknowledged on Capitol Hill in December 1982 when a Senate resolution was adopted to deny 10 percent investment tax credits to U.S. companies wishing to purchase computerized machine tools from Japan. If granted by the president, the resolution would have had the same effect as a 10 to 15 percent tariff on imported machine tools. Robert B. Reich, professor of business and public policy at Harvard University, said that denying the investment tax credit would be "another in a long line of steps we are taking down the road of protectionism."

In Reich's view, the resolution represented the wrong way to respond to international competition. A U.S. manufacturing industry would be protected at the expense of U.S. buyers, and more important, nothing would be done to ensure that the industry became more competitive or efficient.

Opposing Policy Recommendations

Reich was one voice in a growing chorus of economists, business school professors, former government officials and members of Congress calling for an industrial policy to improve the United States' competitive standing in international markets. The scope of the proposals varied greatly.

Some proponents of an industrial policy aimed at promoting high-technology products argued that many of the ailing traditional industries, characteristically labor-intensive as opposed to knowledge-intensive, should be allowed to fade away without further draining financial resources needed to prop them up so that high-technology industries, with large government and industry-supported R & D programs, could capture and control the global markets of the future. To support their argument, the advocates of emphasizing "high-tech" development pointed to the fact that the United States continued to enjoy an overall favorable trade balance in R & D-intensive products and in technical information.

In contrast, other economists stressed the importance of rebuilding traditional "smokestack" industries, recommending large capital investments to restructure ailing businesses. The "smokestack" school pointed to the massive turn-around of the Chrysler Corporation. Deeply in debt in

1979, Chrysler obtained $1.5 billion in federal loan guarantees in return for labor and product concessions. The loan program proved to be a success, with financial returns that enabled the corporation to return the loans years before they were due. *(See box, pp. 226-227.)*

But critics of industrial policies involving federal loans claimed government intervention was not necessarily required to put industries back on their feet again. The growth of "mini-mills" in the traditional steel-producing cities of Cleveland and Pittsburgh was an example. More modern and efficient and with lower labor costs than the larger, older plants, they accounted for approximately 18 percent of U.S. steel output in 1983, an adaptation accomplished without federal financing.

Some economists considered such industry-induced and conducted changes more attuned to the American capitalistic system. Charles Schultze, chairman of the Council of Economic Advisers during the Jimmy Carter administration, shared that opinion. In an October 24, 1983, issue of *Newsweek* magazine, he stated, "We have no basic structural deficiency in American industry. . . . What we have got is exorbitant interest rates and an overvalued dollar caused by tight money and loose budgets." International competitiveness could be improved through improved monetary and fiscal policies, Schultze said. "Imposing an industrial policy is just an irrelevant waste."

Government's Role Already Large

Despite an ad hoc assortment of loan guarantee programs, tax breaks and outright grants that benefited narrow sectors of the economy, both the U.S. government and the private sector did fund R & D programs on a large scale. In fact, total national investment in research and development measured in dollars was more than twice as large in the United States as that in Japan, according to National Science Foundation figures. Of that total, approximately 47 percent was funded by the federal government and 50 percent by private industry in 1982. But of the total federal R & D funding, more than 60 percent was allocated to the Defense Department and another 10 percent went to space research. Measured as a percentage of GNP, both the Japanese and West German total national investments in civilian research have exceeded those of the United States since 1965. However, Reich noted that the large U.S. defense commitment was equivalent to a de facto industrial policy.

Many observers believed that U.S. industry had consistently under-invested its funds in the long-term research required as the foundation for future high-tech products, relying too much on federally-financed short-term development projects intended for defense purposes. Beginning in 1980 several industries — including semiconductors and chemicals — formed consortia to conduct joint research and to encourage research cooperation between industrial firms and universities. Presidents Carter and Reagan encouraged that cooperation by issuing guidelines intended to allay industry's fears that long-term research agreements violated antitrust laws.

The fact that the federal government played a pivotal role in R & D supported arguments that it also should participate actively in long-range industrial policy planning and analyses. According to Reich, the federal government in the early 1980s supported more than 33 percent of U.S. industrial R & D and either employed directly or supported through government contracts more than 35 percent of the country's scientists and engineers.

The U.S. government's impact on industry through its vast purchasing power — particularly of military items — was equally as broad as its role in research and development. According to the Electronic Industries Association and the Defense Department, the federal government bought more than half of all aircraft, television and radio communications equipment, almost one-fourth of all engineering and scientific instruments, and one-third of all electron tubes manufactured in the United States in 1979. These enormous purchases within certain industries prompted charges that the government distorted the market by its needs and did not encourage the development of consumer-related industries.

The federal government's international role in protecting U.S. markets at home and abroad was comprised of protectionist measures such as tariffs, voluntary quotas and embargoes. In ailing, often older industries, the practice may have succeeded in merely bolstering inefficient industries. But Reich pointed out in the Jan.-Feb. 1982 edition of *Harvard Business Review* that well-intentioned protectionist measures might prevent those industries from the restructuring needed if they were to be internationally competitive.

Congressional Policy Proposals

Congressional interest in industrial policy was growing in the early 1980s. Although U.S. inflation had slowed and unemployment rates had improved by the end of 1983, the nation's massive trade deficit continued

Government Loans to Chrysler . . .

The story of Chrysler Corp.'s remarkable turnaround reads something like a children's tale, with the federal government cast in the role of fairy godmother.

At the end of 1979 the company was on the verge of collapse. The sharp increase in gas prices that followed the Iranian oil embargo had saddled it with an enormous unsold inventory of big, gas-guzzling cars. It was projecting cash shortfalls of more than $2 billion.

Faced with the disastrous impact a Chrysler failure would have on the economy, Congress agreed to guarantee $1.5 billion in loans for the ailing firm, provided certain conditions were met. The United Auto Workers union had to give up $462 million in pay raises, company suppliers chipped in $180 million, state and local governments gave $250 million, and the company's banks provided $500 million in new loans and renegotiated debt. The package was unprecedented in the history of federal assistance to private industry, both because of its size — a controversial 1971 Lockheed Aircraft Corp. loan had totaled only $250 million in federal guarantees — and because of the detailed and stringent conditions it included.

The rescue effort apparently worked. It enabled Chrysler Chairman Lee A. Iacocca to conduct a massive reorganization without going into bankruptcy courts. The company cut its workforce almost in half, cut its productive capacity by one-third, cut costs and concentrated its efforts on a new line of small, fuel-efficient cars.

As a result, a leaner Chrysler was basking in the beneficial effects of the overall economic recovery in 1983. It had such an abundance of cash that it planned to pay off the remaining $800 million of its federally backed loans seven years early, and it was expected to earn a profit of close to $1 billion in 1983.

The government also made out well in the deal. Not only were the loans being paid off ahead of schedule, but stock warrants the government received in return for its assistance were expected to sell for as much as $300 million.

Industrial policy enthusiasts cited the Chrysler loan as proof that government had a useful role to play in industry. And they thought it might provide a model for future federal efforts.

"I think it is a good example of what can be done when there is a negotiation between government, business and labor," said Rep. Stan

... Precursor of an Industrial Policy?

Lundine, D-N.Y. Lundine was involved in congressional negotiations over the Chrysler loan package and also sponsored a bill to create a National Industrial Development Bank to help troubled companies like Chrysler, as well as firms in key emerging industries.

Chrysler management deserved principal credit for turning the company around, but the government's role also was critical. "Government needed to be involved to provide the money," Lundine said. "And the government's involvement allowed for various parties to make the compromises they might not have been able to make otherwise."

For Chrysler itself, the government loan in many ways was like a scarlet letter, singling it out from its competitors. With a federal loan guarantee board watching over its shoulder, Chrysler management found it difficult to deal with private lenders and potential foreign partners.

But in spite of its desire to wean itself from government support, Chrysler had become a fervent proponent of industrial policy.

The Chrysler loan package was bitterly contested by those who believed that companies should be allowed to rise and fall as the free market dictated. The bailout eventually won Congress' approval, however, because members felt a Chrysler bankruptcy could be even more costly — in terms of unemployment benefits, tax losses and social disruption — than a loan guarantee.

Chrysler's remarkable turnaround convinced some Chrysler loan critics that they were wrong. But others insisted Chrysler should have been allowed to fail. "Presumably Chrysler was in trouble because of its own inefficiencies. Most basic economic theories suggest more jobs would have been created, greater productivity would have resulted if the capital had gone to an area of greater efficiency," said Rep. Dan Lungren, R-Calif.

Despite continued criticisms from loan opponents, Lundine remained firm in his support for the loan program. "[Chrysler] was working on a fuel-efficient car," he said. "They had a good business plan, in fact they were three or four years ahead of Ford in getting to that market." Lundine acknowledged, however, that the Chrysler rescue may have been partially at the expense of General Motors and Ford.

"What I would rather do is look at industries as a whole," he said, "and then allow whatever companies that want to come in [for loans] to do so, more on a free-market banking basis."

to rise. And the fact that many industries seemed to have lost their ability to compete effectively in world markets made the Reagan administration's opposition to a defined industrial policy a popular political issue for presidential Democratic hopefuls in the 1984 election campaign.

At the very least, supporters of industrial policy legislation before Congress in 1983 claimed more clearcut guidelines would establish a means of analyzing the economic impact of the government's assorted industry-assistance programs and how they fit in with broader economic goals.

Industrial Policy Forum. A proposal introduced in 1983 by Rep. Timothy E. Wirth, D-Colo., and Rep. Richard A. Gephardt, D-Mo., would establish an Economic Cooperation Council to provide "a national arena for clarifying complex economic choices and building broad support for public initiatives." As a forum for developing a national industrial policy, the nine-member council would convene subcouncils composed of government, business and labor representatives to develop strategies for specific industries. It also would operate a new Bureau of Economic Analysis to analyze economic trends and attempt to chart the overall direction of U.S. industry.

The New York Times quickly dubbed the proposal "MITI-minus," after the Japanese Ministry of International Trade and Industry. Like MITI, the council would devise industrial policies by building a consensus among those involved in an industry. But unlike MITI, the council would have no independent power to implement its proposals.

"There isn't a single industrial policy," Wirth said. "American politics and the American press love to look for that one-paragraph answer.... Well we don't have anything like that. What the Economic Cooperation Council is, really, is a *process.*"

Industrial Development Bank. Another bill, sponsored by Rep. Stan Lundine, D-N.Y., and Rep. David E. Bonior, D-Mich., would take the Wirth-Gephardt proposal a step further by adding to the cooperation council concept a National Industrial Development Bank that would make low-cost loans to key industries as it determined. The bank would be authorized to provide at least $12 billion in direct loans and up to $24 billion in federal guarantees. The Economic Cooperation Council would help develop the "conditions" that a company had to agree to before receiving a loan.

The proposed council would have 20 members: five each from business, labor and government and five from academia, consumer groups and other segments of society. That allocation of seats was particularly favored by labor unions, who feared they might be under-represented on Wirth's panel.

To Bonior, the bank was the heart of the legislation. "You can have all the cooperation you want between management, labor and government," said Bonior. "But without the blood to infuse into the patient, the patient will be dormant. You won't have the tools to do the job."

The development bank was designed to provide half of its assistance to mature industries that needed to invest in new manufacturing equipment and half to emerging high-tech industries. Although the bank could not create capital, it would raise money in private financial markets and then make loans to its customers. As a result, the bank would not be adding to the pool of capital, but merely reallocating it.

Lundine pointed out that the U.S. government already was heavily involved in the allocation of credit. According to the Office of Management and Budget, the federal government provided an estimated $130 billion worth of credit to the private sector in fiscal 1982, via direct government loans, guaranteed loans and tax-exempt loans. That amounted to almost one-third of all loans made in U.S. markets. But few of the loans went to help manufacturing industries; most of them were given to home buyers and farmers.

International Trade and Industry Department. Sen. William V. Roth Jr., R-Del., was promoting an administration-supported plan in late 1983 to reorganize the Department of Commerce and the Office of the U.S. Trade Representative into a new Department of International Trade and Industry (DITI). According to Roth, U.S. trade policy had been directed by a "two-headed monster," with the Office of the U.S. Trade Representative setting policy and conducting negotiations and the Commerce Department gathering data and enforcing and administering trade laws. The secretary of the new department would be the president's principal adviser on international trade policy, and would assume most of the responsibilities of the commerce secretary and the U.S. trade representative. *(See Trade Department box, Chapter 1, p. 21.)*

But Senate Democrats, who viewed the bill as an insufficient answer to U.S. trade and industrial problems, pressed Roth to include provisions emphasizing an industrial policy approach to U.S. trade concerns. Sens. Thomas F. Eagleton, D-Mo., and Carl Levin, D-Mich., sponsored two amendments that assured the bill's approval in committee. The first amendment would create an Office of Competitive Analysis within the new department to collect data on the competitive positions of particular industries in international markets and provide a thorough analysis of the information.

The second, more controversial amendment would require the Office of Competitive Analysis to prepare an annual report describing actual and foreseeable economic and technological developments that could affect the competitive positions of particular industries. The secretary of the new DITI then would be charged with convening temporary industry "competitive councils" for established U.S. industries that were likely to face foreign challenges or large risks in competing successfully in "significant future markets."

"Our trade problems are symptoms, for the most part, of our industrial problems," contended Eagleton. "A department which does not provide a reasonable framework for government decisions about our industrial problems will not accomplish very much for our trade problems either."

Although approved by the Senate Governmental Affairs Committee Oct. 4, 1983, the Senate did not act on the measure that year.

House Proposal. House Democrats countered the Senate's reorganization proposal with one of their own. Rep. Don L. Bonker, D-Wash., introduced in November 1983 an alternative that would create a Department of International Trade and Industry with a stronger role in industrial policy than that contained in the Senate version. The Bonker bill would create an assistant to the president for international trade, similar to the powerful position of the national security adviser. In contrast, the secretary of DITI would assume the responsibility of presidential trade adviser under the Roth/administration proposal. The House reorganization measure also included the Industrial Competitive Council plan that was similar to the Senate proposal. The 30-member council would consist of representatives of business, labor, government and public interest groups.

Cautious Approach. Despite the fact that approximately 30 industrial policy proposals had been introduced in 1983, many members of Congress remained skeptical of industrial policy proposals, a sentiment that ran particularly strong in the Senate.

However, some members philosophically opposed to any government role in industry had begun to see industrial policy as necessary to give the United States leverage in bargaining with other nations. A congressional staff member, expressing that view said, "Industrial policy is like the MX; you got to have one so you can phase it down while your trading partners are phasing theirs down."

Glossary of Trade Terms and Organizations

Adjustment assistance. Originally provided by the Trade Act of 1962, extended under the Trade Act of 1974 and renewed several times thereafter (the latest, through September 1985), trade adjustment assistance provides workers whose jobs are terminated because of increased competition from imports with job training and financial benefits to help them find new employment.

Ad valorem duties. Tariff duties calculated on the basis of a fixed percentage of the wholesale value of a good, as, for example, a tax of 6 percent on every dollar's worth of value of an item. Most imports are subject to ad valorem, rather than specific, duties. *Specific duties* are levied on the basis of some physical unit, that is, 10 cents a pound, 4 cents a yard. An advantage of ad valorem duties is that they automatically adjust for inflation, whereas the worth of specific duties can be eroded by inflation.

American Selling Price (ASP). A pricing system used by the United States under which the tariff rate on imported goods, principally benzenoid chemicals, was based on the price of the competitively produced U.S. product rather than on the actual import price. The ASP was abolished in 1979.

Balance of payments. A record of all economic transactions between one country and the rest of the world in a given period, usually one year. Included in the calculation are the movement of goods, services, interest and dividends, long- and short-term investments, currency shipments and gold. The transactions are either in the form of a foreign claim for payment (a debit) from imports and capital outflows; or a foreign obligation to pay (a credit), resulting from exports and capital inflows.

The *capital account* is a record of capital (financial) transactions, both government and private, appearing on the balance-of-payments account. Capital transactions include long- and short-term loans and credits made or received. The account is shown in terms of net increases or decreases in assets (a country's investments abroad) and liabilities (foreign investment in the reporting country).

The *current account* is a summary of the balance-of-payments account of all international transactions. The current account includes exports and imports of goods (merchandise) and services (shipping, air

233

transportation, interest and dividends on investments and so forth) by individuals and governments.

Balance of trade (merchandise balance). The difference between the value of the goods that a nation exports and the value of the goods that it imports during a given period. Unlike balance-of-payments calculations, it excludes capital transactions, payments for services and shipments of gold.

Beggar-my-neighbor tactics. A method of increasing the exports of one country at the expense of those of other countries. Such actions could include unwarranted currency depreciation or unprovoked tariff increases.

Capital flight. A massive transfer of currency from one country to another due to adverse economic, political or international developments.

COCOM (Coordinating Committee). An informal grouping of 14 members of the North Atlantic Treaty Organization (Britain, France, West Germany, Belgium, Luxembourg, the Netherlands, Norway, Denmark, Italy, Portugal, Canada, the United States, Greece and Turkey) and Japan that attempts to coordinate controls on exports to other nations, primarily communist countries. NATO members not a part of the group are Iceland and Spain.

COMECON (Council of Mutual Economic Cooperation, also referred to as the Council for Mutual Economic Assistance, or CMEA). The international organization that coordinates trade and other forms of economic relations between the centrally planned economies of Eastern Europe (Bulgaria, Czechoslovakia, East Germany, Hungary, Poland, Romania and the U.S.S.R.). Yugoslavia is an associate member; Albania is not a member. The group also includes Cuba, Vietnam and Mongolia. It was established in 1949 but did not receive a formal charter until 1969.

Customs union. An agreement among countries to abolish all tariffs among the members of the union and to adopt a uniform tariff vis-a-vis other nations. The European Economic Community (EEC), for example, is a customs union.

Devaluation. The lowering of the value of a nation's currency relative to gold or to the currency of other countries. Devaluation often occurs when a country is having serious balance-of-payments problems.

Domestic International Sales Corporation (DISC). A form of business organization permitted by the Treasury Department that allows a U.S.

exporting firm to postpone payment of federal taxes on income from export profits until the dividends from the profits are distributed to its shareholders. Previously, exporting companies had to pay federal income taxes on export revenues immediately.

Dumping. The sale of a product in another country for less than that charged in the home market in order to gain a competitive advantage over other foreign suppliers. The General Agreement on Tariffs and Trade (GATT) prohibits this practice.

Escape clause. A provision in the U.S. Trade Agreements Act that enables the United States to terminate or modify a specific trade concession if the concession threatens serious injury to a domestic industry.

European Economic Community (EEC). Established in 1957, the EEC, or Common Market, currently consists of 10 member nations: Belgium, Denmark, West Germany, Greece, France, Ireland, Italy, Luxembourg, the Netherlands and the United Kingdom. All customs duties and quotas on imports and export of goods among member states were abolished, and a common external tariff was established. The community also works to abolish nontariff barriers to trade among members and has developed a common agricultural policy (CAP).

Export-Import Bank (Ex-Im Bank). An independent agency of the U.S. government whose purpose is to help finance and facilitate U.S. foreign trade by arranging loans to finance the purchase by foreign governments or private entities of U.S. capital equipment, materials and services. The loans are repayable in dollars.

Flexible tariff. A duty on foreign-made products that can be raised or lowered quickly. Under current U.S. trade laws, the president can order a flexible-tariff program without the approval of Congress.

Floating exchange rate. A system that allows exchange rates in a single country and for a certain time period to float freely in order for the currency to find its own value in a free market. This device usually anticipates exchange-rate adjustments.

General Agreement on Tariffs and Trade (GATT). An international code of tariffs and trade rules signed in 1947 by the United States and 22 other countries. Several rounds of tariff-cutting negotiations have occurred under GATT. At the end of 1983 there were 90 member countries.

International commodity agreement. An agreement between or among nations exporting and importing a particular product that specifies, either in fixed amounts or in ranges of maximum to minimum, a volume and price at which the commodity will be traded while the agreement is in force. Examples are the International Wheat Agreement, the International Sugar Agreement and the International Coffee Agreement.

International Monetary Fund (IMF). An international financial institution, with headquarters in Washington, D. C., affiliated with the United Nations, that provides assistance to its member nations as it is needed to meet adverse balance-of-payments conditions. IMF financial assistance is in the form of an exchange transaction. Each member pays into the fund an amount of its own currency equivalent to the amount of foreign currency that it wishes to draw. The member is expected to "repurchase" its own currency within 10 years by a payment of Special Drawing Rights (SDRs), dollars, or some other currency acceptable to the Fund. Each member is assigned a quota that determines its voting power and the amount it may withdraw from the fund. The IMF also plays a central role in longer-range international fiscal and monetary policy. It is headed by a board of governors, on which each member country (146 as of 1983) is represented. *(SDRs, below)*

Mercantilism. An economic policy, pursued by most nations during the 17th and early 18th centuries, that aimed at increasing a nation's wealth and power by encouraging exports in return for gold. Governments encouraged export industries, protected domestic industries generally and erected high tariff walls to discourage imports.

Most-favored-nation treatment (MFN). A provision in commercial treaties between two or more countries guaranteeing that all partners will automatically extend to each other any tariff reductions that they might offer to a non-treaty-country. For example, if the United States negotiates an agreement with France to reduce tariffs on tire imports, that tariff reduction is automatically extended to all other nations with which the United States has a reciprocal MFN arrangement. Thus, once the United States grants MFN to country A, any tariff reductions extended by the United States or country A to country B automatically is granted to country A or to the United States. All members of GATT have agreed to extend MFN treatment to each other's exports. The granting of MFN treatment frequently has been used to further the foreign policy objective of gaining a nation's good will, just as the removal or denial of MFN has been used to express criticism of a nation's policies. Extension of MFN to the People's Republic of China was part of U.S. policy to improve relations with the PRC, while rescinding MFN status for Poland in 1982 was used as one means to display the U.S. displeasure with the Polish government's crackdown on the independent Solidarity trade union.

Organization for Economic Cooperation and Development (OECD). The successor to the Organization for European Economic Cooperation (OEEC). Founded in 1960, the OECD has 24 members: Australia, Austria, Belgium, Canada, Denmark, Finland, France, West Germany, Greece, Iceland, Ireland, Italy, Japan, Luxembourg, the Netherlands, New Zealand, Norway, Portugal, Spain, Sweden, Switzerland, Turkey, the United Kingdom and the United States. The OECD Council may meet at the level of ministers or at the level of their alternates (permanent delegations). Within the limits of the convention, the Council is in fact a permanent conference in which the economic problems of the member countries are constantly reviewed. The OECD prepares and distributes publications on general economics, statistics, trade, aid to less developed areas and other topics.

Peril point. The maximum cut in a U.S. import duty that can be made for a given commodity without causing serious injury to domestic producers or to a similar commodity. First included as a provision in the Trade Agreements Extension Act of 1948, the peril-point mechanism remained a part of U.S. law almost continuously until it was eliminated in the Trade Expansion Act of 1962.

Reciprocity. The lowering of trade barriers by one country in return for similar concessions by other countries. The principle of reciprocity has been a major ingredient in U.S. tariff policy since 1934.

Revaluation. The upward or downward change in a currency's value relative to gold or other currencies. It is an important tool in dealing with balance-of-payments problems.

Safeguards. Import controls or restrictions imposed unilaterally by one nation on the grounds that such action is needed to protect a domestic industry from injury. GATT allows a country to withdraw or modify concessions or impose new controls if the country can prove that a product is "being imported in such increased quantities as to cause or threaten serious injury to domestic producers."

Special Drawing Rights (SDRs). A form of international liquid reserves used in the settlement of international payments among the member governments of the International Monetary Fund. The SDR system was established in 1967, and the first allocation of SDRs was made in 1970. Drawing rights were allocated among the IMF members according to their already-established quotas in the Fund.

Tariff (customs duty). A tax on the importation and, rarely, on the exportation of particular goods, levied by a nation's government and payable to it when the item crosses the nation's customs boundary. Formerly, tariff schedules showed an absolute amount of duty to be paid on each imported item. However, modern practice is to establish ad valorem tariffs, which show the duty as a percentage of the imported item's wholesale value.

Trade barrier. A restraint imposed by a government on the free exchange of goods and services between nations. The most common types of trade barriers are tariffs, quotas and exchange controls.

United Nations Conference on Trade and Development (UNCTAD). Composed of all members of the United Nations, UNCTAD is a permanent U.N. organization. It is concerned primarily with improving the relative income position of the developing countries by increasing the growth rates in those countries through better trading conditions, such as obtaining tariff preferences (favorable tariff treatment) from industrialized nations for goods exported by the developing countries.

U.S. International Trade Commission. An independent agency of the U.S. government that serves the president and Congress chiefly as a fact-finding advisory body in tariff and trade matters. Established in 1916, the agency is headed by six commissioners appointed by the president and confirmed by the Senate for nine-year terms.

U.S. Trade Representative. The Office of the United States Trade Representative in the Executive Office of the President was created as the Office of the Special Representative for Trade Negotiations in 1963. It is charged with administering the trade agreements programs under several laws and has responsibility for setting and administering overall trade policy. The U.S. trade representative is the chief U.S. representative for all activities related to GATT as well as the OECD, the United Nations Conference on Trade and Development and other multilateral institutions, when such negotiations deal primarily with trade and commodity issues; and for other bilateral and multilateral negotiations when trade is the primary issue.

Selected Bibliography on U.S. Trade Policy

Articles

Badaracco, Joseph L. Jr., and Yoffie, David B. " 'Industrial Policy': It Can't Happen Here." *Harvard Business Review*, November/December 1983.

Batie, Sandra S., and Healy, Robert G. "The Future of American Agriculture." *Scientific American*, February 1983.

Benjamin, Gerald. "Japan in the World of the 1980s." *Current History*, April 1982.

Bergsten, C. Fred. "The U.S.-Japan Economic Conflict." *Foreign Affairs*, Summer 1982.

Diebold, William. "The United States in the World Economy: A Fifty-Year Perspective." *Foreign Affairs*, Fall 1983.

Drouin, Marie-Josee, and Malmgren, Harald B. "Canada, the United States and the World Economy." *Foreign Affairs*, Winter 1981/82.

Farnsworth, Clyde H. "William Brock: Our Man for Trade." *New York Times Magazine*, Nov. 13, 1983.

Graham, J. L. "Hidden Cause of America's Trade Deficit with Japan." *Columbia Journal of World Business*, Fall 1981, pp. 5-15.

Graham, Thomas R. "Global Trade: War & Peace." *Foreign Policy*, Spring 1983.

Grossman, G. M. "Import Competition from Developed and Developing Countries." *Review of Economics and Statistics*, May 1982.

Guzzardi, Walter Jr. "Cutting Russia's Harvest of U.S. Technology." *Fortune*, May 30, 1983.

Heilbroner, Robert. "Reflections: Economic Prospects." *The New Yorker*, Aug. 29, 1983.

Kissinger, Henry A. "Saving the World Economy." *Newsweek*, Jan. 24, 1983.

Lodge, G. C., and Glass, W. R. "U.S. Trade Policy Needs One Voice." *Harvard Business Review*, May/June 1983.

"Making Industrial Policy." *Newsweek*, October 24, 1983.

Oksenberg, Michel. "Sino-American Relations." *Foreign Policy*, Fall 1982.

Quelch, John A. "It's Time to Make Trade Promotion More Productive." *Harvard Business Review*, May/June 1983.

Reich, Robert B. "Beyond Free Trade." *Foreign Affairs*, Spring 1983.

____. "Industrial Policy." *New Republic*, March 31, 1982, pp. 28-31.

———. "Why the U.S. Needs an Industrial Policy." *Harvard Business Review,* January/February 1982.

———. "Why We Are Losing the Hi-Tech War." *Resource Management,* May 1982, p. 7.

Stein, Herbert, and Thurow, Lester. "Do Modern Times Call for an Industrial Policy?" *Public Opinion,* August/September 1983.

Uri, N.D., and Mixon, J.W. "Effect of Exports and Imports on the Stability of Employment in Manufacturing Industries in the U.S." *Applied Economics,* June 1981, pp. 193-203.

Wadekin, Karl-Eugen. "Soviet Agriculture's Dependence on the West." *Foreign Affairs,* Spring 1982.

Wallich, Paul. "Technology Transfer at Issue: The Industry Viewpoint." *Spectrum,* May 1982.

Books

Atlantic Council Working Group on the United States and Canada. *Canada and the United States: Dependence and Divergence.* Cambridge, Mass.: Ballinger, 1982.

Aubrey, Henry G. *The Dollar in World Affairs: An Essay in International Financial Policy.* New York: Harper & Row, 1964.

Bergsten, C. Fred., and Krause, Lawrence B. *World Politics and International Economics.* Washington, D.C.: The Brookings Institution, 1975.

Botkin, James, et al. *Global Stakes: The Future of High Technology in America.* Cambridge, Mass.: Ballinger Publishing Co., 1982.

Camps, Miriam. *Britain and the European Community, 1955-1963.* London: Oxford University Press, 1964.

Caves, Richard E., and Jones, Ronald W. *World Trade and Payments: An Introduction* (3rd edition). Boston: Little, Brown, 1981.

Center for Strategic and International Studies. *The Export Performance of the United States: Political, Strategic and Economic Implications.* New York: Praeger Publishers, 1981.

Chang, C. S. *The Japanese Auto Industry and the U.S. Market.* New York: Praeger Publishers, 1981.

Cline, William R. *Reciprocity: A New Approach to World Trade Policy?* Washington, D.C.: Institute for International Economics, September 1982.

Cohen, Stephen D. *The Making of United States International Economic Policy.* New York: Praeger Publishers, 1977.

Destler, I. M., and Hideo, Sato. *Coping with U.S.-Japanese Economic Conflicts.* Lexington, Mass.: Lexington Books, 1982.

Diebold, William. *Industrial Policy as an International Issue.* New York: McGraw-Hill Book Co., 1980.

Evans, John W. *The Kennedy Round in American Trade Policy. The Twilight of the GATT?* Cambridge, Mass.: Harvard University Press, 1971.

Feinberg, Richard E. *Subsidizing Success: The Export-Import Bank in the U.S. Economy.* New York: Cambridge University Press, 1982.

Gilmore, Richard. *A Poor Harvest: The Clash of Policies and Interests in the Grain Trade.* New York: Longman, 1982.

Gustafson, Thane. *Selling the Russians the Rope.* Santa Monica, Calif: Rand Corp., 1981.

Hansen, Philip. *Trade and Technology in Soviet-Western Relations.* New York: Columbia University Press, 1981.

Hansen, Roger D., ed. *U.S. Foreign Policy and the Third World: Agenda 1982.* New York: Praeger (for the Overseas Development Council), 1982.

Hinshaw, Randall, ed. *Global Monetary Anarchy.* Beverly Hills, Calif.: Sage, 1981.

Hurtland-Thunberg, Penelope. *Government Support of Exports: A Second Best Alternative.* Lexington, Mass.: Lexington Books, 1982.

Kahn, Herman, and Pepper, Thomas. *The Japanese Challenge: The Success or Failure of Economic Success.* New York: Crowell, 1979.

Kindleberger, Charles P. *International Economics* (5th edition). Homewood, Ill.: Richard D. Irwin, Inc., 1973.

____. *International Money: A Collection of Essays.* Winchester, Mass.: George Allen & Unwin, 1981.

Magaziner, Ira C., and Reich, Robert B. *Minding America's Business.* New York: Harcourt Brace Jovanovich, 1982.

Metzger, Stanley D. *Lowering Nontariff Barriers: U.S. Law, Practice and Negotiating Objectives.* Washington, D.C.: The Brookings Institution, 1974.

Pastor, Robert A. *Congress and the Politics of U.S. Foreign Economic Policy.* Berkeley: University of California Press, 1980.

Pinder, John, ed. *National Industrial Strategies and the World Economy.* Totowa, N.J.: Allanheld, Osmun, 1982.

Reischel, Klaus-Walter. *Economic Effects of Exchange-Rate Changes.* Lexington, Mass.: Lexington Books, 1978.

Salamon, Robert. *The International Monetary System, 1945-1981.* New York: Harper & Row, 1982.

Yeats, Alexander J. *Trade and Development Policies: Leading Issues for the 1980s.* New York: St. Martins, 1981.

Reports and Studies

American Enterprise Institute. *U.S.-Japanese Relations: What Should the Future Hold?* Washington, D.C., July 1981.

Bergsten, C. Fred. *The Outlook for the Dollar.* Washington, D.C.: Institute for International Economics, December 1982.

Bergsten, C. Fred, and Cline, William R. *Trade Policy in the 1980s.* Washington, D.C.: Institute for International Economics, November 1982.

Brock, William E. III. *Assessment of the GATT Ministerial Meeting.* Statement before the Senate Finance Committee, Jan. 25, 1983.

Institute for Contemporary Studies. *Tariffs, Quotas & Trade: The Politics of Protectionism.* San Francisco, Calif.: 1979.

Japan Economic Institute of America. *Japan's Import Barriers: An Analysis of Divergent Bilateral Views.* Washington, D.C., 1981.

Shafer, Jeffrey R., and Loopesko, Bonnie E. "Floating Exchange Rates after Ten Years." *Brookings Papers on Economic Activity,* 1:1983.

Willett, Thomas D. *Floating Exchange Rates and International Monetary Reform.* Washington, D.C.: American Enterprise Institute for Public Policy Research, 1977.

Government Publications

U.S. Congress. House. Committee on Agriculture, Subcommittee on Department Operations, Research and Foreign Agriculture. *Agricultural Exports. Hearings, June 25-July 28, 1981.* Washington, D.C.: Government Printing Office, 1981.

U.S. Congress. House. Committee on Energy and Commerce. *United States Trade Relations with China and Japan: 1983. Staff Report.* Washington, D.C.: Government Printing Office, 1983.

U.S. Congress. House. Committee on Energy and Commerce, Subcommittee on Oversight and Investigations. *Impact of Canadian Energy and Investment Policies on U.S. Commerce. Report, October, 1982.* Washington, D.C.: Government Printing Office, 1982.

U.S. Congress. House. Committee on Foreign Affairs. *Export Administration Amendments Act of 1983. Report, June 22, 1983.* Washington, D.C.:

Government Printing Office, 1983.

U.S. Congress. House. Committee on Foreign Affairs, Subcommittee on International Economic Policy and Trade. *Overview of U.S. International Competitiveness. Hearings, March 19, 1981-Aug. 11, 1982.* Washington, D.C.: Government Printing Office, 1983.

U.S. Congress. House. Committee on Foreign Affairs and Committee on Agriculture. *Review of Agricultural Trade Issues. Joint Hearing, Aug. 11, 1982.* Washington, D.C.: Government Printing Office, 1982.

U.S. Congress. House. Committee on Ways and Means, Subcommittee on Trade. *Extension of MFN Status to Romania, Hungary, and the People's Republic of China. Hearings, July 12-13, 1982.* Washington, D.C.: Government Printing Office, 1982.

____. *U.S. Trade Policy-Phase II. Hearings, Feb. 1-March 18, 1982.* Washington, D.C.: Government Printing Office, 1982.

U.S. Congress. Joint Economic Committee, Subcommittee on International Trade, Finance and Security Economics. *U.S.-Japanese Economic Relations. Hearings, June 19-July 13, 1981.* Washington, D.C.: Government Printing Office, 1981.

U.S. Congress. Joint Economic Committee, Subcommittee on Monetary and Fiscal Policy and Subcommittee on Trade, Productivity, and Economic Growth. *Japanese and American Economic Policies and U.S. Productivity. Hearings, June 23-July 28, 1981.* Washington, D.C.: Government Printing Office, 1981.

U.S. Congress. Senate. Committee on Agriculture, Nutrition and Forestry. Subcommittee on Foreign Agricultural Policy. *U.S.-European Agricultural Trade. Hearings, Dec. 19-17, 1981.* Washington, D.C.: Government Printing Office, 1982.

Agricultural Export Trade. Hearings, Feb. 17-25, 1983. Washington, D.C.: Government Printing Office, 1983.

U.S. Congress. Senate. Committee on Banking, Housing, and Urban Affairs. *Revitalization of the U.S. Economy. Hearings, Sept. 15-17, Sept. 22-25, 1981.* Washington, D.C.: Government Printing Office, 1981.

U.S. Congress. Senate. Committee on Banking, Housing, and Urban Affairs, Subcommittee on International Finance and Monetary Policy. *Foreign Barriers to U.S. Trade. Hearings, Nov. 9, 1981-March 4, 1982.* 2 Parts. Washington, D.C.: Government Printing Office, 1982.

U.S. Congress. Senate. Committee on Finance, Subcommittee on International Trade, and Committee on Banking, Housing and Urban Affairs, Subcommittee on International Finance and Monetary

Policy. *Oversight of U.S. Trade Policy. Joint Hearings, July 8-28, 1981*. 2 Parts. Washington, D.C.: Government Printing Office, 1981.

U.S. Congress. Senate. Committee on Foreign Relations. *U.S. Trade Relations with Japan. Hearing, Sept. 14, 1982*. Washington, D.C.: Government Printing Office, 1982.

U.S. Congress. Committee on Foreign Relations, Subcommittee on International Economic Policy. *East-West Economic Relations. Hearing Sept. 16, 1981*. Washington, D.C.: Government Printing Office, 1981.

——. *Economic Relations with the Soviet Union. Hearings, July 30, 1982*. Washington, D.C.: Government Printing Office, 1982.

U.S. Congress. Senate. Committee on Governmental Affairs, Subcommittee on Oversight of Government Management. *United States-Canadian Trade Policies: Impact on Border State Industries, Hearing, Nov. 17, 1981*. Washington, D.C.: Government Printing Office, 1982.

U.S. Defense Department. Defense Science Board. "An Analysis of Export Control on U.S. Technology — A DOD Perspective." Washington, D.C.: Government Printing Office, 1976.

U.S. International Economic Policy in the 1980s. Selected essays prepared for the use of the Joint Economic Committee. Committee print. Feb. 11, 1982. Washington, D.C.: Government Printing Office, 1982.

United States International Trade Commission. "The Effect of Changes in the Value of the U.S. Dollar on Trade in Selected Commodities." September 1983. Washington, D.C.: Government Printing Office, 1983.

United States-China Economic Relations: A Reappraisal. A Workshop sponsored by the Senate Committee on Foreign Relations and the Congressional Research Service, Library of Congress. April 1981 (committee print). Washington, D.C.: Government Printing Office, 1982.

INDEX

A

Acid rain - 136
Advanced developing nations - 8, 11, 17, 87, 93-94
Afghanistan - 115-116, 129, 176
AFL-CIO. *See* American Federation of Labor-Congress of Industrial Organizations (AFL-CIO).
Agricultural Trade Development and Assistance Act of 1954 - 103
Agriculture
　Canada - 145, 172, 176
　Competition in world markets - 172, 181, 182
　Contract sanctity - 178-188
　Decline in exports - 4, 171, 172, 175-176, 179
　Developing countries - 46-47, 72, 172
　EEC
　　Common agricultural policy (CAP) - 82, 88, 172
　　Export subsidies - 14, 16, 179, 183, 184
　Egyptian wheat sale - 14, 145, 181
　Embargoes - 4, 116, 120, 175-179
　Export credit subsidies - 195
　Export subsidies
　　Brazil - 182, 184
　　EEC - 14, 16, 179, 183, 184
　　U.S. - 174, 180-184
　Export volumes and values, 1970-1982 (graph) - 173
　Government farm assistance programs - 173-175
　Japan - 11, 175
　Kennedy Round negotiations - 58
　Lobbyists - 175, 177, 178
　Prices - 172-174

Rise in exports, 1970s - 171, 172
Soviet grain embargo - 4, 116, 120, 176
Soviet grain sales - 110-111, 116-117, 171-172, 176, 180
Surpluses - 172-175
Agriculture Department (USDA) - 110, 111
Airline industry deregulation - 144
Alliance for Progress - 46-47
American Farm Bureau Federation - 175, 180, 182
American Federation of Labor-Congress of Industrial Organizations (AFL-CIO) - 19, 68, 87, 90, 162
American Selling Price - 68, 71, 89
Anti-Dumping Act of 1921 - 40, 58
Anti-dumping practices - 40-41, 57, 58, 81, 89
Argentina - 176, 177
Arms export controls - 101, 102, 200
Australia - 172
Auto industry
　Competition from imports - 4-5, 11, 149-150
　Domestic content legislation - 19-20, 138-139, 151-152, 154-155
　Japanese voluntary quotas - 11, 19, 152-153
　Recession impact - 150

B

Balance of payments - 3 (graph), 8, 30, 49-51, 73
Baldrige, Malcolm - 10, 13, 21
Banks
　Export-Import Bank - 187-197

Industrial development bank proposal - 228-229

Reconstruction Finance Corp. - 219, 220-221 (box)

Battle Act - 101-103. (*See also* Mutual Defense Assistance Control Act.)

Battle, Laurie C., D-Ala. - 102

Bingham, Jonathan B., D-N.Y. - 119

Block, John R. - 172, 174, 176, 180

Bonior, David E., D-Mich. - 228, 229

Bonker, Don, D-Wash. - 21, 199, 208-210, 230

Brazil

Agriculture - 172, 175, 182, 184

Debts - 17, 184

Industrial development - 8, 87, 93

Bretton Woods amendments - 80

Bretton Woods system (box) - 48-49

Britain. *See* Great Britain.

Brock, William E., III - 1, 2, 6, 8, 10, 131

Auto industry - 19-20, 151

Free trade-protectionism debate - 25

GATT meeting, 1982, Geneva - 16-17

Reciprocity - 20, 146, 160

Brzezinski, Zbigniew - 127

Business interests

China ties - 128

Export controls - 201-202, 211

Export credit subsidies - 188

Reciprocity - 162

Butz, Earl L. - 110

Buy American Act of 1933 - 40

Buy American provisions - 139

Byrd, Robert C., D-W.Va. - 1, 221

C

Canada - 135-146

Agriculture - 136, 145, 172, 176

Auto domestic content legislation - 138-139

Buy American provisions - 139

Deregulation of U.S. industries - 144

Export credit subsidies - 188, 191

Fishery Agreement - 135

Foreign investment restrictions - 141-143

Government role in economy - 140-141

Natural gas export price - 144-145

Reciprocity bill - 143-144

Telecommunications - 145-146

Trade conflicts - 136-138, 141, 144-146

Trade with U.S. - 136, 137 (table)

U.S. Congress - 135-136, 139-140

Carter, Jimmy - 86, 88, 115, 225

China relations - 98, 126, 128

Soviet grain embargo - 116, 176

Trade reorganization plan - 81

Caterpillar Tractor Co. - 119, 203 (box)

China. *See* People's Republic of China; Taiwan.

Chrysler Corporation - 223-224, 226-227 (box)

Cochran, Thad, R-Miss. - 171

COCOM. *See* Coordinating Committee.

Cohen, William S., R-Maine - 137

COMECON. *See* Council for Mutual Economic Assistance.

Commerce Department - 21, 81, 201, 205, 208, 209, 229

Commission on Foreign Economic Policy (Randall commission) - 39-42

Commodity Control List - 205

Common Market. *See* European Economic Community.

Communist nations - 97-132. (*See also* People's Republic of China; Soviet Union.)

Détente and trade, 1970s - 98-100, 109-115

Economic cooperation within Soviet bloc - 104-105

Overtures to reopen trade with West - 103-104

Technological achievements - 213

Trade restrictions:

Cold War era - 97, 100-103, 107

High technology exports - 98, 205-208

Moves toward relaxation - 105-108

Michel, Robert H., R-Ill. - 119
Military technology - 212, 213
 Arms export controls - 101, 102, 200
Milliken, Eugene D., R-Colo. - 36, 37
Mills, Wilbur D., D-Ark. - 66
Ministry of International Trade and
 Industry (MITI)
 Functions - 228
 Machine tool manufacturing - 222
 Robotics industry - 218
 U.S.-Japanese trade imbalance - 10
MITI. *See* Japan, Ministry of Interna-
 tional Trade and Industry.
Mondale, Walter F. - 127-128
Most-favored-nation status
 China- 126-129
 Origins - 35, 36
 Soviet Union request - 110-112
Motion picture industry - 153, 154, 156
Moynihan, Daniel Patrick, D-N.Y. -
 138, 146, 221
Multinational corporations - 8, 15, 88
Mundt, Karl E., R-S.D. - 105-106
Mutual Defense Assistance Control
 Act - 102. (*See also* Battle Act.)

N

Nakasone, Yashuhio - 164
National security
 Export restrictions - 22, 101-103, 108,
 199, 205, 209-211
 High technology exports - 199, 200
Natural gas
 Alaska pipeline - 145
 Canadian export price - 144-145
 Soviet pipeline - 14, 117-121
Neal, Stephen L., D-N.C. - 190-191,
194, 196-197
Nixon, Richard - 63, 66, 67, 77, 81, 108
 China relations - 98, 123
 Import surcharge - 64, 74
 Soviet Union - 109, 110
 Trade Act of 1974 - 82, 113
Nontariff barriers
 Japan - 156-158
 Tokyo Round code - 84

Trade Act of 1979 - 86, 89 (box)
 Types - 70-71
North Atlantic Treaty Organization
 (NATO) - 100-101
North Korea - 102
North Vietnam - 102, 107
Nuclear technology - 211
Nunn, Sam, D-Ga. - 208, 209

O

Obey, David R., D-Wis. - 187
OECD. *See* Organization for Economic
 Cooperation and Development.
Office of Export Administration -
 205, 208
Office of Technology Assessment
 (OTA) - 120-121, 212
Office of the U.S. Trade Representa-
 tive - 20-22, 81, 229
Oil
 Imported from China - 124
 Price increases - 13, 78-79, 124
OPEC. *See* Organization of Petroleum
 Exporting Countries (OPEC).
Operation Exodus - 208-209
Organization for Economic Cooper-
 ation and Development (OECD) -
 51, 195
Organization for Trade Cooperation
 (OTC) - 42-44
Organization of Petroleum Export-
 ing Countries (OPEC)- 13, 78-79,
 124
OTC. *See* Organization for Trade Coop-
 eration.

P

Payment-in-kind program (PIK)
 Background - 174
 Export payment-in-kind program -
 181
Payne-Aldrich Tariff of 1909 - 33
Pell, Claiborne, D-R.I. - 135
People's Republic of China - 123-132
 Cold War embargo - 100, 102

Export-Import Bank - 126, 130
High technology - 131
Most-favored-nation status - 126-129
Opening of trade relations with U.S. - 123-124, 126
Textile exports - 127, 130, 131
Trade agreements with U.S. - 126-131
U.S.-China trade 1971-1982 (table) - 125
Pepper, Claude, D-Fla. - 219-221
Peril points - 36-39, 43
Perle, Richard N. - 201, 206, 209
Peterson, Peter G. - 110
Philippines - 8, 65, 93, 164
Poland
Early U.S. trade with - 101, 104
Suspension of most-favored-nation status - 54, 56, 117
U.S. sanctions against Soviet Union - 117, 120, 176, 202
Product standards as trade barriers - 89, 158
Productivity
Japan-U.S. comparison - 165
Pay and productivity, 1960-1982 (table) - 91
U.S. decline - 92-93
Protectionist measures. *See also* Tariffs.
Costliness - 4
Criticism - 223, 225
Developing countries - 90-91
Development of - 33, 43
EEC - 30, 45, 62-64, 82
Nixon administration - 68-69
Types (box) - 40-41
Protectionist sentiment
Late 1960s and early 1970s - 30, 58, 61
Late 1970s - 87, 88, 90
Lobbying - 23-25, 162
1980s - 16, 19

Q

Quotas
Japanese - 157
Steel - 6

Textiles - 6, 7
U.S.-Japanese - 64-66, 68
Voluntary - 11, 19, 46, 65-66, 69, 88, 152-153
Quality standards, Japanese - 158

R

Randall commission. *See* Commission on Foreign Economic Policy.
Reagan, Ronald - 1, 116, 117, 122, 176, 225
Blended credit program - 180, 181
China - 131
Export controls - 209
Export-Import Bank - 22, 187
Free market ideology - 140, 219
Free trade policy - 2, 18-19
Japan - 152
Soviet pipeline sanctions - 118-120, 202, 203
Tariffs and quotas on steel imports - 6
Recession - 1, 78-80
Reciprocal Trade Agreements Act of 1934 - 7
Reciprocity bills - 20, 22, 23
Canada - 143
Japan - 160, 162
Reconstruction Finance Corp. - 219, 220-221 (box)
Reich, Robert B. - 8, 26, 223-225
Research and development - 92, 224-225
Robotics - 9, 166-167, 217-218
Rogers, William P. - 112
Roosevelt, Franklin D. - 33, 34
Rose, Charlie, D-N.C. - 182
Roth, William V., Jr., R-Del. - 21, 81, 229
Royalties, film - 153, 154, 156

S

Sanctions. *See* Export controls.
Schaetzel, J. Robert - 75